THE UNSTEADY STATE

Analytical jurisprudence often proceeds with two key assumptions: that all law is either contained in or traceable back to an authorizing law-state and that states are stable and in full control of the borders of their legal systems. What would a general theory of law be like and do if these long-standing presumptions were loosened? *The Unsteady State* aims to assess the possibilities by enacting a relational approach to an explanation of law, exploring law's relations to environment, security and technology. The account provided here offers a rich and renewed perspective on the preconditions and continuity of legal order in systemic and non-systemic forms and further supports the view that the state remains prominent yet is now less dominant in the normative lives of norm-subjects and as an object of legal theory.

Keith Culver is Professor of Management at the University of British Columbia, Canada. His research blends jurisprudential scholarship with professional contributions to regional innovation capacity.

Michael Giudice is Associate Professor in the Department of Philosophy at York University, Canada. His research focusses on philosophy of law and associated areas in political and moral philosophy.

The Unsteady State

GENERAL JURISPRUDENCE FOR DYNAMIC SOCIAL PHENOMENA

KEITH CULVER
University of British Columbia

MICHAEL GIUDICE
York University

CAMBRIDGE
UNIVERSITY PRESS

CAMBRIDGE
UNIVERSITY PRESS

University Printing House, Cambridge CB2 8BS, United Kingdom

One Liberty Plaza, 20th Floor, New York, NY 10006, USA

477 Williamstown Road, Port Melbourne, VIC 3207, Australia

4843/24, 2nd Floor, Ansari Road, Daryaganj, Delhi - 110002, India

79 Anson Road, #06-04/06, Singapore 079906

Cambridge University Press is part of the University of Cambridge.

It furthers the University's mission by disseminating knowledge in the pursuit of education, learning and research at the highest international levels of excellence.

www.cambridge.org
Information on this title: www.cambridge.org/9781107134805
DOI: 10.1017/9781316471203

First published 2017

A catalogue record for this publication is available from the British Library.

ISBN 978-1-107-13480-5 Hardback

Contents

Acknowledgements

This book, like its predecessor, *Legality's Borders*, is the product of many conversations with many people in many places. We are grateful to colleagues and students who have responded to our interest in this book's topics with their own questions, criticisms, examples and counter-examples and sometimes even agreement. Amongst the many contributors to our thinking, we owe particular thanks to several who followed us into the sometimes murky realm of draft written work, providing thoughtful reactions which nonetheless leave us solely responsible for errors in our arguments. Stefan Sciaraffa provided substantial and expert advice on an earlier version of Chapter 2. Maks Del Mar and Roger Cotterrell read and responded to a version of Chapter 3. Two excellent PhD students in philosophy, Max Leonov (McMaster University) and Sam Steadman (York University), discussed an early version of Chapter 3 at a workshop and meeting of the legal philosophy reading group at York University. William Twining published a response to our arguments in a paper whose core occupies the beginning of Chapter 5 and, in personal discussion, generously offered sound suggestions we have tried to absorb. Brian Tamanaha tread through an early version of the nearly complete manuscript and provided valuable correctives and insights. Dennis Patterson is owed special thanks as an enthusiastic discussant of even our most embryonic ideas, through to reading of individual chapters and providing criticism and encouragement in the right measures and at the right moments. Julie Dickson also deserves special mention, as her thoughtful objections to our earlier work have in many ways shaped the objectives of this book. We owe an ongoing debt of gratitude to Wil Waluchow, whose patience with former students who disagree with him is surely the stuff of legend. Finally, we must not forget to thank our families, and particularly our daughters Gwen and Sophia, since they are the ones who show the greatest patience when co-author dads say they'll be ready 'in one more minute', just as soon as yet another Skype chat about the current chapter is brought to an end. The patience of our colleagues, students and families will be drawn upon yet again, and soon, as we are warming up for another run at persistent jurisprudential questions not yet addressed in work to date.

Most of the chapters in this book draw to some extent on material previously published or forthcoming. We gratefully acknowledge prior publication of the following articles and book chapters:

K. Culver and M. Giudice, 'Pulling off the mask of law: a renewed research agenda for analytical legal theory', *Problema*, 5 (2012), pp. 81–116. (Chapter 1)

K. Culver and M. Giudice, 'Old questions made new: law, legal system, and state', in S. Sciaraffa and W. Waluchow (eds.), *Philosophical Foundations of the Nature of Law* (Oxford: Oxford University Press, 2013), pp. 279–300. (Chapter 2)

K. Culver and M. Giudice, 'Claims to authority, legal systems, and dynamic social phenomena', in R. Cotterrell and M. Del Mar (eds.), *Authority in Transnational Legal Theory* (Cheltenham, UK: Edward Elgar, 2016). (Chapter 3)

K. Culver and M. Giudice, 'Complementing comparison: renewing analytical legal theory to meet the explanatory challenge of globalisation', *Transnational Legal Theory*, 4 (2013), pp. 700–713. (Chapter 5)

K. Culver, 'How the new ICTs matter to the theory of law', *Canadian Journal of Law and Jurisprudence*, 17 (2004), pp. 255–268. (Chapter 7)

Introduction

This book is in many ways a continuation of our earlier effort, *Legality's Borders*.[1] There we focussed on state-centred descriptive-explanatory theories of law and their weaknesses as approaches that purport to be meaningfully descriptive yet fail to account adequately for novel prima facie legal phenomena beyond the state. We offered what we took to be an improvement to analytical approaches to legality by amplifying suggestions made by H. L. A. Hart and Neil MacCormick, amongst others, to arrive at an inter-institutional approach. That approach accounts for varieties of legality within and beyond the state and further offers a clearer and deeper account of the nature of a theory of law as a contribution to human self-knowledge.

As a continuation of the argument of *Legality's Borders*, this book is of a particular kind. Whereas in *Legality's Borders*, we strove to show that state-focussed legal theory is impoverished to the extent that it ignores other legal phenomena for which it ought to account, we now presume that readers share our interest in characterizing what is spoken of and thought to be legality in non-state-centric situations as diverse as international law, trans-boundary law and supranational law, as visible in the European Union. Here we aim to deepen the inter-institutional account using a 'relational' approach derived from Hart. Our approach will serve the explanatory interests of the inquiring ordinary citizen of the twenty-first century as that citizen encounters social and physical phenomena challenging state-based explanations of law, while enabling us to offer new insights into long-standing jurisprudential questions. Where Hart and others began from the ordinary educated person's understanding of the municipal state and explored the relations between law and coercion, law and morality and law and rules, here we start from the broader

[1] K. Culver and M. Giudice, *Legality's Borders* (Oxford: Oxford University Press, 2010).

viewpoint of our contemporary ordinary citizen who travels across legality's old borders. Our ordinary citizen is concerned both with the relations Hart explored in many of the systems of law he examined and, for reasons we explore below, now with law's relation to environment, security and technology in state and non-state contexts. As we add to the relational approach in the context of both state legal systems and non-state legal orders, the phenomena we examine will enable us to provide a renewed appreciation of the problem of continuity, allowing and perhaps demanding characterization of legality in more than the 'momentary' way typical of analytical approaches to explanation of legal system. This extended and enriched view is intended to be dynamic, offering a means to approaching legality which is constantly re-informed by changing phenomena in the social and physical contexts in which legality is found, resulting in an explanation of legality and life under law which is apt in light of the gradually evolving interests of law's subjects. Our approach in this book, as in *Legality's Borders*, is evolutionary rather than revolutionary, extending and amplifying methods and insights of predecessor analytical legal theorists, while admitting the need for corrections where demonstrable errors have been made and attempting to supply those corrections.

SALIENT PHENOMENA

The social and physical phenomena we have chosen to investigate in relation to law have been chosen for their interest to an inquirer whose experience of law reaches beyond experience of legal systems and because they serve as a challenge to explanations of law which depart from presumption that legality is found in or authorized by states making exclusive claims to authority over normative life within their borders. Our introduction and exploration of environment, security and technology in Chapter 1 and Part II treat these areas of investigation independently while acknowledging their overlap. In discussion of law's relation to environment, we shall explore natural and human-caused environmental disasters which significantly affect the ability of states to maintain life under law for their subjects. In examination of law's relation to security, we shall explore the ways in which conceptions of security as a form of personal safety enabled by state-based law are outmoded by challenges of collective security in the face of threats beyond the historic prominence of human coercion of other humans. And in discussion of law's relation to technology, we shall explore some of the possibilities of legal-normative life found in cyberspace and the internet of things, focussing in particular on the ways new communications technologies are growing arguably legal practices beyond the control of single sovereign states.

Our inquirer's interest in law's relation to these social and physical facts is not surprising. They are, after all, associated with major practical concerns of the early twenty-first century. Yet, there is a further, and more important, reason why we chose environment, security and technology as salient categories of phenomena which analytical legal theory ought to address. We assume that none will dispute the fact that environment, security and technology are categories of events or forces capable of rapid elimination of a legal system. A sufficiently large earthquake could collapse a state's social order and bring an end to a legal system. A sufficiently large-scale nuclear attack could also destroy the physical and social security of a state and its legal system. Similarly, it is not difficult to imagine applications or perhaps breakdowns of technology that bring an end to legal order. It is also beyond dispute, we suggest, that smaller-scale events, such as natural disasters prompting temporary suspension of certain laws, or insurrections after which states later regain control, pose problems for the normal operation of law and legal-normative expectations of subjects. The effective persistence of state legal systems is not immune to changes in natural and social conditions in which legal systems exist. However, while it can be agreed that such changes can affect the existence and operation of legal order, we wish to explore what might lie beyond such agreement and ask whether exploration of environment, security and technology in relation to law might also merit re-thinking our ideas of law and legal order themselves, as continuity of legality involves forms of legal order beyond the legal system. Our view is that investigation of such phenomena does warrant a kind of conceptual revision or, at the very least, consideration of conceptual alternatives to those that have dominated analytical legal theory. Here we do expect disagreement, but disagreement of the sort that will nonetheless advance the goals and reach of analytical legal theory in much-needed ways.

Our use of exploration of law's relation to environment, security and technology to further explore legality beyond the state may be novel in the context of state-focussed contemporary analytical legal theory, but it has deep roots in historic choices in analytical jurisprudence. Nearly all of analytical jurisprudence offers what Joseph Raz calls 'momentary' or 'static' accounts of legal systems – accounts of the structures and interrelationships of rules and norms which compose legal systems – viewed as if drawn from a snapshot fixed in time.[2] Raz acknowledges that his and adjacent theories, such as Hart's, are limited in this way and suggests work on the dynamic or temporally extended dimension of legal systems, so their continuity is best left to 'other social

[2] J. Raz, *The Concept of a Legal System*, 2nd edn (Oxford: Clarendon Press, 1980), esp. Chapter 8.

sciences'.[3] As we explain in later chapters, we view this as an invitation to think about the preconditions of legal order which bear on questions of continuity and have chosen security, environment and technology as particularly significant types of phenomena serving as preconditions to continuity of legal order. Attention to these phenomena in this role will enable us to challenge Raz's indifference to the problem of continuity in its dynamic dimensions as a problem of analytical jurisprudence and his view that such an investigation has little or no potential to disrupt core claims and presumptions about the nature of law – particularly core claims and presumptions about the centrality of state legal systems as evidentiary bases for inferences about the nature of law. Contrary to Raz, we hold that exploration of the preconditions of legal order understood as the means to continuity of a given legal order will show such claims and presumptions to be far from stable and will demonstrate the new unsteadiness of the state's role in authoritatively regulating the social lives of subjects by means of law. A different approach is needed, we shall argue, learning from characterizations of law beyond the state just how legal orders continue and change identity, looking eventually to an understanding of law which does not presume and examine the consequences of hierarchically organized state systems of law as the main object of legal experience worth examining and is instead sensitive to legality's traces from early appearance to sophisticated expression in legal orders such as state systems of law.

A NOTE ON METHODOLOGY

Our attention to social and physical phenomena in relation to law and exploration of the implications of that relational approach to law for legal concepts raises questions as to just what our total approach is and what it delivers. As a second preliminary step, we must therefore introduce and explain more precisely the kind of conceptual explanation we employ and situate that explanation in relation to more familiar methods of analytical jurisprudence (though we will leave full explanation of our method to Chapter 1). What we can summarize as our approach to 'contextualized conceptual explanation' begins from but does not end with conceptual analysis. Conceptual analysis in legal theory, as employed by Hart and explained by Raz, refers to the exercise of trying to make explicit what is already implicit in some community's or culture's self-understanding, of trying to help people understand how they already understand themselves. As Raz puts it on the final page of his celebrated article 'Authority, Law, and Morality', 'it is a major task of legal theory to advance our

[3] Ibid., p. 189.

understanding of society by helping us understand how people understand themselves'.[4] While conceptual analysis forms an important beginning in any theoretical investigation of law, it cannot mark the end or objective, since the resulting concept, i.e., the result of the exercise of analysis, might reveal a view of law that is parochial, distorting or even contradictory when compared against social reality. The concept of law delivered by largely Anglophone conceptual analysis to date has revealed a concept which suffers, we think, from many of these flaws. More specifically, conceptual analysis of law as practiced so far has revealed that the dominant and pervasive way in which people have understood law is, as we argued in *Legality's Borders*, unacceptably state limited. To move beyond the limitations of the state-based approach to understanding law, we need to move beyond conceptual analysis as previously practiced. We offer an improvement we call *contextualized conceptual explanation*. This, as we shall explain, is the exercise of building new conceptual tools which aspire to general application and which respond to the defects of existing concepts when tested against observationally available evidence and phenomena.[5] Seeking to construct concepts in this phenomena-responsive way follows in the footsteps of prior legal theorists while insisting on examination of novel phenomena and permitting the explanatory demands of those phenomena to motivate use of new explanatory concepts and categories. We can do no less once we recognize that characterization of legality drawn from a frozen moment of a state system of law is incomplete in terms of both the phenomena examined and its change over time. Whether law is found in state-based legal systems changing with the societies which constitute them or in non-state legal orders interacting with state legal systems and one another, law's promise to protect expectations is always in tension with social and natural change, giving rise to law's always unsteady state.

CHAPTER OVERVIEW

Our argument is set out in two parts, the first part establishing the need for contextualized conceptual explanation, the second exemplifying our approach. We begin Chapter 1 by exploring what we think our antecedent, Hart, meant by a relational approach to law, together with further examination of how such an approach offers a distinctively philosophical contribution to understanding

[4] J. Raz, 'Authority, law, and morality', in *Ethics in the Public Domain*, rev. edn (Oxford: Clarendon Press), p. 237.

[5] Contextualized conceptual explanation is essentially a particular form of what one of us has termed in previous work *constructive conceptual explanation*. See M. Giudice, *Understanding the Nature of Law* (Cheltenham, UK: Edward Elgar, 2015).

of law, and how such an approach is valuable, even if it is only partial and needs connection to other investigations of law both theoretical and empirical.

In Chapters 2 and 3 we begin our analysis of the relation between the state and legality. In Chapter 2 we analyse the first half of the relation, the state, as the presumed primary and natural social context of law. We argue that while law must have a social foundation for its existence, it is not necessary to suppose that such a foundation must be the modern sovereign state and that there is contrary evidence suggesting that legality is found in other social settings. One consequence of this view is the remarkable continuity it reveals between analytical legal theory and socio-legal theories of legal pluralism. Such continuity helps to show where analytical legal theorists might look for observationally available phenomena to which their theories must respond to keep pace with the dynamic nature of law in a globalizing world.

In Chapter 3 we turn to the second half of the relation and investigate the adequacy of the conception of law which is typically presumed in the relation between the state and legality. This is the idea of the state legal system, conceived as a special union of different types of rules, which, in the hands of its officials and institutions, makes special normative claims of authority over the lives of its subjects. Just as the idea of the state is only one way – and probably not the best way – of understanding the social foundation of law, so we argue in this chapter that the idea of the state legal system is only one way – and probably not the best way – of understanding the nature of law. This analysis yields the conclusion that the relation between modern sovereign states and state legal systems is only one way of conceiving the relation between society and law and that other conceptions might be better suited for analytical legal theory's task of offering phenomena- and interest-responsive conceptual explanations of law.

In Chapter 4 we proceed to offer what we take to be a better way of conceiving of law which avoids many of the pitfalls faced by a system-centred account. We recapitulate and extend the inter-institutional view articulated in *Legality's Borders*, responding in that discussion to critics who claimed that our positive argument for the existence of legal orders alongside well-established legal systems was less thorough than the criticism we offered contra the idea of legal system. Our discussion of the nature of legal order leads us to further discussion of the purpose of conceptual explanation and its relation to social phenomena, as a contribution to self-understanding which may make its contribution in a phenomena-responsive way, while falling short of providing demarcation criteria distinguishing each instance of legality from moral, religious or aesthetic norms.

In the second part of the book we turn away from questions regarding the need for new approaches to phenomena beyond state systems of law, towards and beyond a challenge William Twining first proposed for legal theory: to understand the implications of globalization for law. Twining suggests that the argument of his *Globalization and Legal Theory*[6] has three main consequences for legal theory. First, it is no longer possible, or advisable, to treat legal systems, societies or states as black boxes, immune from interaction with outside influences and forces. Second, legal theorists concerned to offer general explanations of law must include within their subject matter more types of law than simply the Westphalian duo of state law and public international law. Third, greater effort must be devoted to cross-cultural comparison, or comparative law more generally, to see which legal concepts travel well and which do not. For his part, Twining has recently renewed his commitment to comparative law, attaching to it a special prominence for legal theory and globalization scholars. In Chapters 5, 6 and 7 we accept and respond to Twining's first two claims, while challenging the third claim regarding the centrality of comparative law as a first response to the implications of globalization for law. We argue instead that amongst the clear and unmistakable demands globalization makes of legal theory, we must not just compare various conditions of legality but reach further to attempt to understand the social and physical *preconditions* of legality, an issue which earlier analytical legal theorists have acknowledged but not investigated in detail. In Chapter 5 we offer a general account of the importance of analysis of preconditions of legality for legal theory, before turning to an account of law's relation to environment. We argue that if part of analytical legal theory's task is to offer a morally neutral account of the nature and limits of law as a means of social organization, it cannot afford to avoid analysis of the relation between environmental conditions and the aspirations of legal order. We give particular attention to the effects of the 2004 Indian Ocean tsunami on legality in the Indonesian province of Aceh and to the possible legal effects of sea-level rise for the Pacific island state of Kiribati.

In Chapter 6 we turn to a further relation of interest to our ordinary citizen who travels: the relation between law and security. When security is little discussed by legal and political theorists, the range of questions and issues receiving attention tends to narrow rapidly to questions of the obligation of states to their own and other states' citizens, in matters such as state limitation of rights and freedoms in times of emergency. Our aim in this chapter is to broaden this discussion to include investigation of the conditions of security

[6] W. Twining, *Globalisation and Legal Theory* (London: Butterworths, 2000).

which constitute and so make legal order possible. While individual security might have primary or intrinsic moral value, from an analytical and explanatory perspective, individual security presumes conditions of stability. Such conditions might be provided at the state level, but often the conditions of security and stability are satisfied (and compromised) at diverse levels, both within and beyond particular states. We take up with particular interest the question of what may be learned about legality from pandemics such as Ebola, and Joseph Raz's observation that facts arising from state and international organizations' responses to Ebola may give reasons for a negative response to the question: 'Is the state likely to remain the most comprehensive legal social organization within its domain?'[7] We suggest in a subsequent argument that the idea of legal systems may now be most usefully understood as an ideal roughly analogous to the rule of law insofar as achievement of each is distinctive of a particular kind of legal order, yet legal orders can exist without them.

In Chapter 7 we conclude our exploration of the social and physical preconditions of law, turning to the way new information communication technologies present the possibility that states may undermine their own claims to sovereignty as they embrace some technologies, while other technologies create legal order beyond states and with little need for them. We begin by examining the case of trans-boundary electricity grids enabled by the joint choice of states deploying legal norms to enact that choice, creating a subsequent trans-boundary web of legality in which state sovereignty is supplanted by a technological legal order supported but not determined by individual states. We then explore the development of virtual currencies, focussing on Bitcoin, occurring with and without recognition by state legal systems. Both examples compel re-thinking of legal concepts, and perhaps even jurisprudential problems, as the intersection and interaction of legal system, technology and legal order lead us to ask whether the problem of continuity, once conceived largely as a matter of legal system replacing legal system, has now become the problem of continuity and transition amongst legal orders.

We close this volume in traditional fashion in Chapter 8, encapsulating prior argument in summary terms we can only deploy once readers have journeyed through the preceding chapters. We may nonetheless offer here a 'sequel teaser'. *Legality's Borders* developed an inter-institutional view of legality and urged its application beyond the state. Here, in *The Unsteady State*, we have extended application of that view to new phenomena and, in facing familiar jurisprudential problems, have re-framed them in light of new phenomena.

[7] J. Raz, 'Why the state?', King's College London Law School Research Paper No. 2014-38, p. 13. Available from http://ssrn.com/abstract=2339522.

We intend in our next steps to follow phenomena and problems into the most prominent non-state instances of legality in the twenty-first century – legality's place in territorial and virtual *regions*. But first, let us invite you to explore with us in the following chapters the nature and jurisprudential consequences of law's unsteady state.

PART I

Preparing Analytical Legal Theory for New Challenges

1

Pulling Off the Mask of Law

A Renewed Research Agenda for Analytical Legal Theory

The goals of this book make it a contribution to an unfortunately neglected genre of analytical legal theory: sympathetic yet comprehensive renovation of its research agenda. This renovation is motivated in part by the fact that analytical legal theory is in the midst of an identity crisis – or, at least according to its critics, it certainly ought to be. In the aftermath of Ronald Dworkin's celebrated response in 'The Model of Rules I' to Hart's magisterial *The Concept of Law*, analytical legal theory appeared to have lost track of its reason for being. The historical task of analytical legal theory is perhaps best expressed by its most colourful forefather, Jeremy Bentham. In a characteristically vivid use of metaphor, Bentham advises that we must 'draw aside that curtain of mystery which fiction and formality have spread so extensively over the Law' and, in criticism of Blackstone, suggests that while 'Law shews itself in a mask . . . this mask our author instead of putting off has varnished'.[1] Bentham decried, for example, Blackstone's approving report of the fiction contained in the doctrine that there was no need to publicize widely the acts of Parliament, since 'every man in England is, *in judgement of Law*, party to the making of an Act of Parliament, being thereat *by his representative*'.[2] This might make good legal sense, Bentham writes, but it is an affront to common sense. The job of legal theory is to confront the affront: to clarify what remains obscure about law, using morally neutral methods. While analytical legal theory continues to accept as the kernel of its task the job of pulling off the mask of law, the

[1] J. Bentham, 'A comment on the commentaries', Chapter 2, Section 1 in *The Collected Works of Jeremy Bentham* (London: Clarendon Press, 1968), p. 124. This particular setting of Bentham's remarks is of course used in an essay by H. L. A. Hart, out of which some of our argument grows: 'The demystification of the law', in *Essays on Bentham* (Oxford: Clarendon Press, 1982), p. 23.

[2] J. Bentham, *A Fragment on Government*, ed. J. H. Burns and H. L. A. Hart (Cambridge: Cambridge University Press, 1998), p. 17.

reasons why this goal is sought have varied, as have the methods deployed in pursuit of the goal. Disputes regarding the proper motivations and methods of analytical legal theory have taken so much effort that analytical legal theory gives the appearance of being in a state of perpetual preparation to reach its goal, with little demonstrable progress.

Some analytical legal theorists, such as Leslie Green, see a mixed record of progress in response to persistent questions of legal theory: 'some broadening' of understanding in investigation of the relation between law and social rules; 'some narrowing, some deepening' of understanding in investigation of the relation between law and morality; and 'some paralysis'[3] and a 'depressing' point of 'stasis'[4] in study of the relation between law and coercion. Yet Green does not advocate any great departure from past methods or questions and is seemingly content for analytical legal theory to continue work on its persistent questions, no matter the reactions of the 'plain lawyers' who might never be convinced of the interest of those questions.[5] Few, however, are persuaded that this will result in the needed breakthroughs. David Dyzenhaus, for example, has called analytical legal theory a 'stagnant research programme'[6] whose increased precision in specification of claims and methods has generated increasingly sophisticated defence of increasingly limited theoretical ambitions. As Jeremy Waldron put it, 'most of those who bask in Hart's glory prefer to fiddle with issues about exclusive and inclusive legal positivism, a discussion that has been following the law of diminishing returns since Jules Coleman initiated it in 1988, rather than address . . . more urgent and compelling issues'.[7] Others are less kind in their assessment of the sophisticated parochialism they see, charging that the enterprise of analytical legal theory risks collapsing into itself, leaving little more than a goal and endless quibbles over method. As Brian Simpson memorably assesses the post-*Concept* progress of analytical legal theory,

3 L. Green, 'General jurisprudence: a 25th anniversary essay', *Oxford Journal of Legal Studies*, 25 (2005), p. 575.

4 Ibid., p. 573.

5 As Green explains at the conclusion of 'General Jurisprudence', 'there have always been jurisprudence books that didn't discuss much law; now there are jurisprudence books that don't discuss much jurisprudence. Will plain lawyers find them interesting? Perhaps not; but we should remember that the editors of the *Quarterly Review* urged Charles Darwin to abandon the manuscript of *The Origin of Species* and instead write about pigeons, because "everyone is interested in pigeons". And perhaps we should be glad the advice was ignored'. Ibid., p. 580.

6 D. Dyzenhaus, 'Positivism's stagnant research programme', *Oxford Journal of Legal Studies*, 20 (2000), pp. 703–722.

7 J. Waldron, 'Hart and the principles of legality', in M. H. Kramer et al. (eds), *The Legacy of H. L. A. Hart* (Oxford: Oxford University Press, 2008), p. 69.

> in a sense it has been downhill all the way – downhill, that is, from the lucidity and elegance of Herbert's writing to the unattractive elaborations of some of his critics and defenders, downhill from Herbert's direct analysis of law and legal institutions to writings about what other people have said about what other people have written about law and legal institutions. In British military circles there was, in my time, a bawdy monologue, much recited in pubs, which took the form of a bestiary. One of the creatures featured in it was the Fu-Fu Fly, which was said to fly in ever diminishing circles until it finally vanished up its own bottom, from which secure if unsanitary location it looked out at the world with scorn and derision. That, leaving on one side scorn and derision, is more or less the present picture in relation to much of the secondary literature on *The Concept of Law*.[8]

Simpson's despairing picture leads us to a simple question: what next for those intrigued by analytical legal theory yet frustrated by its offering of deflections and defences rather than advances? One option is to adopt an entirely new research agenda, perhaps taking a direction like that pioneered by Brian Tamanaha in his 'socio-legal positivism'.[9] A rather more promising option, we shall argue, lies in a line of argument we began in our recent *Legality's Borders*.[10] The inter-institutional theory of law elaborated there is an attempt to marshal overlooked insights of analytical legal theory in support of sympathetic yet ground-up renovation of analytical legal theory sufficient to enable explanation of legality in diverse forms within and beyond the state. The argument of *Legality's Borders* contributes, we believe, to the extrication of analytical legal theory from stagnation and to a re-orientation towards pressing problems whose salience is rooted in the experience of ordinary citizens encountering diverse forms of legality in a world in which the law-state appears prominent yet no longer dominant. This book continues the methodological amplification started in *Legality's Borders*, turning from the expanded range of legal phenomena we investigated in *Legality's Borders* to an attempt to deepen the analytical account of legality as it is found in those diverse phenomenal contexts. Where our inter-institutional theory was developed and deployed to enable characterization of prominent forms of legality in addition to the law-state, this next, complementary step is an attempt to better understand the nature of legality in some of those extra-state situations. This approach is not, however, straightforwardly a continued investigation of intra-state, trans-state, supra-state and super-state legal phenomena. Rather, it is an attempt to deepen understanding

8 B. Simpson, 'Herbert Hart elucidated', *Michigan Law Review*, 104 (2006), pp. 1455–1456.

9 B. Tamanaha, 'Socio-legal positivism and a general jurisprudence', *Oxford Journal of Legal Studies*, 21 (2001), pp. 1–32.

10 See K. Culver and M. Giudice, *Legality's Borders* (Oxford: Oxford University Press, 2010).

of prominent manifestations of legality, in whatever state or non-state form they occur, by expansion of an approach begun by Hart yet left behind as enthusiasms led elsewhere. What has been called Hart's 'relational approach' to the concept of law sought to explain that concept by way of its relation to social rules, morality and coercion. The results of this investigation are well known, as are the results of its newer champions. What is less well recognized is the fact that Hart did not suppose that his choice of these particular relations was in any way exhaustive, and it was certainly not exclusive. Rather, these relations appeared salient from the point of view of the ordinary educated person to whom his theory was nominally addressed. Hart might have done otherwise. He might, for example, have chosen the relation between law and religion, or he might have added the relation between law and liberty, which he treated later in the celebrated Hart–Devlin debate. His choice of the focal relations of *The Concept of Law* was just that: a choice, made in light of the interests of a particular audience engaged from a particular explanatory and historical perspective, in which the relations explored matter not just individually but also collectively. We aim here to take up Hart's approach and insight to further develop the relational approach, renewed in the context and perspective of the citizen in the age of globalization. In that context we turn from Hart's chosen relations to those relations individually and collectively salient to our citizen's perspective as a member of a state made unsteady by dynamic mixtures of social and natural pressures: the relations between law and environment, law and security and law and technology. The precise way in which we engage those relations will produce a contextualized concept of law capable of serving as a bridge between descriptive-explanatory approaches to legal theory and the empirical phenomena those theories engage.

Before we explore those relations and their product, however, we must take up the prior question of the nature and benefits of a renewed relational approach to the concept of law and the still earlier question of how such an approach might be divorced from the dismal mis-steps which have led to analytical legal theory's stagnation. We should aim, at the very least, to see where analytical legal theory went wrong, so we might attempt to replace present stagnation with a renovated research agenda giving fresh life to Bentham's clarity of purpose and ambition.

ANALYTICAL LEGAL THEORY: FUNCTIONS, METHODS, OBJECTS AND EVIDENCE

It is probably impossible to conduct a kind of social archaeology which might reveal precisely the chain of events leading from Bentham's confident goal setting through Hart's inspiring re-statement of legal positivism and on to the present state. Fortunately, for our purposes, no such archaeology is necessary. We are seeking less to isolate a point of error from which the correct path might be rejoined and rather more to understand where the debate lost its way as a dialogue amongst scholars. With this purpose in mind, let us explore a suggestion visible in Brian Simpson's remark that analytical legal theory has become too little concerned with 'direct analysis' and too much a debate regarding 'what other people have said about what other people have written'. What Waldron and Simpson see as a distracting preoccupation with words about words, rather than words about things, is perhaps nobler than suggested by the Fu-Fu fly's backwards trajectory. It may be that analytical legal theory has been something of a victim of its own openness to criticism, launching too eagerly into dialogue regarding questions adjacent to its main job. This possibility is visible in the way debate has been drawn into response to questions it should perhaps have rejected as secondary questions to be answered after further efforts at theory building, not *in medias res*. Entanglement in these questions has resulted, we argue below, in a dialogue which has left analytical legal theory simultaneously too narrow and too broad, in need of a substantial middle we aim to supply. More specifically, and as we have argued elsewhere,[11] analytical legal theory has been distracted by an attempted response to three, sometimes concurrent demands it demonstrably need not engage. The 'practicality demand' asks that analytical legal theory become a kind of practical philosophy aimed at least partially at giving tools of understanding to lawyers and private citizens – a demand associated with Green's 'plain lawyers'. The practicality demand sometimes arrives in the company of the 'normativity demand', the demand that any theory of law capture law's distinctive normative function in a wholly theoretical way, independently of any particular system. Both practicality and normativity demands are sometimes found in conjunction with a third demand, the insistence that analytical legal theory must somehow be total, exhaustive and utterly self-sufficient, a contender for the title of 'best comprehensive understanding of law as a whole'. These demands are hardly unreasonable as representations of the diverse interests inquirers may bring to the activity of understanding legality; yet from the fact that these are reasonable interests, nothing follows about whether a valuable contribution to our understanding of legality must satisfy any one or all of these interests. These are not the only justifiable interests in legality – a valuable contribution to understanding legality might address altogether different

[11] K. Culver, 'Leaving the Hart-Dworkin debate', *University of Toronto Law Journal*, 50 (2001), pp. 367–397.

interests. More importantly, there is little reason to suppose that a response to these interests must come from analytical legal theory. In fact, as we aim to show below, the greatest value in these demands may lie not in their value as demonstrations of the shortcomings of analytical legal theory but in their pointing the way towards needed renovations of analytical legal theory sufficient to enable it to connect appropriately with other data, arguments and insights into legality in its many forms.

In suggesting that analytical legal theory has become both too narrow and too broad, we are identifying coincident problems whose origin is more an epiphenomena of a dialogue than a consequence of theory-building goals or methodological commitments and operations. The roots of these problems in dialogue is key to understanding how analytical legal theory has strayed from its motivating goal and descriptive-explanatory methods and, in turn, key to understanding how renovation of the approach might take up and extend its original insights. In this context, what is perhaps most surprising about the crippling narrowness identified by Green, Waldron, Simpson and others is the fact that the criticism is not new. In fact, it is a danger explicitly acknowledged by analytical legal theorists, particularly in handling the phenomena of adjudication in response to the practicality demand. As Hart lists the accusations evident in the demand, 'the sin imputed to positivist conceptions of the judicial function was "formalism", "conceptualism", "mechanical" or "slot machine" jurisprudence or an excessive belief in the use of "logic" in reaching decisions'.[12] In early response to these charges, legal realists took up the new methods available from psychology and sociology to throw light on the all-too-human dimension of judges as flesh-and-blood reasoners capable of misinterpretation, political bias and other motivations with the potential to limit the likelihood of impartial application of rules with determinate meaning. A few of these realists took theorists to task for omitting other dimensions of courtroom life, as Jerome Frank did in chiding his colleagues 'for forgetting "juriesprudence"',[13] which might additionally take account of the role of juries. Yet, for the most part, response to the practicality demand led to an unquestioned focus on the pivotal role of the judge, and surrounding investigation of the nature of legal concepts treated judicial use of legal norms as the crucible for theories of law. Later in the century, Hart's attempt to avoid undue narrowness by means of a broader theory of social rules soon collapsed

[12] H. L. A. Hart, 'Law in the perspective of philosophy', in *Essays in Jurisprudence and Philosophy* (Oxford: Clarendon Press, 1983), p. 152.

[13] J. Frank, 'Preface to the sixth printing', in *Law and the Modern Mind* (Gloucester, MA: Peter Smith, 1970). First published in 1930.

to a similar fate. Hart's pioneering use of the idea of social rules accepted and applied by generically identified 'officials' became enmeshed in the deep but narrow Dworkin-initiated debates regarding judicial discretion. Here our purpose is limited to diagnosis of just where the dialogue fell away from the purportedly central goals of analytical legal theory, so we will not fall back into discussion of theoretical characterization of adjudication. It is worthwhile nonetheless to quickly illustrate the deficiencies of the judge-centred approach to the adjudicative enterprise, beyond Frank's pointed observation about the importance of juries.

It seems to be easily forgotten that judges do not operate in isolation. Other players within and without the courtroom can influence very significantly the context in which judges carry out their work. With the advent of the *Charter of Rights and Freedoms* in Canada, for example, interveners play a role in Supreme Court decision making which is only now beginning to be examined by scholars, who note that

> despite the frequency of activity and the resources contributed to the collective intervention effort, the effects on the Court's decision making are poorly understood. A growing body of empirical literature examines the effects of *amicus curiae* at the US Supreme Court. The empirical literature is not as developed regarding the effects of intervention on the decision making of the Supreme Court of Canada, although interventions at the Court have been repeatedly discussed in the literature.[14]

[14] B. R. D. Alarie and A. J. Green, 'Interventions at the Supreme Court of Canada: accuracy, affiliation, and acceptance', *Osgoode Hall Law Journal*, 48 (2010), p. 381. Alarie and Green cite US evidence as follows in note 3:

> J.D. Kearney and T.W. Merrill, 'The Influence of Amicus Briefs on the Supreme Court', *University of Pennsylvania Law Review*, 148 (2000), p. 743 (amicus briefs were filed in approximately 85 per cent of appeals before the US Supreme Court in the period from 1986–1995); P.M. Collins Jr., *Friend of the Supreme Court: Interest Groups and Judicial Decision-Making* (Oxford University Press, 2008).
>
> Canadian evidence is characterized in note 4 as tending not to be empirical and focuses on discussing issues surrounding the practice of intervention and the role of interveners. See Bernard M. Dickens, 'A Canadian Development: Non-Party Intervention' (1977) 40 *Mod. L. Rev.* 666; Jillian Welch, 'No Room at the Top: Interest Group Intervenors and *Charter* Litigation in the Supreme Court of Canada' (1985) 43 *U.T. Fac. L. Rev.* 204; Kenneth P. Swan, 'Intervention and Amicus Curiae Status in Charter Litigation' in Robert J. Sharpe, ed., *Charter Litigation* (Toronto: Butterworths, 1987) 27; Philip L. Bryden, 'Public Interest Intervention in the Courts' (1987) 66 *Can. Bar Rev.* 490; John Koch, 'Making Room: New Directions in Third Party Intervention' (1990) 48 *U.T. Fac. L. Rev.* 151; Eugene Meehan, 'Intervening in the Supreme Court of Canada' (1994) 16 *Advocates' Q.* 137; Gregory Hein, 'Interest Group Litigation and Canadian Democracy' in Paul Howe & Peter H. Russell, eds., *Judicial Power and Canadian Democracy* (Montreal: McGill-Queen's University Press, 2001) 214; Ian Brodie, *Friends of*

There may be still other factors only a little beyond the courtroom which directly influence judges' tasks. Prosecutorial discretion, for example, determines which laws are in fact applied and brought before judicial interpreters. Unpopular laws may become functionally obsolete as prosecutors consciously cease relying on them, all without judicial attention to the nature of the norm expressed in the obsolete law. (We might call this desuetude in fact as opposed to desuetude by rule of positive law, as is permitted in, e.g., Scotland). None of these facts are novel or unavailable to analytical legal theorists, and these sorts of facts were top of mind in Frank's and Hart's response to accusations of formalism. Later analytical legal theorists' entanglement in narrow questions of judicial activity is almost incomprehensible in light of the availability of earlier warning against just this sort of narrowness. Yet seen from the point of view of theorists peppered by versions of the practicality demand by 'plain lawyers' and their sympathizers, it is entirely understandable that these theorists have paused to extinguish this kind of flaring up of criticism, before pressing on with pulling off the mask of law in a way more sensitive to the wide range of phenomena properly examined by a descriptive-explanatory theory. The derailing of a research agenda by the practicality demand is interesting in itself as a tale of changing enthusiasms and misplaced effort, but what is far more interesting about the drain of philosophical energies towards questions about judges comes in the effect of this work on arguments addressing more general questions about the nature of the concept of law and legal system, the nature of legal obligation, acceptance and fidelity to law, and associated concepts of duty, permission, right and so forth.

There is a curious knock-on effect from analytical legal philosophy's deep but narrow response to accusations of arid conceptualism. The general-level picture of the nature of law and legal system built on the back of the Anglo-American judge-focussed picture of brute phenomena overemphasizes the importance of judges as legal officials at the cost of losing touch with legal phenomena purportedly captured by these pictures, particularly with the addition of the inclusive vs exclusive positivism debate and its devolution into a debate over the logic of intra-theory differences. The key features of the general picture are quite simple: a legal system may be said to exist when officials accept and private citizens at least obey certain authorized norms as

the Court: The Privileging of Interest Group Litigants in Canada (Albany: State University of New York Press, 2002); and Donald R. Songer, *The Transformation of the Supreme Court of Canada* (Toronto: University of Toronto Press, 2008) (particularly Chapter 5, 'Understanding the Decision-Making Process').

non-optional standards of conduct. The validity of authoritative norms is expressed by the collective commitment and practice of officials, whose recognition of certain norms as authoritative provides a master rule of validity for the system. This picture is placed under serious theoretical strain by two empirical factors: the increasingly elusive nature of the class of officials, and the increasingly porous nature of nominally discrete legal systems.

Hart's famous sketch of a primitive legal society under the rule of Rex I was meant as a notional construction, yet at some points in history reality bore a substantial resemblance to theory. The most famous of the Icelandic sagas, *Njal's Saga*, tells of a rudimentary legal order in which authoritative legal norms were verified by the law-speaker, who could be consulted by disputing parties to confirm the existence of a particular legal norm.[15] The rule of recognition was maintained and passed on by the requirement that the law-speaker provide an annual recitation of all of the laws, so the system was evidently quite simple, or the law-speaker possessed remarkable skills of memorization. Modern municipal systems of law are significantly different from this isolated island society and its slim set of authoritative norms. As we have already observed, a wide range of complex forces – some local, and some apparently universal – bear on judges making determinations of law. These forces are poorly represented by the kinds of model officials, nearly always model judges, depicted in general theories of law delivered by analytical legal theory and its interlocutors. Dworkin's Hercules,[16] and Jules Coleman's development of the Swede,[17] seem to resemble more closely the kind of official envisioned in the Icelandic sagas than the diverse range of officials evident in modern municipal systems of law. Both Dworkin's Hercules and Coleman's Swede function as model authorities at a crucial nexus point, Dworkin's in the context of a court, and Coleman's as a kind of special epistemic authority regarding the identity of legal norms in a system which is not the object of the Swede's normative allegiance. These choices of illustrative character each refer to a nexus point of testing for normative authority which is under threat by empirical change from within the fragile borders of discrete municipal systems, and from without. As William Twining has argued, 'globalisation and interdependence challenge "black box theories" that treat nation-states or societies or legal systems as discrete, impervious entities that can be studied in isolation either internally

[15] *Njal's Saga*, trans. C. F. Bayerschmidt and L. M. Hollander (Hertfordshire, UK: Wordsworth Editions, 1998), Chapter 97, note 5.

[16] Dworkin's fictional judge of superhuman powers is most prominently used in his *Law's Empire* (Cambridge, MA: Harvard University Press, 1986).

[17] J. Coleman, *The Practice of Principle* (Oxford: Oxford University Press, 2001).

or externally'.[18] Familiar examples of penetration of municipal legal systems can be seen in the effect of international trade law on domestic legal practices, and the demands placed on states by international law-governed human rights violations in other states. The collapse of state isolation has been illustrated in the conduct of the United States, the global leviathan historically tempted towards an isolationist stance. The BBC World Service reported that declassified US documents show that senior American officials were warned in plain terms of impending genocide in Rwanda, yet chose nonetheless to vote with the remainder of the United Nations (UN) Security Council to withdraw troops from Rwanda. According to the BBC, 'In May [1994], a Pentagon memo cautioned against using the term "genocide" to describe the Rwandan massacres, as under the 1948 Genocide Treaty, this could legally oblige the UN, and by extension the US, to act. "Genocide finding could commit USG (US Government) to actually 'do something'", the memo warned'.[19] This example illustrates neatly the extent to which identification of officials of a particular discrete legal system is increasingly difficult, and perhaps more importantly, how judge-focussed accounts of officials in general-level analytical pictures of law as an inhabitant of discrete legal systems omit demonstrably important phenomena. In the instance cited, the US plainly feared a kind of external legal source and legal official triggering a significant change to its legal position, and in turn its policy position. Of course, it is entirely possible for a critic sympathetic to a rule of recognition plus official acceptance account of the concept of law to respond in various ways including insistence that the events of the example are interesting not because they show the interdependence of the American legal system with other sources of legality, but because the talk of a trigger to action shows precisely how that system remains autonomous to the extent that there is some final choice to be made by officials in the event that the trigger is tripped. Or perhaps one might say there was some antecedent recognition-carrying choice to join a treaty which foresaw just this sort of event. Yet as we argued at length in *Legality's Borders*, while this style of response might be effective against occasionally encountered challenges to the explanatory power of the orthodox view, the rise of intra-state, trans-state,

[18] W. Twining, *Globalisation and Legal Theory* (London: Butterworths, 2000), p. 51. See also W. Twining, *General Jurisprudence* (Cambridge: Cambridge University Press, 2009).

[19] BBC World Service, 21 August 2001, Africa page, 'US warned about Rwanda Genocide', http://news.bbc.co.uk/2/hi/africa/1502708.stm. The poignancy of this example is underscored by the fact that the International Criminal Tribunal for Rwanda, established to address the crimes committed in the Rwandan genocide, took more than twenty years from the time of the genocide to complete its work, handing down its last judgement in December 2015: http://unictr.unmict.org/en/news/appeals-chamber-delivers-judgement-nyiramasuhuko-et-al-case.

supra-state and super-state legality is so extensive and so pervasive that a theory which fails to engage those novel phenomena risks losing any claim to being meaningfully descriptive-explanatory. Instead of pulling off the mask of law, such an approach risks becoming an apologist for fictions.[20] Worse yet, a state-centric rule of recognition plus official acceptance approach risks embracing a fiction which Hart saw and railed against in Austin – the misleading view that law-states are or ever have been autonomous in the sense required by Austin's Uncommanded Commander. The deep but narrow gains made in exploration of social rules appear to have given rise to a general jurisprudence whose attempts at response to comprehensiveness and normativity demands lead them to a picture of law so broad and abstract that it is no longer clear just how they are descriptive-explanatory, and still less clear how these investigations are connected to the remainder of Hart's original investigation of the relations between law, social rules, morality and coercion, all in aid of a richer picture of law developed from the perspective of the ordinary citizen. The results may be satisfying to some,[21] bravely holding their analytical course and ignoring calls to do otherwise. Yet it seems to us that this amounts to bravely holding to a course which has been subtly altered by the force of a dialogue which has left its original goal, motivation and audience behind, forgetting Bentham's and Hart's urging clarity in understanding law as a social institution, practice and experience. We have tried to indicate above some ways in which narrowness and over-breadth are evident in the careers of devices such as Hercules, the Swede and the Uncommanded Commander. Still more pressing shortcomings are evident in the fact that even if all were well with investigation of law and social rules and morality, there is still the 'stasis' observed by Green with respect to coercion, and worse yet, as Green writes, 'What we have not had is convergence'.[22] The absence of convergence in investigation of social rules, morality and coercion is particularly troubling in light of the contingent relevance of these relations to an understanding of law satisfactory to inquirers' interests. The relation of law to those particular relations was judged important by Hart in his deepening of a picture of those features of legality particularly salient to ordinary citizens. We have already suggested that Hart might have

[20] We are not alone in this assessment. See, e.g., B. Tamanaha, *A General Jurisprudence of Law and Society* (Oxford: Oxford University Press, 2001); Twining, *General Jurisprudence*; D. Von Daniels, *The Concept of Law from a Transnational Perspective* (Surrey, UK: Ashgate, 2010); and B. de Sousa Santos, *Toward a New Legal Common Sense*, 2nd edn (London: Butterworths, 2002).

[21] Perhaps those who suppose they are the Darwins in Green's metaphor. See Green, 'General jurisprudence'.

[22] Ibid., p. 575.

chosen other relations to investigate, and in other work did so. What does it say about the progress of analytical jurisprudence that it has made little headway towards an integrated picture of just three of the contingent relations relevant to a citizen whose interests may well change? As we suggested in *Legality's Borders*, we would do well to conduct legal theory from the perspective and interests of the ordinary citizen who travels in a globalizing world whose effects are felt at home and when travelling. The interests of that citizen are at best partially satisfied by the partial advances of Hercules, the Swede and friends in a subset of the relations between legality and its wider social context. The citizen of *Legality's Borders* demands more: a wider relational approach, with better integration, resulting in a concept of law whose claim to be descriptive-explanatory is grounded in a clear account of the responsiveness the theory owes to social evidence, and fidelity to its goal of clarification such that practicality, normativity and comprehensiveness demands can each be given their proper space and no more. In a phrase, the ordinary citizen of the twenty-first century demands 'contextualized conceptual explanation' whose deployment of Hart's relational approach renews analytical jurisprudence in a way which overcomes its narrowness and over-breadth while acknowledging the limits of analytical jurisprudence and the value of other theoretical and empirical approaches to law.

CONTEXTUALIZED CONCEPTUAL EXPLANATION

In this section we shall explain the nature and role of the kind of contextualized conceptual explanation we suppose needs to be developed. This type of explanation is a continuation of the approach begun in *Legality's Borders*. There we sought to develop a 'bottom-up' phenomena-sensitive explanation in which our account of legality as agglomerations of institutions of law operated as a kind of radar or detection device. Our inter-institutional account is capable of detecting manifestations of legality in both familiar areas of social life such as the law-state, and in less familiar areas of trans- and super-state legality. That account is intended as one kind of contribution to the broadest possible picture of law, surfacing for further examination several instances of legality given insufficient attention by contemporary analytical jurisprudence. The difference between our inter-institutional theory and our present effort is usefully expressed by way of a spatial metaphor: where our inter-institutional theory enables detection of peaks and promontories of legality on the terrain of social life, this book and contextualized conceptual explanation aim to enrich our account of those promontories by beginning to examine the relations between legality as found there, and other social forces salient from the perspective of our ordinary citizen who travels and finds legality in the law-state, intra-state, trans-state and super-state situations we have previously characterized. The resulting conceptual explanation is contextualized in three ways. First, in our advancing the relational approach towards previously underexamined relations between law and other social phenomena, we aim to be responsive to social phenomena salient from the point of view of the ordinary citizen who travels, undertaking what in *Legality's Borders* we called 're-socializing a descriptive-explanatory view of law'.[23] Contextualized conceptual explanation aims in this way to fill the hole left by overly narrow theorizing generating a distorted general jurisprudence whose claims to descriptive-explanatory relevance are at best difficult to credit, as discussed above. Second, our use of an expanded relational approach is intended to contribute to contextualized conceptual explanation by conducting a history-sensitive style of analysis, not just narrowly sensitive to legal history or the history of salient social phenomena in relation to legality, but to the fact that our concepts have histories as they have evolved in our understanding and as reflections of practice. Third, our expanded relational approach is contextualized in the sense that it follows and is complementary to our inter-institutional analysis, and is situated as one component of a broader conceptual-explanatory context, in which we claim we are not liable for direct response to practicality, normativity and comprehensiveness demands, yet we accept that we are reasonably held liable for the intersection of our view with theories responding directly to those demands. It will be characteristic of this expanded relational approach that it produces a concept of law which is vague, yet tolerably vague, as the story of law's relations to salient social forces is a story of a dynamic concept constantly under renewal in response to novel phenomena.

The remainder of this chapter is devoted to exploration of these three aspects of contextualized conceptual explanation, motivated by the shortcomings of analytical theory, identified as a kind of narrowness in engagement of social phenomena, mistaken inference to generality from that limited set of data, and failure to situate analytical theory relative to other reasonable demands made of legal theory considered *in toto* and not just in its pre-censorial, clarificatory and expository mode. The very last part of this chapter will discuss the particular relations we propose to engage in later chapters as a way to broaden the phenomenal basis of analytical legal theory. It will be useful to approach that discussion via further consideration of the sense in which contextualized conceptual explanation is historically sensitive and self-consciously a partial contribution to the broadest possible picture of legality, by way of beginning to

[23] Culver and Giudice, *Legality's Borders*, pp. 184–185.

respond to the problem of unselfconscious abstractness evident in analytical legal theory to date.

HISTORY

Analytical jurisprudence has long attempted to take history seriously in various ways, but those attempts have been arguably unselfconscious: history has mattered as an input to jurisprudential reasoning, not as an aspect of it. We propose a broader role for history in contextualized conceptual explanation, understanding that the concept of law and subordinate concepts have a more than etymological history, and that this history matters to the way we understand them now, particularly when aiming at something like a universal concept of law applicable to all societies at all times. Let us explain this claim *in situ*. One of the problems which has vexed analytical legal philosophy is understanding of the nature of legal obligation – how laws obligate, why subjects obey laws and so forth. A typical analytical approach to the question of the nature of legal obligation is to examine first the meaning of obligation, and then to rely on that rich understanding of the meaning of the concept to try to understand the place of that concept in the surrounding web of legal concepts such as duty and permission. Lon Fuller, for example, writes of fidelity to law as a kind of translation of the attitude of acceptance of law, and builds the notion of faith, the Latin *fide*, into the account of how law presents itself to subjects in a way which secures their acceptance.[24] Hart contributes the observation that 'obligation' seems to have its roots in the Latin *ligare*, to bind, and works from there towards ideas developed in a better known, and likely better worked fashion by Joseph Raz, in his understanding of legal norms as a special variety of exclusionary reasons.[25] Yet all of this seems to be a half-step where a full step is needed. Some concepts have deeper historical roots than others, and the changes some concepts undergo over the course of their history may reflect special characteristics of that concept. Those special characteristics may in

[24] L. Fuller, *The Morality of Law*, 2nd edn (New Haven, CT: Yale University Press, 1969), pp. 38–41.

[25] See H. L. A. Hart, *The Concept of Law*, 2nd edn (Oxford: Clarendon Press, 1994), p. 87; Hart, 'Commands and authoritative reasons', in *Essays on Bentham* (Oxford: Clarendon Press, 1982), pp. 243–268. See also J. Raz, *The Authority of Law*, 2nd edn (Oxford: Oxford University Press, 2009); Raz, 'Authority, law and morality', *The Monist*, 68 (1985), pp. 295–324; Raz, 'Authority and justification', *Philosophy and Public Affairs*, 14 (1985), pp. 3–29; Raz, 'Postscript to the second edition: rethinking exclusionary reasons', in *Practical Reason and Norms*, 2nd edn (Princeton, NJ: Princeton University Press, 1990), pp. 178–199; Raz, 'Explaining normativity: on rationality and the justification of reason', *Ratio*, 12 (1999), pp. 354–379; Raz, *Engaging Reason* (Oxford: Oxford University Press, 2000).

turn require special handling in any understanding of that concept and the conditions under which it is applied. Legal obligation seems to us to be one of these concepts whose historical career presents variations in meaning which are more than surface deep.

Understanding obligation as rooted in *ligare*, a binding tie, may capture a subtly yet importantly different dimension of the practice thought to be represented by descriptive-explanatory accounts of lived experience which inform the concept. To understand choice of conduct consistent with legal obligation as a choice to which one is bound is to invoke a metaphor which captures a sense of helpless involuntariness, and a constraint imposed from without. It may well be true that this understanding of legal obligation, built out of Roman use of *obligatio* generated from *ligare*, represents adequately the historical development of one use of the term and one contribution of experience to the shared concept. Yet this understanding may be unduly narrow, and a poor basis for an understanding of the concept of legal obligation as part of a broader understanding of adjoining legal concepts of permission, duty and so forth. In Bertram Wyatt-Brown's essays on the ideal of honour in the antebellum American South,[26] he remarks on the arguments made by pre-revolution Americans seeking some form of self-rule that taxes sought by the English crown 'were supposed to be considered as "free gifts", and as such could be offered only by the elected representatives of those who possessed the property thus given'.[27] As Edmund Morgan reads Wyatt's argument, 'In depriving them of the sole right to tax themselves, the right to offer whatever they gave in taxes as a free gift to their king, Parliament deprived them of honour'[28] and collapsed the relationship which served as the precondition of a legal obligation to pay tax. These pre-revolution Americans seem to have understood legal obligation as something quite different from an externally imposed tie that binds. For these Americans, legal obligation sprung from an internally generated sense of honour as the autonomously chosen, internally generated entering into a liberty-limiting obligation. Any externally coerced compliance to some norm was to be resisted as strongly as possible.

We do not aim to suggest that either of these examples – *ligare* or free 'gifts' – illustrates the uniquely correct understanding of the concept of legal obligation, yet at the same time we do not wish to discard either one as an historical anomaly. It may be possible to integrate these ideas into some part

[26] B. Wyatt-Brown, *The Shaping of Southern Culture* (Chapel Hill: University of North Carolina Press, 2000). See also E. Morgan's review 'The price of honour', New York Review of Books, XLVIII, No. 9 (31 May 2001), pp. 36–38.

[27] Morgan, 'Price of Honour', p. 37.

[28] Ibid.

of the contemporary analytical account of legal obligations as a special kind of reason, excluding other reasons for action, and accepted in that role for any reason at all, as Hart supposes, or because the exclusionary reason expresses some normally justified course of action, as Raz supposes. Yet even if these ideas cannot be incorporated into the contemporary account, it is far from clear that we are justified in discarding one as anomalous or an outlier and simply picking the other, perhaps *ligare*, as the etymologically nearest cousin to what we mean by legal obligation today. At least two options are opened by the historical wariness we think ought to be characteristic of an appropriately contextualized conceptual explanation. We might choose to modify the account of legal obligations as exclusionary reasons accepted by legal subjects for certain kinds of reasons, choosing to understand historical accounts of the binding force of legal obligations as indications of contextually variable perceptions of what counts as a normal reason for action, capable of bearing special force once recognized as a legal reason for action. Or we might choose to revisit the adequacy of this account of legal obligations. We might recognize that the contemporary social situation reflected in doctrines such as Raz's exclusionary reasons approach to legal obligation is itself a historical product concerned with a concept which is evolving through its use. Or we might imagine still further options for response. Yet doing nothing about the deep historical roots of these varying ideas about legal obligation would be a mistake which we ought to resist on the grounds that doing so would lead into acceptance of an undesirable descriptive-explanatory dissonance: we ought not to accept those pictures of legal obligation which capture some aspect of contemporary practice while making it difficult or impossible for us to understand at the same time the practice of legal obligation in these historical contexts. Laws are conventional products, and the conventions which produce them have histories which are part of a full understanding of the product. Historically sensitive, perhaps historically 'inclusive' theorizing may result in an understanding of the concept which is capacious and vague as it incorporates quite different societies and times, but that is scarcely an objection if possession of that concept enables us to understand better the very wide variety of ways of living life under law, avoiding the well-known trap of undue narrowness giving rise to Hercules, the Swede and the Fu-Fu fly.

THE CONTEXTUALIZED CONCEPT IN LEGAL THEORY AS A WHOLE

Having gone this far to emphasize the importance of history in understanding the meaning of concepts, we must be clear that our contextualized approach to the concept of law requires further methodological innovation beyond recognition that concepts do not arrive history-free. The second element of contextualized conceptual explanation is derived from an argument one of us made in a characterization of H. L. A. Hart's picture of the concept of law.[29] That argument attributed to Hart what Culver called 'relational legal positivism', a method of concept-reconstruction which begins from what might be called a folk understanding of the concept of law, and builds a dynamic, changeable concept out of its relations to other phenomena.[30] This concept of law is a kind of reflection of changes beneath it, a concept modified according to the results of ebbing and flowing changes in life under law. This approach, which Hart once recognized as 'hermeneutic',[31] has been taken up by some analytical theorists, including, for example, Jules Coleman, whose support of a pragmatic method for analytical legal philosophy extends to acceptance of the need for our concepts to be revisable, and continuous with the social sciences, while not being supplanted by them.[32] Coleman's powerful pragmatism is, however, hampered by a lack of clarity about its place relative to the normativity, practicality and comprehensiveness demands. His assertion that the pragmatic method is always responsive to all of these concerns seems to leave his theory aiming to capture absolutely everything, which is plainly at odds with the nearly total absence of empirical data in his analysis, and his use of abstract devices such as the Swede, nominally independent of particular legal systems. Contextualized conceptual explanation aims to improve upon Coleman's pragmatism by being clear about its sources, the limits of its aims, and clear about the reasons why those aims are properly sought using the descriptive-explanatory relational approach. This analysis recognizes the incompleteness of the relational approach as a way of understanding social phenomena, and rests its value on the clarificatory power it can bring to our otherwise potentially confused understandings of the concept of law and subordinate legal concepts, all contributing to the widest possible understanding of the promise and limits of law as a mode of organizing social life. This limits the relational approach and contextualized concept of law to a role which is admittedly impractical and non-comprehensive. Contextualized conceptual explanation recognizes that it is not an attempt to provide the best

[29] Culver, 'Leaving the Hart-Dworkin debate'.

[30] On the general idea of modifying and constructing concepts in legal theory, see Michael Giudice, *Understanding the Nature of Law* (Cheltenham: Edward Elgar Press, 2015).

[31] See N. MacCormick, *H.L.A. Hart*, 2nd edn (Oxford: Oxford University Press, 2008), pp. 46 and 184, and P. M. S. Hacker, 'Hart's philosophy of law', in P. M. S. Hacker and J. Raz (eds), *Law, Morality, and Society* (Oxford: Clarendon Press, 1977).

[32] Coleman, *Practice*, p. 201. See also B. Leiter, *Naturalizing Jurisprudence* (Oxford: Oxford University Press, 2007), Part II.

comprehensive theory of law as a whole, and remains agnostic regarding the character of non-philosophical investigations best suited to carrying out empirical and local-level theoretical investigations which inform the project of conceptual explanation. Investigations in sociology and anthropology of law, for example, are welcomed by contextualized conceptual explanation, yet this type of explanation holds no particular view regarding the methodology of sociology or anthropology. This explanation is nonetheless cautiously universal about the concept of law, in the sense of attempting to construct a universally applicable concept. The constructive power of the contextualized concept of law is derived from two dimensions of its method, together with a careful admission about its explanatory limits. Contextualized conceptual explanation understands through its sensitivity to history that while legal philosophy can be concerned with general or universal concepts, life under law is fundamentally local. Historical sensitivity allows contextualized conceptual explanation to recognize the historical variability of legal practices. This might be called the vertical richness of contextualized conceptual explanation, matched by the horizontal reach of the relational method, whose focus in Hart's hands on relations between law and coercion, morality, and social rules required us to look broadly at the function of what is said to be law and persuades us away from excessive reliance on observed data from particular situations which are local both to a particular legal culture and to a particular time. The relational method reminds us to look beyond the massive figures of judges in Anglo-American legal life to other officials and other experiences of life under law, and to avoid moving too quickly from local experience, particularly judicial experience and constitutional experience, to general conclusions about the nature of the concept of law. In this way contextualized conceptual explanation occupies a middle ground which admits the importance of local experience, yet attempts also to widen our understanding of that experience. This analysis reminds us of the importance of history to concept-formation, and the importance of working broadly and thoroughly with local investigations to constantly re-inform the concept of law. The resulting concept is contextualized because it is inclusive of a wide range of experience of life under law, yet it is admittedly theoretically and practically thin because it is a reflection of empirical investigations and locally situated conceptual investigations (into, e.g., interpretive principles accepted by judges in the context of Canadian Charter adjudication).

The historically sensitive, partial contribution to general jurisprudence made by the contextualized concept may ultimately be a vague concept whose edges are not easily delineated. This vagueness is, however, both tolerable and expected of a concept emerging from relational study, and serving as a constantly revised conceptual backdrop for understanding of life under law, a prelude or constant accompaniment to normatively committed and social scientific investigations of law. Unsurprisingly, then, given the emergent, reconstructed character of this clarificatory concept, it is not the only one. It is the particular result of one method calculated to reveal law as it is for the sake of the ordinary citizen who travels, pulling off the mask of law not by being practical or comprehensive, but by filling the gap between practically oriented, often judicially focussed legal philosophy, and general accounts of the logic of norms. Contextualized conceptual explanation is then truly a middle way, its virtues identifiable only through its co-operation with accompanying investigations. It is nonetheless a powerful middle way, since it opens the possibility of analytical legal philosophy coming to terms with changes in social life judged by our observer's perspective in a world where the importance of law's morality, social rules, and coercion is changed, and changing. In the pluralist world inhabited by our citizen who travels, law's relation to morality is far more varied and complex than the relation claimed by Lord Devlin in the Hart–Devlin debate as he celebratedly claimed that a sense of sin in a society where morality and religion are conjoined is essential to effective administration of criminal law.[33] The social rules to which our ordinary citizen is subject may be no more logically complex than those of Hart's generation, but the diversity of their sources and their force is ever-more bewildering in the globalizing world. And while the relation between law and coercion remains of fundamental interest as a persistent question, the way in which the ordinary citizen experiences this question has likely changed, as our citizen's mobility enables both evasion and sudden meetings with coercion.

CONCLUSION

The aim of this chapter has been to launch a renewed research agenda for analytical jurisprudence, advocating a return to an expanded version of Hart's descriptive-explanatory, relational approach to characterization of the concept of law. In bringing this approach to bear on law's relation to environment, security and technology in later chapters, we aim simultaneously to offer a contextualized concept of law relevant to the interests of contemporary inquirers, and to redirect explanatory efforts away from an excessively narrow focus

[33] 'As a judge who administers the criminal law and who has often to pass sentence in a criminal court, I should feel handicapped in my task if I thought that I was addressing an audience which had no sense of sin or which thought of crime as something quite different'. P. Devlin, *The Enforcement of Morals* (Oxford: Oxford University Press, 1965), p. 4.

on the phenomena of adjudication, towards a broader range of phenomena from which a broad concept of law may be abstracted, adequately reflective of the full range of relevant empirical phenomena. This contextualized concept of law may additionally put old problems in fresh perspective, encouraging us to see, for example, the questions of continuity and identity as pressing matters. A contextualized concept of law responsive to the concerns of our modern citizen may escape from the illusion fostered by state-centred jurisprudence that the continuous, identity-stable state is legality's standard manifestation, whose interior needs further investigation while its exterior shell – its continuity of identity – may be taken for granted. As we begin to develop a contextualized concept of law via our investigation of new relations, the question of identity and continuity of legal orders gains a renewed prominence it has not had since the early 1970s, when John Finnis investigated identity and continuity in decolonization of Africa, in his 'Revolutions and the Continuity of Law'.[34] Pessimists might view this as analytical legal theory coming full circle in its enthusiasms, looking once again to the phenomena of revolution as a reason to engage the persistent question of the identity and continuity of legal order. Optimists like us see the possibility of new and better answers to the persistent question, which is not just persistent but of new importance in the new era of the state made unsteady not just by revolution but by other developments as well. The relation of law to coercion, explored by Finnis as the relation of law to security, remains important to our worldly citizen, albeit increasingly at the scale of a given legal order, and not just legal obligation by legal obligation in a single law-state. As the state's role as a law-giver is increasingly shared with other legal orders, and those orders and the state's role in the community of legal orders is affected by changing relations between law and environment, and law and technology, the question of the identity and continuity of legal orders is justifiably regarded as demanding attention at least equal to that historically given the persistent questions of the nature of municipal legal systems and legal obligation within them, and the relation of legality in that context to morality, coercion and social rules. If we succeed in subsequent chapters in carrying out the research agenda we have advocated in this introductory chapter, via a renewed relational approach taking the persistence of legal orders as a major challenge to descriptive-explanatory legal theory, we may contribute to the destruction of the fiction of the centrality of the state to the nature of legality, and in that way, contribute one step to pulling the mask off law. In the

[34] J. Finnis, 'Revolutions and continuity of law', in *Philosophy of Law*, vol. IV (Oxford: Oxford University Press, 2011), pp. 407–435.

next chapter we shall begin the particular project of this book of reconstruction and modification of the state- and system-centred approach of analytical legal theory by assessing the extent to which legal pluralist challenges to such an approach are successful in destabilizing the long prominent role of state legal systems in understanding the existence and character of law.

2

Making Old Questions New

Legality, Legal System and State

From the first steps of what is now regarded as the analytical tradition of legal theory, from Hobbes to Hart and beyond, analytical legal theorists have long taken the law of the sovereign state as the primary example of legality.[1] Their theories of the nature of law have been firmly rooted in what Joseph Raz has described as the 'assumption of the importance of municipal law', which 'reflects our, or at least my, intuitive perception that municipal legal systems are sufficiently important and sufficiently different from most other normative systems to deserve being studied for their own sake'.[2] On this widely shared view, state legality is sufficiently prominent and familiar that its correct explanation also serves as a criterion of adequacy for any general theory of law.

The power of this view rests on much more than the intuitive perception that modern municipal legal systems are important and distinctive. Post-Westphalian sovereign states and their operation of systems of laws have in fact played a dominant role in shaping forms of social life – the organization of political communities, markets, educational practices and so on. No theoretical study of social life can ignore the role of the law-state without opening itself to serious objections as to its completeness. Yet at the same time it is clear that the role of the law-state in social life can be overstated, or simply given more than due attention at the expense of an adequately comprehensive

[1] By way of admitting that this is identification of a dominant trend to which there has been some opposition, it is worth noting Hans Kelsen as an exception. See H. Kelsen, *Principles of International Law*, 2nd edn (Toronto, Canada: Holt, Rinehart and Winston, 1966). Also, a note on terminology: for the most part we will use 'legality', instead of 'law', to emphasize the variety of types of social situations which display elements of legal order or lawfulness. 'Law', we believe, is too strongly associated with the idea of state law and so for this reason is undesirable. On the elements of legality and legal order, see K. Culver and M. Giudice, *Legality's Borders* (Oxford: Oxford University Press, 2010), Chapter 4.

[2] J. Raz, *The Authority of Law*, 2nd edn (Oxford: Oxford University Press, 2009), p. 105.

and nuanced account of contemporary social life. In recent years analytical legal theory has been charged with just this sort of overstatement of the importance of the law-state to characterization of social life. Legal pluralists such as William Twining and Brian Tamanaha, for example, who are deeply knowledgeable about analytical jurisprudence, have repeatedly pointed out that state legality is simply one variety of legality, and has only ever been one variety of legality amongst others.[3] Twining and Tamanaha both maintain that the existence of other varieties of legality demonstrates the limited scope of analytical jurisprudence, and further, shows why its aim to provide a general theory of law is likely misguided. Where analytical legal theory seeks to explain the essence or nature of law as an ultimately unitary or monolithic phenomenon intrinsically linked to the career of the law-state, no such phenomenon exists in law's actual habitat. Instead observers find only diversity of phenomena and diverse legal concepts serving diverse purposes.[4] This may be called the legal pluralist challenge to state-centred theories of legality.[5]

To date the legal pluralist challenge has elicited little interest and little reaction from analytical and state-centred legal theorists.[6] It might even be

3 See W. Twining, *Globalization and Legal Theory* (London: Butterworths, 2000); Twining, *General Jurisprudence* (Cambridge: Cambridge University Press, 2009); B. Tamanaha, *A General Jurisprudence of Law and Society* (Oxford: Oxford University Press, 2001); and Tamanaha, 'Understanding legal pluralism: past to present, local to global', *Sydney Law Review*, 30 (2008), pp. 375–411.

4 Tamanaha writes: 'The long history of failed attempts at articulating an essentialist concept of law should be taken as instructive – there is something wrong with the ways in which the question of what law is has been posed and answered. The source of the intractable difficulty lies in the fact that law is a thoroughly cultural construct. What law is and what law does cannot be captured in any single concept, or by any single definition. Law *is* whatever we attach the label *law* to, and we have attached it to a variety of multifaceted, multifunctional phenomena: natural law, international law, state law, religious law, and customary law on the general level, and an almost infinite variety on the specific level, from lex mercatoria to the state law of Massachusetts and the law of the Barotse, from the law of Nazi Germany to the Nuremberg Trials, to the Universal Declaration of Human Rights and the International Court of Justice. Despite the shared label 'law', these are diverse phenomena, not variations of a single phenomenon, and each one of these does many different things and/or is used to do many things. There is no law *is* . . . ; there are these kinds of law and those kinds of law; there are these phenomena called law and those phenomena called law; there are these manifestations of law and those manifestations of law. No wonder, then, that the multitude of concepts of law circulating in the literature have failed to capture the essence of law – it has no essence'. Tamanaha, *A General Jurisprudence*, p. 193.

5 For other types of challenges to essentialist theorizing about law, see D. Priel, 'Jurisprudence and necessity', *Canadian Journal of Law and Jurisprudence*, 20 (2007), pp. 173–200, and B. Leiter, 'Beyond the Hart/Dworkin debate: the methodology problem in jurisprudence', *American Journal of Jurisprudence*, 48 (2003), pp. 17–51.

6 For a recent exception, see W. Waluchow, 'Legality's frontier', *Transnational Legal Theory*, 1 (2010), pp. 575–585.

wondered whether there really is any challenge to be met. The debate between state-centred legal theory and legal pluralism might not really be a debate at all, and might instead be better read as an awkward comparison of two different kinds of theories addressing two very different subject-matters. State-centred legal theory, it might be said, is analytical in method and focussed on the most general possible explanation of state legal systems, even at the occasional cost of declaring some phenomena to be outliers. Legal pluralism, by contrast, can be said to use analytical tools of the same sort, yet in its sensitivity to diversity of legal phenomena, legal pluralism is more content to tolerate conceptual-explanatory tensions while capturing descriptively the widest possible range of diverse manifestations of legality at all levels of social organization. We may have found a new Janus-faced figure in jurisprudence: to assert that legal theory captures legality is to say that analytical theorists look abstractly in one direction, asking how general a theory of municipally originating law can be, while legal pluralists look pointedly in another, asking what municipally originating legal theory might be overlooking.

Could this really be the end of the matter? Possibly so, but even if this is the end, such a conclusion can only be asserted once the legal pluralist challenge has been taken seriously. Our investigation will show that the Janus-faced image is quite misleading: there is in fact much to gain from close comparison of legal pluralism with state-centred analytical legal theory. The comparison shows more points of common orientation than might be initially supposed, and more importantly for our purposes as defenders of a variety of analytical approach, the comparison shows that the presumptive centrality of state legality to analytical jurisprudence ought to be reconsidered, and can be reconsidered without damage to the enduring insights of analytical legal theory.

Here is our plan. First, we shall identify three characteristic features of the core commitments of state-centred legal theory and contrast those commitments with the legal pluralist challenge to them. The second part of the chapter examines the ways in which the legal pluralist challenge – regardless of its independent merits as a theory of law – shows that state-centred legal theory is incomplete on own its terms. We intend to show in particular that state-centred legal theory lacks a satisfactory solution to the problem of the continuity of legal systems because it lacks an adequate explanation of the relation between law and state. Third, we will then take some initial steps towards specification of the characteristics of an adequate account of the relation between law and state. Here legal pluralist insights are most relevant, and show most clearly the limitations of state-centred legal theory. In the fourth part of our discussion we shall identify areas of remaining disagreement between state-centred legal theory and legal pluralism, arguing that the challenge of legal pluralism can be taken seriously even without accepting all of its insights. In particular, we shall argue that even if legal pluralists are ultimately correct in their contention that law does not have an essence, that conclusion requires more support than is provided by the legal pluralist challenge. In the fifth and final part of our discussion we shall attempt to make good on the promise identified in the title of our chapter, showing how some old jurisprudential questions can be made new for the next set of challenges we believe analytical jurisprudence must face.

STATE-CENTRED LEGAL THEORY AND THE LEGAL PLURALIST CHALLENGE

State-centred theorizing about law embodies three main features. The first is so familiar that it risks being regarded as beneath analytical notice: it is the view that the legality of the law-state is a systemic legality. That is, there are no free-floating state laws: all laws in the law-state are members of its system of laws. While there are important variations amongst theorists regarded as members of the analytical camp, all of Bentham, Austin, Kelsen, Hart and Raz agree that legality as found in the law-state is systemic. Raz's expression of this view is particularly instructive. Raz suggests that state legal systems can be identified in terms of three characteristic claims they exhibit: *comprehensiveness*, *supremacy* and *openness*.[7] In attributing claims to legal systems, Raz is not simply personifying what are in fact better regarded as emergent properties of the complex collection of norms and institutions giving rise to a legal system. Rather, on Raz's view, the claims of legal systems are found in the attitudes and practices of a class of law-applying officials and institutions. So the systemic claims of comprehensiveness, supremacy and openness are epiphenomena of the attitudes and practices of law-applying officials and institutions, detectable in their operation of institutions in application of laws. In exhibiting a claim of *comprehensiveness* a legal system (or more properly, its officials in action) claims authority to regulate all aspects of social life within the self-declared boundaries of that system, whether by prohibition, requirement or permission. Legal systems differ in this way from other normative systems, such as sports associations and universities, which have limited purposes and so limited spheres of regulation within their broader social situation and legal system. A claim to *supremacy* can be seen in a legal system's self-understanding that its standards provide the ultimate foundation or authority for all other normative

[7] Raz, *Authority*, pp. 116–120.

standards recognized by the system. In states with a written constitution, the hierarchy of rules and procedures which embodies a legal system's claim to supremacy is readily apparent: constitutions typically claim to be the supreme law of the state, and authorize and empower institutions and officials to create, vary and extinguish laws. A claim to supremacy can also be detected in the way a legal system views conflicts between its legal norms and other types of normative standards. Where legal norms conflict with religious norms or moral norms, for example, legal norms hold priority unless otherwise stipulated by the legal system, whose authority over such special stipulations preserves and demonstrates its claim to supremacy. Finally, a legal system typically claims to be *open*: the norms of other systems – e.g., sports leagues, trade unions, universities, etc. – can be supported by legal systems and 'adopted' or certified as permitted to operate in certain ways within a given legal system. Examples of such certification include use of legislation to establish subsequently largely self-governing institutions such as universities or professional bodies. Examples of adoption are most typically seen when norms of other systems are applied by courts to resolve disputes arising within their own systems.[8] Taken together, the features of comprehensiveness, supremacy and openness serve well to explain the way in which, as Raz puts it, 'we feel that legal systems not only happen to be the most important institutionalized system governing human society, but that that is part of their nature'.[9]

The state-centred view's identification of the law-state with systemic legality does not, as the 'openness' claim demonstrates, preclude the state-centred view from forming further views about non-state forms of legality which might exist within, between or across states. Such views make up the second main feature of state-centred legal theory as it views all other forms of legality from the perspective of the presumptively basic form and perspective of state legality. This view typically results in either an adverse comparison identifying non-state legality as deficient in one way or another or revelation that what appears to be non-state legality is in fact ultimately authorized by and so a creature of state legality. For example, both Hart and Kelsen thought that international legality was a defective kind of state legality. In Hart's view, international legality lacked a system-constituting rule of recognition, and so amounted to a primitive or non-systemic form of legality. Kelsen also thought that international

8 Ibid., p. 120. Raz also views conflict of laws cases in terms of the relation of adoption, in which domestic courts apply the norms of a foreign system to resolve a dispute, but without the foreign norms thereby becoming part of the domestic system.

9 Ibid., p. 116. Here we are only presenting Raz's view of state law, and we ought to note that we do not think it is true that all state legal systems exhibit claims of comprehensiveness, supremacy, and openness. Federal systems, e.g., pose a particular problem. See Culver and Giudice, *Legality's Borders*, Chapter 2.

legality was primitive, though mainly because it lacked effective centralized institutions of enforcement. Yet this assessment of international legality did not rule out the possibility, via the openness characteristic of the law-state's systemic legality, that at least some of what is called international law might be or become legal via support in the form of state practice or recognition.[10] For example, there seems to be nothing in Hart's account of a rule of recognition which would rule out the possibility that a state legal system's rule of recognition might come to include religious, international, transnational, Aboriginal or customary legality amongst its authoritative sources of law.[11]

The third feature of state-centred legal theory is its view, manifested in the tendencies of state-centred legal theorists, that state legality is not just sufficiently important to warrant study, but so central that study and explanation of inherently systemic state legality amounts to study and explanation of the nature or essence of law full stop. This view is readily apparent in the views of Austin, Hart and Raz. In *The Province of Jurisprudence Determined*, for example, Austin proceeds by narrowing the class of true law[12] (laws 'properly so called') until he settles on the theory that only commands issued by state sovereigns are laws. And where Austin thought that he had found the 'key to the science of jurisprudence' in the idea of a command, Hart sought to show that the real 'key' lies in the union of primary and secondary rules, amongst which there is a single rule of recognition which validates all the norms of the legal system and claims supremacy.[13] Notice that neither Austin nor Hart specified or qualified their claims as claims to have found the key to the science of jurisprudence of state legality; they appear content for their views to be understood as scoping over all legality. It remains possible, of course, to suppose on a charitable reading of Austin, Hart and Raz that they have simply *chosen* to focus exclusively on state legality without much emphasis of the fact of that choice. These choices have nonetheless had the tendency of over-reaching and turning into claims about the nature or essence of law,[14] or what might

[10] Roger Cotterrell puts the assumption like this: 'all law is created by the state or derives authority and validity from its recognition by agencies of the state, and that its guarantee is its enforceability by the state'. R. Cotterrell, 'Transnational communities and the concept of law', *Ratio Juris*, 21 (2008), p. 10.

[11] See N. MacCormick, *Questioning Sovereignty* (Oxford: Oxford University Press, 1999).

[12] Sometimes with surprising results. Constitutional law, e.g., was only really positive morality. See J. Austin, *The Province of Jurisprudence Determined* (New York: Prometheus, 2000), pp. 253–261. On this score Austin's view has been echoed more recently by theorists wishing to deny legal status to negotiated or cooperative orders. See S. Roberts, 'After government? On representing law without the state', *The Modern Law Review*, 68 (2005), pp. 1–24.

[13] H. L. A. Hart, *The Concept of Law*, 3rd edn (Oxford: Oxford University Press, 2012), Chapters 5 and 6.

[14] See Tamanaha on 'analytical imperialism'. Tamanaha, *A General Jurisprudence*, p. 146.

be overly quick dismissal of those who aim to take non-state legal phenomena seriously. It is precisely this combination of state-based over-reaching and under-sensitivity to additional *prima facie* legal phenomena that legal pluralists contend has severely limited the scope of analytical jurisprudence.

It may seem from the preceding discussion that exactly those aspects of the state-centred analytical view of legality which enable it to characterize systemic yet absorptive state legality are at the same time weaknesses of the view in the event that it can be shown that there really are non-state legal phenomena whose legality cannot plausibly be attributed to state-sponsored certification, temporary adoption or similar processes. Legal pluralists assert just this challenge, contending that state-centred analytical legal theory proceeds with two crucial – and ultimately mistaken – assumptions in the construction of general theories of law: (1) that all law is either contained in or traceable back to an authorizing law-state[15] and (2) that for the purposes of analysis, states are stable and their legal systems have meaningful boundaries, which is to say that legal norms operating in a given legal system are only those authorized by the given state legal system. As legal pluralists attempt to demonstrate with observationally available evidence, both recent and historical phenomena cast significant doubt on these assumptions.

Since the emergence of legal pluralism as a theoretical approach in the hands of anthropologists studying social life in colonial and post-colonial states, it has been widely adopted by socio-legal theorists to explain law within and across states in a variety of contexts. Indeed, legal pluralism is used to explain the diversity and interaction of all forms and levels of social order.[16] Amongst legal pluralists, Twining and Tamanaha are perhaps most relevant to investigation of the possibly Janus-faced relation between legal pluralism and analytical jurisprudence, in significant part because both begin from and are well aware of the explanatory merits of analytical approaches. Two main features of their views are useful to understanding the contrasting approaches of legal pluralism and analytical jurisprudence. Both Twining and Tamanaha maintain (1) that a general jurisprudence, to be genuinely general, must take as its subject matter legality wherever and whenever it exists, and since state legality is only one kind of legality, it cannot be given any special theoretical priority. In this way, both Twining and Tamanaha are *pluralists about the sources or types of legality*. Twining and Tamanaha also both maintain (2) that the diversity of sources and types of legality makes it impossible or at least

[15] This assumption goes hand in hand with the assumption that states divide the normative order of the world without remainder and with the view that state legal systems necessarily claim supremacy.

[16] For a recent and useful overview of legal pluralist literature, see Tamanaha, 'Understanding legal pluralism'.

unproductive to settle on an essence or nature of law: legality's manifestations are simply too diverse.[17] In this way, both Twining and Tamanaha are *pluralists about the concept of law itself*.

As we remarked earlier, it is relatively easy at this point to see how the conversation between state-centred legal theorists and legal pluralists might come to an end and settle into an agreement to co-habit within the metaphor of a new kind of Janus-faced jurisprudence. In this co-habitation, state-centred legal theorists might insist that state legality is still very much prominent, yet still incompletely understood so warranting the continued centrality of the law-state in legal theory (though it might be more accurate to call itself a theory of state legality[18]). Legal pluralists in this context might be said to simply exhibit a different preference, maintaining that all forms of legality ought to be explored in a general jurisprudence. Each approach's conclusions about the nature of legality would of course be very different, but only because the two types of theories began with very different aims and subject-matters.

Our central concern here is not with the possibility of a genuinely general theory of law, so we shall leave that question to one side as we consider more thoroughly an avenue of investigation opened by consideration of the metaphor of a Janus-faced discipline of jurisprudence. Here we shall investigate whether the legal pluralist challenge to the analytical assumption of the fundamentally systemic nature of legality raises an explanatory challenge for analytical theory, as it encounters the question of continuity of legal systems over time. We take up this question in part because legal pluralists have drawn attention to a tension in analytical approaches as they attempt to reconcile the apparently closed nature of legal systems with conditional openness to absorption or adoption of norms from without, and in part because analytical attention to the phenomena driving this explanation and tension takes the analytical approach closer to legal pluralists' preoccupations with consideration, identification and characterization of diverse forms of legality. The results of the investigation are of immediate relevance to the fate of the Janus-faced standoff between rival approaches to characterization of legality, and eventually, to the possibility of a truly general jurisprudence.

THE PROBLEM OF CONTINUITY OF LEGAL SYSTEMS

As we noted earlier, one of the key features of state-centred legal theory is the view that state legality is always and everywhere systemic. Analytical theorists have developed increasingly sophisticated explanatory devices to capture the

[17] See Twining, *General Jurisprudence*, p. 117, and Tamanaha, *A General Jurisprudence*.
[18] See Tamanaha, *A General Jurisprudence*.

systemic nature of law, deploying the ideas of sovereignty, basic norm, rule of recognition and comprehensiveness, supremacy and openness. These devices are well-suited to static legal systems or those made momentarily stationary for purposes of analysis, enabling explanation of how it is that, at some given moment, the norms and laws of a particular state form one legal system. The explanatory formulae are familiar: norms and laws form one legal system if they are all issued as commands by the sovereign, or authorized by a single basic norm, or validated by a single rule of recognition, or consist of all those standards law-applying institutions are under a duty to apply as standards of the comprehensive, supreme and open legal system.

These explanations are not, however, complete explanations, to the extent that they capture legal systems frozen in time for analysis. The second part of the explanatory task arrives with the question of how to explain the continuity, or dynamic nature of state legal systems. This is a multi-part question of how to identify and explain the conditions under which a legal system comes into existence, persists and ceases to exist as it is displaced by another, falls prey to natural disaster, or another of the perils of social life. As Raz observed in 1998, the problem of continuity remains amongst the unsolved problems of analytical jurisprudence,[19] but not only that, there has been little interest in bridging the gap between explanations of systematic legality in static and dynamic forms.[20] As Raz suggests, interest has simply 'shifted elsewhere'.[21] This lack of interest is somewhat remarkable given widespread acknowledgement of the inability of available theories to provide a solution, a series of failures worth reviewing as a source of salutary lessons regarding the explanatory challenge posed by the problem of continuity.

Austin thought that the conditions of creation, persistence and disintegration of legal systems mirrored the conditions of creation, persistence and disintegration of independent political societies, of which Austin had states primarily in mind. Yet such a view, Raz argues, cannot explain how it is that independent political societies can come to recognize the jurisdiction or legal authority of outside institutions yet still remain meaningfully independent, a possibility which might do well in explaining the character of member states within the European Union.

[19] Though here it might depend on who you ask. John Finnis argues that the problem is unsolvable on the terms set by legal positivism, but a solution is available from natural law theory. See J. Finnis, 'Revolutions and continuity of law', in *Philosophy of Law* (Oxford: Oxford University Press, 2011), pp. 407–435.

[20] J. Raz, 'Two views of the nature of the theory of law: a partial comparison', in *Between Authority and Interpretation* (Oxford: Oxford University Press, 2009), p. 58.

[21] Ibid.

Kelsen thought that the problem of continuity was to be solved by seeing that a legal system's identity and continuity rested with authorization by a historically first constitution. The problem with Kelsen's view, however, is that it does not provide the means to explain how legal systems (such as Canada's) can become independent through legal authorization, such as constitutional devolution of power.[22] Canada, for example, reached its present stage of independence from the United Kingdom by virtue of its *Constitution Act, 1982*, an act of the Canadian Parliament, which established domestic constitutional amendment power and the *Charter of Rights and Freedoms*. The *Constitution Act, 1982*, however, is also Schedule B of the *Canada Act, 1982*, an act passed by the UK Parliament, which grants – or perhaps recognizes – Canada's independence. On Kelsen's view, there are least two possible explanations. The *Constitution Act, 1982* might be considered the historically first constitution of the now independent Canadian legal system. Or it might be the case that Canada does not yet have an independent legal system since its historically first constitution still lies somewhere in the constitutional history of the United Kingdom. The trouble is that there seems to be no way to decide in Kelsen's view between these two very different possibilities.

Hart's views might seem to fare somewhat better than those of Kelsen, as Hart developed one dimension of a solution to the problem of the continuity of law-making rules by introduction of the idea of a rule of recognition, an analytical device whose invention was motivated by observation of the defects of Austin's habit-based account of sovereignty.[23] Surely the idea of a system-constituting rule of recognition, rooted in admittedly dynamic official practices, at least points the way towards explanation of continuity of legal systems? Perhaps not. Raz provides reason to doubt that explanation of the rule of recognition is in part also an explanation of the continuity of legal systems. Hart's explanation is disturbingly thin, Raz explains, exactly where it ought to be thick. Raz asks:

> What changes are consistent with the continued existence of the same rule, and what changes compel the admission that a new rule has replaced the old one? It is easy to bring examples for either situation, as well as examples of borderline cases. However, it is not the existence of borderline cases, which are inevitable, that is disturbing. The disturbing fact is that Hart's theory provides no clue as to *how* to draw the conceptual distinction.[24]

[22] See Finnis, 'Revolutions and continuity of law'.

[23] Recall that in Hart's view, Austin's account of sovereignty, which was based on the habitual obedience of subjects to particular sovereigns, would signal the end of a legal system once a sovereign died, since it would take time for habits of obedience to a new sovereign to form. See Hart, *Concept*, pp. 51–61.

[24] Raz, *Authority*, p. 98.

In Raz's view, the diagnosis of Hart's oversight is simple:

> If his theory fails to provide a complete solution to the problem of identity it is because he overlooked not only part of the answer but also a whole question: that of the relation of law and state.[25]

We will suggest later that Hart's oversight may not actually be a deficiency of his theory, but instead a decisive strength: his apparent omission of explanation of an obviously close tie between legality and the state is in fact a strength enabling his view to more closely approach full-blooded generality as a general jurisprudence. But let us first follow Raz's suggestion further, since his reasons for supposing legality and state systems to be one and the same are relevant to our evaluation of whether analytical legal theory and legal pluralism really are in a Janus-faced relation. If we are to solve the problem of continuity, according to Raz, we must raise the question of the relation of legality and state in a way which avoids the extremes of Austin's and Kelsen's views. Whereas Austin attempted to reduce or define law entirely in terms of political facts of sovereigns, habits of obedience and coercion, Kelsen explained the state entirely in legal terms, as a juristic entity, without reference to political facts of any kind. Raz rejects both views, asserting instead that the solution lies somewhere between them:

> A theory of law must be based, at least partly, on a theory of the state, and denying this has been one of Kelsen's gravest mistakes. A theory of state, however, is partly based on a theory of law – the two are intimately connected.[26]

Raz has not, however, provided a theory of the state which would explain the continuity of legal systems, even while observing, as we noted above, that the problem remains unresolved – a situation which still stands, so far as we are aware.[27] Raz's brief remarks in 1971 on a strategy for solving the problem are nonetheless instructive: 'A state is the political organization of a society, it is a political system that is a subsystem of a more comprehensive social system'.[28] Legal systems, in particular, are themselves sub-systems of the political systems of the states of which they form a part. It follows, then, 'that since the continuity of a legal system is tied to the continuity of the political system, the former

25 Ibid.

26 Ibid., p. 99. But of course Kelsen was never aiming at a social theory of law. If his theory is interpreted in this way, it should not come as a surprise that it will look mistaken.

27 But for a recent account on the relation between law and state, see MacCormick, *Questioning Sovereignty*, Chapter 2.

28 Raz, *Authority*, p. 100.

is affected by the fate of the non-legal norms that happen to form part of the political system concerned'.[29]

In the next section we shall explore some of the assumptions in Raz's suggestion. It will be useful in advance of that discussion to attempt to explore further the meaning of the suggestion, couched as it is in open-textured phrases asserting that there is an 'intimate relation' between law and state, in which the legal system as a 'sub-system' is 'affected by the fate' of norms in the larger political system. Intimacy and fate, in particular, demand further explanation, as they are little in evidence elsewhere in Raz's jurisprudence. These terms connote a kind of blending of interests and purposes characteristic of interdependence: but interdependence of what kind, with what points of connection and bearing on which less-intimate relations with other social and legal systems? It may be initially tempting to think of the relation as quasi-isomorphic, a reflexive relation between two norm systems which likely vary principally in terms of their claim to supreme authority: where a is a norm of the state system with property g, there is a corresponding norm p of the social system with property g; and where there is a norm p of the social system with property g, there is a corresponding norm a of the legal system with property g. So where there is a legal norm that swimming in the lake is permitted, there is a corresponding social norm that swimming in the lake is permitted; and where there is a social norm that swimming in the lake is permitted, there is a corresponding legal norm that swimming in the lake is permitted. While perhaps *prima facie* trivial, this reading of Raz's view is actually revealing to the extent that it asserts a relation of interdependence between social and legal systems which might serve as a reminder in the event of finding a social norm without a corresponding legal norm that one might need to look harder, or question whether the social norm really is a social norm. Yet the relation between social and legal systems cannot be quite so intimate, since as Raz observes in the passage immediately quoted above, the legal system is a 'subsystem of a more comprehensive social system', meaning that the more comprehensive social system is larger so there is no simple one-to-one relation of social to legal norms. The intimacy involved is evidently rather more complex. It may be helpful for at least heuristic, exploratory purposes to conceive of the inter-systemic relation as a variety of supervenience: a non-symmetric supervenience in which properties of the smaller system of authoritative, exclusionary legal norms supervene on the system of non-authoritative, non-exclusionary norms of the larger social system. So for a given state system with norms (a, b, c) exhibiting respectively properties (g, h, i), those norms and their

[29] Ibid.

properties supervene on corresponding norms of the broader social system (*p*, *q*, *r*) exhibiting respectively properties (*g*, *h*, *i*). So *a* swimming in the lake *b* on Sundays *c* may be *g* legally permitted only with *h* supervision and *i* prohibited after dusk, and this situation corresponds to social norms (*p*, *q*, *r*) with properties (*g*, *h*, *i*) permitting supervised Sunday swimming before dark. Yet the supervenience is non-symmetric, to the extent that while the social system may exhibit both supervening associations of legal norms (*a*, *b*, *c*) with corresponding social norms (*p*, *q*, *r*) with common properties (*g*, *h*, *i*), the social system may exhibit further norms which lack corresponding legal norms and properties. So the social system may exhibit, e.g., norms (*l*, *m*, *n*) and associated properties bearing no further relation to the legal system. The supervenience relation between these non-symmetric systems is nonetheless reflexive to the extent that changes to legal system norms and properties supervene on social system norms and properties. If this is a plausible rendering of Raz's view of an 'intimate relation' as in effect an assertion of non-symmetric supervenience of legal systems on their associated social systems, what is perhaps surprising at this juncture is what is left incomplete. An assertion of supervenience is an assertion that for some set of property-bearing objects under consideration, a certain pattern or variation is evident.[30] An assertion of supervenience is not at the same time an explanation of why the supervenience occurs – such an explanation amounts to 'superdupervenience'.[31] Without pushing beyond plausibility the exploratory suggestion that Raz's view is usefully viewed as a kind of assertion of supervenience, it is nonetheless worth noting what application of the distinction between supervenience and superdupervenience helps us to see in the nature and reach of Raz's view. Raz's explanation following assertion of an 'intimate' relation between legal and social systems does not appear to extend on towards superdupervenience, in explanation of the ontological priority of elements of legal or supporting social systems. Nor do his views contain assertions regarding dependence between elements of legal and social systems. This is perhaps sensible to the extent that his view is left open to supervening legal norms' originating in either the legal system or the social system; but it does leave a possible dependency relation unexplained, as the 'intimate relation' explored above does not appear to arrive with any further explanation of how the legal system can be 'affected by the fate' of non-legal norms of the social system. In short, relations of dependence between social

[30] B. McLaughlin and K. Bennett, 'Supervenience', in E. N. Zalta (ed.), *The Stanford Encyclopedia of Philosophy* (2011), esp. Section 3.7. Available at plato.stanford.edu/archives/win2011/entries/supervenience/.

[31] T. Horgan, 'From supervenience to superdupervenience: meeting the demands of a material world', *Mind*, 102 (1993), pp. 555–586.

and legal systems seem to be presumed rather than explained. We are offered a static snapshot of the intimate relationship with little understanding of how it changes, and how, if intimacy collapses, we are to detect that collapse.

THE RELATION BETWEEN LAW AND STATE

We have arrived at a puzzling position. Hart's use of the rule of recognition to account for continuity may be problematic to the extent that it does too little to explain the relation of law and state, but Raz's view sets us only a little ahead, and raises other problems along the way. No analytical legal theorist, it seems, is willing to deny that the continuity of legal systems depends on the continuity of surrounding and encompassing political and social conditions. That is, none want to deny that the existence and persistence of law depends upon political and social facts. Any theory of law which attempts to identify and explain the social nature of law must explain how law sits upon social foundations. And surely if the social conditions of existence of a political community fail, its legal system will fail as well. Yet as preceding analysis showed, if these are plausible explanatory propositions, their plausibility is not an output of Raz's explanation of the relation between law and state via explanation of the interaction between a state legal system and a statewide social and political system. As we saw, while Raz's view states or maps the pattern of shared properties of norms in a state legal system and a social system, he offers no explanation of their interaction with one another, or their interaction with other systems – explanations including, perhaps, how a given social system rejects as an imposter the claim of a non-corresponding legal system to authorize a supervening norm. What is instead evident is that what leads Raz to focus on state legal systems as the object of continuity are his assumptions about the state. In particular, Raz relies on the assumptions that the social and political systems which encompass legal systems and constitute the state must be both (1) unified systems of norms and, more importantly, (2) bounded by state borders. In what follows we shall contend that neither assumption is safe. States sometimes may internally embody multiple and possibly conflicting political and social systems in various relations with one another, and may tend towards fragmentation and instability rather than unity and stability. Even states with meaningfully independent legal systems may depend to a significant extent on the existence and stability of international political and social norms, which themselves might not be systemic, unified and stable.

Let us look within the state first. Is there a social system – a system of norms, in Raz's view – of a state which partly constitutes and is partly constituted by the state's legal system, standing in an 'intimate relation' with the legal system and affecting its fate? Here a number of perplexing questions immediately arise.

First, if there is a social system of norms, is it a system of norms in the same way or sense that a legal system is a system of norms which, as we have noted, claims through the attitudes and actions of norm-applying institutions to be comprehensive, supreme and open? And if it is a system of the same kind, what are its norm-applying institutions determining the membership of the norms of the system?[32] These questions may on reflection seem wrongheaded: perhaps, since the relation between law and state is intimate, we ought not to look for distinct norm-applying institutions of the social system. These social institutions might just be the same institutions as the norm-applying institutions of the legal system. So just as, e.g., courts apply the norms of the legal system, they are also social actors who apply the norms of the social system. This suggestion has more than trivial plausibility to the extent that actors within different institutions may be members of both, as officials in courts applying legal norms are simultaneously members of a broader system of social norms. Yet this suggestion carries an unacceptable explanatory cost, as it seems to leave us with no means of distinguishing the norms of the social system from the norms of the legal system, since we can no longer distinguish these by pointing to their distinct owners and operators. More importantly, this isomorphic relation seems to be inconsistent with the implication of Raz's claim that a legal system is nested in a political system, in turn nested in a social system, supporting a reading of Raz's view as admitting some but likely not complete overlap in the institutions of legal and broader political and social systems. While Raz does not offer anything approaching a theory of social systems confirming this reading, other related remarks are consistent with this reading, as, for example, he suggests that Dicey's constitutional conventions are good examples of non-legal political norms whose continued existence and acceptance matters for the continuity of the legal system.[33] What is distinctive about constitutional conventions is that they are not enforced by courts,[34] but are maintained by a state's political institutions, especially its executive,

[32] Notice that if it were a system of the same kind as a legal system, in every state we would have competing claims of supremacy, as both the social system and the legal system would each be claiming supremacy over each other.

[33] A. V. Dicey, *Introduction to the Study of the Law of the Constitution*, 9th edn (London: Macmillan, 1952), Chapter 14.

[34] Courts will, however, often recognize the existence of conventions. See, e.g., the Canadian patriation reference case *Reference re a Resolution to amend the Constitution*, [1981] 1 S.C.R. 753.

legislature(s), political parties and other actors. Yet even this observation does not deliver an explanation of the systemic character of the social system whose operations affect the fate of the legal system – it remains to be explained just what binds the social system as a system.

Second, we might also wonder whether the social system is really, or necessarily, or entirely a system of *norms*. Raz's discussion of constitutional conventions certainly points in this direction. He also offers as an example of non-legal norms that matter for the continuity of a legal system what he calls 'norms of respect', which are general norms held by society in general, or 'some important sections in the society', 'for at least some of the laws and some authorities'.[35] Yet no explanation of why respect must take the form of a norm or norms is given. It certainly seems possible that attitudes of acceptance and recognition towards the legal norms or legal system, which do not themselves exist as norms,[36] legal or otherwise, could explain how and when legal systems and their norms persist, such that if the attitudes of acceptance and recognition come to an end, so does the legal system. Notice, however, that such attitudes of acceptance and recognition, as a matter of social fact about the existence and continuity of legal systems, are likely very diffuse, as legal systems typically need a very wide social base to exist. The social base likely overlaps but more importantly probably extends beyond the base of legal officials and norm-applying institutions of the legal system.[37]

Third, and most importantly, do these social norms or attitudes always point towards and support the laws of the state legal system? In a stable and well-functioning state, the answer is usually yes; but there are instances where even in relatively stable states the social base of norms and attitudes may additionally or conflictingly support non-state norms. Consider, for example, instances of market-driven norms and industry standards, which depend upon their acceptance and practice by market and industry institutions and businesses. Often these norms are more stringent than state laws,[38] and sometimes they are

[35] Raz, *Authority*, p. 100.

[36] Such attitudes might simply exist as a matter of habit, with no critical or normative features.

[37] For a sample of recent work on questions of popular acceptance and efficacy, see L. Alexander and F. Schauer, 'Rules of recognition, constitutional controversies, and the dizzying dependence of law on acceptance', in M. D. Adler and K. Himma (eds), *The Rule of Recognition and the US Constitution* (Oxford: Oxford University Press, 2009); M. D. Adler, 'Popular constitutionalism and the rule of recognition: whose practices ground US law?', *Northwestern University Law Review*, 100 (2006), pp. 719–805; and G. Postema, 'Conformity, custom, and congruence: rethinking the efficacy of law', in M. H. Kramer et al. (eds), *The legacy of H. L. A. Hart* (Oxford: Oxford University Press, 2008), pp. 45–65.

[38] See, e.g., B. Cashore, 'Legitimacy and the privatization of environmental governance: how non-state market-driven (NSMD) governance systems gain rule-making authority', *Governance: An*

norms of a transnational (and so again, non-state) nature.[39] Consider as well states in which entire regions or sections are effectively self-governing, despite the claims or pretensions of the centralized government and legal system. Tamanaha has written extensively about social life and law in the federated states of Micronesia,[40] and Boaventura de Sousa Santos has observed the relative isolation of favelas in Brazil[41]. In Micronesia indigenous communities operate mainly according to indigenous customary laws, even when these conflict with state laws, and such a social situation is widely recognized and accepted by both state officials and the indigenous communities themselves.[42] Similarly, favelas are effectively governed by internal leaders, not state officials (who rarely venture into such areas), and this relatively stable state of affairs is recognized and accepted by both state officials and the relevant actors in the favelas. In each instance, there are wider social norms which support both state as well as non-state (and sometimes outlaw) norms. What Tamanaha's and Santos's examples have in common is not just identification of the possibility, but in fact evidence of the reality of failure of a state legal system's claims to supremacy and comprehensiveness. (We will explore this theme more fully in the next chapter.)

Now let us turn to the state's external legal-normative environment. It may be easily seen just why the nature of state legal systems might not be adequately explained in isolation from international law, or at least in isolation from an account of international conditions. All principles of sovereignty in international law define or regard sovereign statehood partially in relational terms. For instance, consider the elements of statehood laid out in the Montevideo Convention of 1933, formalizing in a North and South American treaty various elements of sovereignty gradually emerging in practice and state vs. state international litigation, such as the locus classicus *Lotus* case of the Permanent Court of International Justice.[43] Article 1 of the Convention provides that to be a state there must be a territory, a permanent population and an effective government capable of governing the territory and population and

International Journal of Policy and Administration, 15 (2002), pp. 503–529; and B. Cashore, G. Auld, and D. Newsom, *Governing through Markets* (New Haven, CT: Yale University Press, 2004).

39 The lex mercatoria is the best known example.

40 See Tamanaha, *General Jurisprudence*, pp. 145–146.

41 See B. Santos, *Towards a New Common Legal Sense* (London: Butterworths, 2002), pp. 99–162.

42 So we might say that such self-governance and conflicts are preserved by wider social norms, i.e., norms which encompass both state and non-state norms.

43 Available at www.taiwandocuments.org/montevideo01.htm. See also S.S. *Lotus* (Fr. v. Turk.), 1927 P.C.I.J. (ser. A) No. 10 (7 September). Available at www.worldcourts.com/pcij/eng/decisions/1927.09.07_lotus.htm.

entering into international relations.[44] The benefits of sovereignty so conceived include the rights to territorial integrity and freedom from intervention, which arrive with recognition by other states (although such freedom is increasingly becoming subject to institutionally recognized moral conditions, especially human rights conditions[45]). Under this conception of sovereignty, the social practices of surrounding states, especially their recognition and cooperation, matter very much to the existence and operation of state legal systems. There can be little doubt, for example, that the sovereignty of Mexico, and so the existence of its legal system (while perhaps not the content of its particular legal norms, though even here there is likely influence), depends a great deal on the US government's recognition of Mexico's government, borders and citizens, amongst other things. Any social fact account of a state legal system must admit as much: if the practice of recognition of state sovereignty were to end, state legal systems would come to an end as well.[46]

Taken together, these questions amount to a demand for explanation of the various interactions which might occur amongst the elements of the independent and internally unified yet corresponding legal and broader social systems mapped and distinguished by Raz. In the absence of such an explanation, we are left with an account of a momentary legal system, and no means by which to approach the problem of continuity. Perhaps surprisingly, this result is consistent with Raz's own account of at least early iterations of his view: in *The Concept of a Legal System* he restricts his account to investigation of momentary legal systems: 'Apart from a few remarks in this section, this chapter is concerned only with the problem of identity of momentary systems'.[47] More importantly, he explicitly disavows as a task of analytical jurisprudence the investigation of social phenomena needed to explain the interaction between legal and social systems where the former is 'affected by the fate' of the latter, writing somewhat enigmatically of a dependency relation between legal

44 The Montevideo Convention is discussed in A. Buchanan, *Justice, Legitimacy, and Self-Determination* (Oxford: Oxford University Press, 2004), p. 264. On the essentially relational quality of sovereignty, see also T. Endicott, 'The logic of freedom and power', in S. Besson and J. Tasioulas (eds), *The Philosophy of International Law* (Oxford: Oxford University Press, 2010).

45 See, e.g., M. Reisman, 'Sovereignty and human rights in contemporary international law', *American Journal of International Law*, 84 (1990), pp. 866–876. For illuminating discussion, see J. Raz, 'Human rights without foundations', in Besson and Tasioulas, *Philosophy of International Law*, pp. 321–337, and Raz, 'Human rights in the emerging world order', *Transnational Legal Theory*, 1 (2010), pp. 31–47.

46 In fact, where the recognition of the sovereignty of particular states has been withheld, the legal as well as social order of those states often collapses as well.

47 J. Raz, *The Concept of a Legal System*, 2nd edn (Oxford: Clarendon Press, 1980), p. 187.

system and 'social forms': 'The identity of legal systems depends on the identity of the social forms to which they belong'.[48] Exploration of the relation between legal system and broader social system or 'social form' is outwith the responsibilities or capacities of analytical jurisprudence, according to Raz, pressing on to claim that:

> The criterion of identity of legal systems is therefore determined not only by jurisprudential or legal considerations but by other considerations as well, considerations belonging to other social sciences . . . . Not wishing to trespass on other fields, I shall confine myself to the problem of the identity of momentary systems.[49]

While this deference to the methods and insights of other disciplines may seem sensible on general grounds of methodological modesty, Raz's omission of even an attempt to borrow constructively from 'other fields' leaves his view short of precisely the evidence or 'other considerations' needed to transform his account of the legal system-social system relation from map to explanation. In light of this apparent acceptance that resolution of the problem of continuity lies in the hands of others outside analytical jurisprudence, it is quite striking that Raz claims in 1998 that the problem of continuity remains for analytical jurisprudence, and remains unsolved because interest has 'shifted elsewhere'.[50] It is difficult to avoid concluding that Raz aims to have it both ways: to claim simultaneously that the explanation of the legal system-social system relation key to resolution of the problem of continuity must be left to 'other' social sciences, while maintaining nonetheless that the problem of continuity is a jurisprudential problem. If this is the case, it is no surprise that analytical legal theory has yet to develop or receive a solution to the problem of continuity: resolution requires a kind of interdisciplinary diplomacy which is acknowledged as necessary yet shunned as somehow requiring a presumably wrongful or at least undesirable 'trespass'.

What can we draw from the preceding observations? One conclusion stands out: by seeing how the project of state-centred legal theory needs to complete itself – by investigating the relation between law and state as mediated and represented by the legal system-social system relation, it becomes easier to see where the intersection, rather than opposition, between state-centred legal theory and legal pluralism lies. If the social norms and conditions which are necessary to support law can be seen, in some contexts, to be disparate and not a unified system, not restricted within the borders of single states, and to support non-state legality as well as state legality, the tight association between

[48] Ibid., p. 189. [49] Ibid. [50] Raz, 'Two views', p. 58.

law and state begins to loosen. And this is precisely the destination at which the legal pluralists arrive, albeit by a different route, one which never shared the core commitments of analytical, state-centred legal theory.

A further set of insights regarding analytical legal theory can be drawn from observation of how the limitations of Raz's views point towards convergence with legal pluralism regarding the subject or subjects of legal theory. We presented in an earlier section Raz's contention that Hart had no solution to the problem of the continuity of legal systems, because Hart did not ask the question to which the solution would be the answer: the question of the relation between law and state. Our subsequent analysis and extension of Raz's view now enables us to reconsider the plausibility of this criticism of Hart. In *The Concept of Law* and elsewhere, Hart attempted to take seriously the social conditions of law's existence, in ways especially evident in his development of a system-constituting rule of recognition whose existence and scope is to be determined by observing the social practices of recognition of the various officials of a particular system. What is missing from Hart's view is an account of how these social practices amount to a wider social and political system of norms, a single sovereign state, in effect, which stands in a necessary and one-to-one relation with the state legal system.[51] *Contra* Raz, however, this is plausibly regarded not as a weakness but as a strength of Hart's theory. Hart's view escapes the questions and problems we have noted in Raz's view, to the extent that Hart's conception of legality is not inherently state-centred and thus compelled to view legality in terms of a state in correspondence with a geographically bounded and unified social and political system of norms. Amongst the views of analytical legal theorists, Hart's position seems most likely to be able to make sense of non-state forms of legality, such as international legality and transnational legality.[52]

REMAINING DISAGREEMENT

Discussion in the last section might give rise to the impression that the difficulties faced by Raz's state-centred view should incline analytical jurisprudes towards a Hartian approach which in turn leads to a convergence with legal pluralism and collapse of the possibility of a Janus-faced relation between pluralism and analytical jurisprudence. This is not, however, the view we aim to

[51] Raz: 'Every state – by which is meant a form of political system and not a juristic person – has one legal system that constitutes the law of that state, and every municipal legal system is the law of one state'. Raz, *Authority*, pp. 98–99.

[52] Though not without some modification. See Culver and Giudice, *Legality's Borders*.

convey or support. While all should welcome joint acknowledgement between analytical and pluralist theorists regarding the existence and importance of non-state legal phenomena, at least one key issue signals that disagreement is likely to remain: the question of just how inclusive the concept of legality ought to be. For legal pluralists, there is little reason why non-state social norms ought not to be considered law. Often they are spoken of, thought of and function as law in creating and maintaining social order. For state-centred legal theorists, however, this extends the concept of law far too broadly and empties it of all meaning. The goal of analytical jurisprudence – or at least one of its goals – is, after all, to explain how legality and laws are related to but also different from normativity generally and a wider class of social norms.[53] It is beyond the scope of this chapter to resolve this disagreement here; yet it is safe to say that it is not a disagreement that can be resolved by simply adducing more facts or by appealing to any shared or ordinary understanding of law or shared concept of law. Rather, resolution of this disagreement will likely require a return to a much more extensive investigation of the theoretical aims of descriptive-explanatory theories of law. We can, however, briefly return to Hart's account of the difference between wide and narrow concepts of law for some clues as to the ingredients of a resolution of the question of the proper degree of inclusiveness of an explanation of the concept of law. As Hart notes in explaining the 'choice' between a wide positivist concept of law, which includes within the category of law morally evil but legally valid rules, and a narrow natural law concept of law, which excludes morally evil rules from the category of law, he appeals to two success criteria for theories or concepts of law:

> If we are to make a reasoned choice between these concepts, it must be because one is superior to the other in the way in which it will assist our theoretical inquiries, or advance and clarify our moral deliberations, or both.[54]

We think it would be difficult to deny the gains for theoretical and moral inquiries by including, e.g., transnational legality within the concept of law. Note here that, in relying on a reasoned choice, what matters most is the best explanation of social phenomena legal theorists can offer, and not what such theorists are willing to consider law at some pre-theoretical, intuitive or linguistic level. We tend to side with those who would include a greater diversity of social norms within the concept of law, but we also hope to have shown that the very project of state-centred legal theory, with its need for an account of the relation between law and state, already includes, and

[53] See Waluchow, 'Legality's frontier'. [54] Hart, *Concept*, p. 209.

necessarily, greater investigation of the diversity of social norms within the subject matter of legal theory.

Notice, however, that to accept a greater diversity of types or sources of legality is to accept only a part of the legal pluralist challenge raised by Tamanaha and Twining, namely, that there is a diversity of types and sources of legality. Accepting this does not amount to accepting pluralism about concepts of law. Consider, for example, Tamanaha's claim that the sheer diversity of varieties of legality shows why law can have no essence: that is, that state law, religious law, aboriginal law, transnational law, and other varieties of law are simply too different to warrant any presumption that they share an essence. But how do we know these are all varieties of legality to begin with? Tamanaha's answer is this: they are all law because as a matter of convention and practice we (or some group) have attached the label 'law' to them.[55] The labelling test, however, plainly will not do. As Twining observes, it leads to the following strange conclusion: since we speak of the 'Laws of cricket' but only the 'rules of association football', we must conclude that cricket is regulated by law but football is not.[56] To this insight regarding the insufficiency of an approach too-reliant on lexical use, we can add a further argument against inference from the plurality of types or sources of legality to a plurality of concepts of law. As Tamanaha and Twining admit, analytical jurisprudence has been squarely focussed on explanation of state legality, which in part means that few, if any, have even attempted to find or construct a concept of law which meaningfully illuminates diverse types or sources of legality. With so few or perhaps no substantive attempts on offer, it is likely premature to pass negative judgement on the prospects of a truly general or universal jurisprudence which provides a truly general or universal concept of law, in favour of a usage-tracing approach which leads to highly counter-intuitive, indeed absurd conclusions, depriving us along the way of meaningful characterization of the ways in which legal order is quite plainly distinguished from social order and social practice.

OLD QUESTIONS MADE NEW

The title of this chapter promises renewal of old jurisprudential questions, a renewal whose motivation, it should now be apparent, lies in the need to

55 Tamanaha, *General Jurisprudence*, pp. 151 and 166.

56 Twining, *General Jurisprudence*, p. 101n69. See also W. Twining, 'A post-Westphalian conception of law', *Law and Society Review*, 37 (2003), pp. 199–257; and K. Himma, 'Do philosophy and sociology mix? A non-essentialist socio-legal positivist analysis of the concept of law', *Oxford Journal of Legal Studies*, 24 (2004), pp. 717–738. Yet even Twining is explicitly reluctant to being characterized as holding an essentialist view about law.

respond to the legal pluralist challenge and its surfacing of social phenomena which cannot be ignored by any jurisprudential approach claiming to take social facts seriously. The force of the legal pluralist challenge is particularly evident in the context of the continuity problem, once viewed by analytical jurisprudes as the problem of explaining the existence and persistence of distinct legal systems, and in particular, distinct state legal systems as they are challenged by such phenomena as revolution and devolution.[57] This conception of the problem of continuity is committed to regarding the state legal system as a central unit of analysis. There are several familiar features of the idea of state legal system which characterize this commitment, surveyed above and expressible in digest form: the state legal system contains all the legal norms of the system, claiming supreme and comprehensive authority and organized hierarchically as superior to all other social norms in the broader social system of which the legal system is a member, with legal norms recognizable by their pedigree in particular hierarchically organized institutional sources or official practices.[58] Such a system typically makes its claims of comprehensive, supreme authority with respect to a given geographic territory, and views competing normative claims as either members of entirely separate systems or as in effect subordinate to and within the operational control of the system.

These features are certainly found in – at least the idea of – the modern sovereign state, in which the creation, application, and enforcement of law are centralized, and there is no appeal or reliance on extra-state institutions or rules for validation or authorization. Conceiving the problem of continuity of law in the particular terms of the continuity of state legal systems is, however, just one way of conceiving the problem of the continuity of law. Given the historical prominence of sovereign states, this particular choice has evident merit; but in light of our accumulating argument, there are reasons to suppose that we might need to re-conceive the terms of the problem. Completion of the project of state-centred legal theory, which includes offering a solution to the problem of the continuity of legal systems, requires explanation of the supporting and associated social and political norms and attitudes. These, however, may or may not be systemic, and may or may not be restricted by

[57] See, e.g., Finnis, 'Revolutions'.

[58] There is of course a problem of circularity looming here, as the norms of a legal system appear to determine who the officials and institutions are but the officials and institutions are responsible for determining which norms are legal norms of the system. For an assessment of the problem of circularity, and its associated problem of indeterminacy, see Culver and Giudice, *Legality's Borders*, Chapter 1.

state boundaries.[59] More importantly, such social and political conditions may or may not converge in supporting the laws of the state legal system. They may sometimes support non-state legal orders, which might be contained within single states or converge to create trans-state or supra-state forms of legality. The problem of the continuity of law might then be more aptly understood not as a problem about how to draw clear borders around the edges of state legal systems, but instead how to trace the various ways in which state and non-state legality come into existence, and overlap and interact with each other. Why might this be a better way of conceiving the problem of continuity? Theories of law ought, amongst other achievements, to explain the social reality of law, and the social reality of law might be untidy in ways not amenable to explanation by state-centred legal theory. Perhaps more importantly, we must recover and revisit analytical legal theory's initial motivation for attention to the problem of the continuity of state legal systems, a motivation rooted in the perfectly sensible idea that we ought to be able to track the borders of legality. This motivation has been lost in analysis, stuck in problem subdivision as efforts to grapple with the problem began with 'momentary' legal systems and failed to advance to the full-fledged problem of continuity. Yet any theory of law purporting to be a social fact theory must recognize that while laws may at least appear to be unchanging and so outside of time, the social life of law is ever-dynamic and within time. There can be no fully satisfying theory of law or account of the concept of law which does not face and account for the dynamic relation within legality and between legality and surrounding social phenomena. The problem of continuity is accordingly not secondary, to be resolved once legality is given a foundational characterization; rather, it is co-fundamental, and can never be ignored. Analytical legal theorists owe thanks to legal pluralists for spurring renewed attention to this fact, and owe themselves a redirection of jurisprudential effort.

59 See, e.g., Cotterrell, 'Transnational communities'.

3

Legal Systems and Presumptions of Unity and Validity

For many analytical legal theorists, a claim to authority is amongst the hallmarks of law, so identification and explanation of the nature of law's claim to authority must form part of any adequate theory of the nature of law. Explanation of law's authority has tended to investigate it in two steps, inquiring first into correct explanation of the character of such a claim. Is the law asking us to surrender our judgement? Coercing us? Presenting us with new reasons for action? A second step has come with inquiry into the conditions under which such a claim is legitimate. Is law's obligatory force rooted in its creating moral obligations for its subjects? Or in law's correspondence to sociobiological needs? Or correspondence with God's will? Analytical legal theorists have paid much less attention to questions about what might be learned from present and historic conditions under which claims to authority can and have failed – that is, regardless of their legitimacy, where those claims fail to correspond to the social reality of law in contexts within and across states – and what such failures might teach us about the nature of law itself. This feature of much of recent analytical legal theory is perhaps easily explained, as the claims of authority typically taken up for analysis are those visible in states under conditions of stability, whose centrality in legal theory is well established: if states are part of the fabric of our social and political world, then their claims to authority can in turn be treated as part of the reality of our world as well. Yet once the presumption of the centrality of the state in legal theory is held up to fresh scrutiny, several new lines of inquiry emerge. To what extent have states lost their characteristic power and influence under globalization? Do their limitations as practical and political agents now exceed their strengths? And perhaps most pressingly, was there in fact any period in history when states enjoyed the kind of prominence typically presumed in classic conceptions of state sovereignty, or have analytical theorists actually created a straw man while striving to make their subject 'tractable', as economists sometimes describe simplifications undertaken to enable modelling? These questions cut across several sub-areas of legal theory which we will leave to one side here, using them instead as motivation to address a particular neglected interest in legal theory which they reveal in being asked: the extent to which explanations of claims of authority presume a particular and flawed conception of legality.

The context of our interest in this chapter is the familiar recent practice of many analytical legal theorists who characterize legal systems as the central habitat of legality and treat the problem of the identity and continuity of law as the question of how to explain the identity and continuity of legal systems.[1] This approach is intuitively plausible, yet, as we saw in the last chapter, once examined raises at least as many questions as it answers, particularly in its thin or absent explanation of the relations between legal systems and broader social systems, and the relation between legality and the state qua political entity. This approach is still further challenged by evidence raised by legal pluralists and others. These critics claim that the facts of normative life, including life under law, are poorly represented by analytical legal theorists' picture of norm-guided social life as a global set of local hierarchies of social, political and legal norms. In broad, illustrative terms, where some analytical legal theorists see hierarchies of bordered normative systems, many pluralists see a dynamic interplay of norms and normative orders in a polycentric or polymorphous normative world where overlap and competition amongst normative orders is at least as prominent as firm borders dividing them.[2] Yet as we also suggested, these apparently quite different pictures of normative life have surprising points of convergence. The idea of legal system is perhaps the most obvious point of convergence, insofar as legal pluralists have queried whether legal systems really do exist as more than just-so stories, and analytical legal theorists have less a received view of the nature and fact of legal system than a series of candidate views greeted first with hope then disavowed as inadequate.

We have seen in preceding discussion not just reasons for dissatisfaction with the approaches of early analytical theorists such as Austin and Kelsen in presuming a central authority or basic norm, but further reasons for being wary of even the most sophisticated analytical approaches, such as Raz's account of legal system and its reliance on a seriously incomplete explanation of the relation of the law-state to a supporting social system. While some analytical theorists remain convinced that what is needed is more work to arrive at a better

[1] J. Raz, *The Authority of Law*, 2nd edn (Oxford: Clarendon Press, 2009), Chapter 5.

[2] This characterization is by no means original. R. Cotterrell offers a similar account of the state of legal philosophy's handling of state and transnational law at p. 504ff. of 'What is transnational law?', *Law and Social Inquiry*, 37 (2012).

account of legal system, we suggest considering a different possibility, explored in this chapter. We suggest asking again just what is won by characterizing legality in terms of legal system, and just as importantly, what might be lost by characterizing the most prominent instances of legality in this way. Before this suggestion is dismissed as absurd, it is worth recalling Raz's observation that the idea of legal system is a 'conceptual tool' for use by legal theorists aiming to better understand the nature of law, not a technical legal term whose use in the hands of law's subjects is a matter of definition or other study by legal theorists.[3] 'Legal system', then, is for at least Raz a tool chosen, honed and used to fulfil the interests of particular inquirers in the nature of law, not an observed social fact requiring explanation. Yet this conceptual tool seems to be in constant danger of being mistaken for an object under explanation, particularly as it appears that use of 'legal system' by some theorists to capture certain phenomena of interest to their theoretical inquiries into law has been mistaken as the sole necessary tool for explanation of all social phenomena relevant and of interest to an understanding of the nature of law. Overreliance on legal system as a conceptual tool may then distort rather than clarify our understanding of law, and what is worse, may underwrite poor practical choices made under the presumption of the plausibility of the view of law developed by the misused tool. An instructively similar situation may be seen in an intriguing remark by Italian Prime Minister Mario Monti in 2012, discussing the capacity of Italy to extricate itself from its financial predicament and the assumptions driving reasoning about that capacity. Supposing itself to be sovereign and so meaningfully autonomous in light of its control of tax and

3 Raz writes: 'The term "a legal system" is not a technical legal term. It may occasionally figure in courts' decisions, but any term can appear there. Although it is occasionally used in legal argument, it has not the character of a technical legal term such as "floating charge" or "fee simple" or "consideration". Nor is the concept important to the day-to-day administration of law, as are the concepts of contract, ownership, right, duty, and the like. The term is primarily used in thinking about the law, not in the actual use and application of the law. It is commonly used in books of jurisprudence or comparative law, not in books about property law, torts, or copyright. . . . Therefore, when trying to clarify the notion of a legal system, the legal theorist does not aim at defining clearly the sense in which the term is employed by legislators, judges, or lawyers. He is, rather, attempting to forge a useful conceptual tool, one which will help him to a better understanding of the nature of law. This does not mean that he should not try to model the concept in a way that would be useful to the solution of certain legal problems. Rather, it means only that even if he does this, he will not be trying to elucidate the meaning of a technical legal term, but instead to provide the legal practitioner with a concept that may help him in tackling some nagging legal problems. But should it really be the goal of the legal theorist to help solve legal problems by molding a precise concept of the identity of a legal system? To what kind of legal problems may such a concept be relevant? And if this is not his goal, what is? Providing an answer to these questions is the main purpose of this essay'. Raz, *Authority*, pp. 78–79.

fiscal policy, Italy found itself much less capable of manoeuvre than it had conceived itself to be when what it supposed were practical tools sufficient for enacting its autonomy were instead insufficient. The mistake was a conceptual one regarding the scope of the tools' explanation of the social facts of Italy's political, legal and economic context. As Monti described the situation to Canadian journalist Neil MacDonald, 'We proceeded for many years under the assumption that tax policy and fiscal policy were manifestations of national sovereignty, until we discovered that this was no longer the case, because we had ceded that to the marketplace' dominated by bond traders.[4] Monti's 'tax policy' and 'fiscal policy' and 'sovereignty' turned out to be not actual social states of affairs, and instead were revealed as conceptual tools inappropriate to Monti's interests as an inquirer into practical choices available to him as Prime Minister. Worse, their relation to one another gave the impression of their being sufficient to provide a comprehensive picture of Monti's context, yet they were insufficient, and he found to his detriment that reality and a better explanation of it were more complex than the picture delivered by his tools. A rough lesson for legal theory may be drawn from this example: it is possible that 'legal system' is a poor tool for inquirers' understanding of legality even in states where its descriptive-explanatory merits are most plausible; and its dominance in thinking about legality as manifesting in legal systems may be misleading inquirers to suppose they have characterized all the legality worth characterizing, while in fact much more remains to be explained, with theoretical and practical advantages to being able to do so. If this situation is possible, we must put into question the presumption that legal system is both necessary and sufficient for legality, and even put that presumption into question where it is most plausible: in the law-state. It might well be necessary to ask whether, since Monti's tackling reality with inadequate 'conceptual tools' (as Raz calls them) led him to practically unreliable judgements demonstrating the frailty of their theoretical foundations, we ought to take warning and question whether our familiarity with the theoretical use of the conceptual tool 'legal system' and our daily talk of it are in fact impeding understanding of even our most familiar forms of legality. It is time, perhaps, to re-examine what we understand by legal system, and why and how inquirers' interests are advanced by giving it a central role in explaining legality in state and non-state manifestations. Without this re-examination we are trusting to presumption of the identity between legal system and legality, and rule out by fiat rather than by argument the possibility that other forms of legality exist and may require other conceptual tools for their explanation in satisfaction of inquirers'

4 www.cbc.ca/news/world/story/2012/04/20/f-power-shift-italy.html.

interests. Let us turn, then, to an investigation of the role of legal system in prominent analytical legal theorists' work, and the question of whether it might require supplementation by other conceptual tools appropriate to other legal phenomena.

THE ROLE OF LEGAL SYSTEM IN EXPLANATION OF LEGALITY

As we have seen in preceding discussion, the concept of a legal system has played an arguably central role in analytical legal theory's attempt to characterize the nature of law and law's familiar claim to authority. Kelsen, Hart and Raz, for example, have all maintained in various ways that there is nothing special about the form or content of legal norms which distinguishes them from other types of norms, including norms of etiquette, moral norms and religious norms. Instead, each maintains that what makes legal norms distinctively legal – and so what is distinctive about legality as a form of social order – is to be found in their relation to a particular sort of system of norms. Kelsen, for his part, introduced the idea of a 'basic norm', a foundational, system-constituting norm which provides the reason for the validity (i.e., validates) all the legal norms of the system.[5] For Kelsen, the basic norm of every system is not to be characterized as a kind of logical axiom, from which other, less general norms are derived or deduced. Rather, the basic norm is a necessary postulate of reason: for norms of a system to be conceived as legally valid, a validity-conferring norm which sits at their ultimate base must be presumed.[6] Hart identified a similar idea for a system-constituting rule,[7] but with one important difference. In Hart's view the foundational 'rule of recognition' in every legal system is not a postulate of reason: it is, rather, a social rule observable in the practices and attitudes of the legal system's officials.[8] Raz follows Hart in focussing on the social nature of legal systems as key to explanation of the existence and nature of legal norms,[9] but adds a further twist: he does not suppose that a single,

5 H. Kelsen, *Pure Theory of Law*, 2nd edn, trans. M. Knight (Berkeley: University of California Press, 1967), pp. 193–217.

6 Ibid., p. 200.

7 The rule of recognition provides a test for the 'conclusive affirmative indication' that some norm is indeed part of the legal system. H. L. A. Hart, *The Concept of Law*, 3rd edn (Oxford: Clarendon Press, 2012), p. 94.

8 Hart, *Concept*, p. 101.

9 Raz explains: 'It may be useful to begin by confessing to some of my prejudices and to make explicit a few of the assumptions underlying my reflections. One of them can be dubbed the assumption of the primacy of the social. . . . Whether or not a system is in force in a society depends on its impact on the behaviour of people in the society'. Raz, *Authority*, p. 103.

unitary rule rests at the foundation of a legal system.[10] Raz argues instead that the legal norms of a system are better understood as the set of all norms that the law-applying institutions of the system are under a duty to apply as norms of the system, a set whose membership neatly embodies a single legal system which can nonetheless practically overlap with norms of other systems, norms which law-applying institutions are under a duty to apply, but nonetheless do not by their borrowing and application certify as members of the legal system.

Kelsen, Hart and Raz also share the view that the function of a theory of legal system is essentially to explain the membership conditions a given system applies to its constituent legal norms.[11] Again they hold similar views but with important differences. Kelsen argues that a legal system consists of all those norms which are validated by its historically first constitution, which is itself validated by the system's basic norm.[12] Hart explains that a legal system consists of a union of primary rules of obligation and secondary rules of change, adjudication and recognition.[13] The rule of recognition of course plays a special, perhaps tertiary role: all those norms validated by the rule of recognition are members of the legal system. For Raz, since there is no single basic norm or rule of recognition at the foundation of a legal system, the membership conditions of legal norms in systems are to be determined by viewing which norms form part of a supreme, comprehensive and open normative system which law-applying institutions are under a duty to apply as norms of the system.[14] As we saw in the last chapter, state legal systems are the most prominent example of legal system discussed by Raz.

Even amongst sympathizers, however, these influential views regarding the systematic nature of legality have faced substantial objections. As we saw in the last chapter, Kelsen's account of the foundation of a legal system resting in a historically first constitution seems unable to explain how new, independent legal systems can be created by legal devolution.[15] His conclusion that there must be only one, unified world legal system which validates (or is validated by, depending on the perspective taken[16]) all state legal systems is an implication

[10] Ibid., pp. 95–96.

[11] For each the concept of legal validity is essentially explained as a relation of membership of norms in systems.

[12] Kelsen, *Pure Theory*, pp. 200–201.

[13] Hart, *Concept*, pp. 91–99.

[14] Raz, *Authority*, pp. 116–120.

[15] See J. Raz, *The Concept of a Legal System*, 2nd edn (Oxford: Clarendon Press, 1980), pp. 102–103.

[16] H. Kelsen, *General Theory of Law and State*, trans. Anders Wedberg (Cambridge, MA: Harvard University Press, 1945), p. 388. See also H. Kelsen, *Principles of International Law*, R. W. Tucker (ed.) (Toronto, Canada: Holt, Rinehard and Winston, 1966), p. 587, and Kelsen, 'Sovereignty',

of this view. Yet that conclusion is highly contentious, at least in part because it lacks observed evidence in its support; and as we shall see below, his explanation of how a chain of legal validity is maintained faces a similarly serious difficulty to the extent that it is offered without provision of supporting social facts, even at a very general level of factual claim. Hart's practice-based account of the rule of recognition has achieved greater influence, perhaps because it at least attempted to indicate its relation to empirical evidence located in legal officials' practice. Hart's influence has waned, however, first under the determined objections of Ronald Dworkin, and now as even those once sympathetic now question not just the idea itself, but the centrality of its role in a broadly Hartian approach to the foundations of law. In 'Who Needs Rules of Recognition?'[17] Jeremy Waldron suggests that we might do away with the idea of the rule of recognition altogether, since all the work it is meant to do – in identifying the authoritative sources of law of a legal system – seems to be equally well accomplished by another of Hart's ideas, the idea of rules of change.[18] And finally, Raz's view that legal systems necessarily claim comprehensive, supreme and open authority is also challenged on empirical grounds, that such claims not only happen to fail in some circumstances, but more importantly, that they are not necessarily or universally made in all legal systems.[19] It might be thought that such empirical challenges miss the mark here, since Raz's argument is conceptual, not empirical. But it is worth remembering that his view has an evidential base in experience: the claim that law necessarily claims authority is rooted in the generally observable or widely observed practices and attitudes of law-applying officials and institutions.[20] Yet if the evidential base can be seen to fail to support the conceptual claim about

in S. L. Paulson and B. L. Paulson (eds), *Normativity and Norms* (Oxford: Oxford University Press, 1998), pp. 535–536.

[17] J. Waldron, 'Who needs rules of recognition?', in M. Adler and K. Himma (eds), *The Rule of Recognition and the U.S. Constitution* (Oxford: Oxford University Press, 2009), pp. 327–349.

[18] See Hart, *Concept*, pp. 95–96.

[19] See A. Marmor, *Positive Law and Objective Values* (Oxford: Oxford University Press, 2001), pp. 39–42, and B. Tamanaha, *A General Jurisprudence of Law and Society* (Oxford: Oxford University Press, 2001), p. 140.

[20] J. Raz, 'Authority, law, and morality', in *Ethics in the Public Domain*, rev. edn (Oxford: Clarendon Press, 1995), pp. 215–216: 'The claims the law makes for itself are evident from the language it adopts and from the opinions expressed by its spokesmen, i.e., by the institutions of the law. The law's claim to authority is manifested by the fact that legal institutions are officially designated as "authorities", by the fact that they regard themselves as having the right to impose obligations on their subjects, by their claims that their subjects owe them allegiance, and that their subjects ought to obey the law as it requires to be obeyed (i.e. in all cases except those in which some legal doctrine justifies breach of duty. Even a bad law, is the inevitable official doctrine, should be obeyed for as long as it is in force, while lawful action is taken to try and bring about its amendment or repeal'.

law in more than merely borderline cases, then we must doubt the truth of the conceptual claim, even if understood not as a fixed and fundamental truth about the nature of law, and instead merely as an inquirer-satisfying means of ordering our experience of law.

The capacity of these views of legal system to explain and distinguish modern municipal systems of law from one another and other forms of legal order has been thoroughly discussed. We do not plan to add here to our prior contribution to that discussion.[21] Rather, we shall continue on to an issue which we believe is given too little attention as debate has often circled around the internal logic and consistency of pictures of legal system, accepting as givens the set of conceptual tools and judgements arising from initial assertion of a particular picture of legal system. The issue we aim to address is at the juncture of practice and theory, at the point of the relation between official practice and legal systems. More specifically, we wish to investigate analytical legal theorists' response to the ontological question of whether there is such a thing as a legal system beyond the collection of officials' practices. It is one thing to assert a constitutive relationship between officials and legal system – that there is no legal system without official practice – and it is quite another thing to give an account of the ontology of the constituted thing. Is there anything more to the existence of a legal system than official practice? If so, what?

TRANSCENDENCE: SYSTEMIC VALIDITY BEYOND PRACTICE

Some analytical theorists assert the existence of legal system ontologically beyond official practice, and further purport to supply observable evidence supporting their ontological claims of something like a transcendent sense of legal validity and systemic existence. For example, in a recent article attempting to resolve the sibling rivalry between inclusive and exclusive legal positivists,[22] Wil Waluchow argues for a two-part understanding of legal 'validity' which subsequently underpins an ontological distinction of legal system from its constitutive official practice.[23] Waluchow argues that inclusive and exclusive positivists can be seen to be talking past one another once we recognize the

[21] See K. Culver and M. Giudice, *Legality's Borders* (Oxford: Oxford University Press, 2010), Chapters 1 and 2.

[22] For book-length discussions of the debate, see W. Waluchow, *Inclusive Legal Positivism* (Oxford: Clarendon Press, 1994), and J. Coleman, *The Practice of Principle* (Oxford: Oxford University Press, 2001).

[23] W. Waluchow, 'Four concepts of validity: reflections on inclusive and exclusive positivism', in Adler and Himma, *Rule of Recognition*, pp. 123–144.

difference between validity as 'existence' and validity as 'systemic validity'. He makes the distinction as follows:

1. Legal Validity as Existence (or Acceptance)
   R is officially accepted and practiced in legal system *L* as a norm that fully satisfies all systemic criteria of legal validity (both pedigree- and merit-based) included within *L*'s rule(s) of recognition.
2. Systemic Validity
   R is officially accepted and practiced in legal system *L* as a norm that fully satisfies all systemic criteria of legal validity (both pedigree- and merit-based) included within *L*'s rule(s) of recognition, *and does, as a matter of objective fact, satisfy all such systemic criteria of validity* [emphasis added].[24]

Waluchow urges this distinction to highlight the fact that officials might accept and practice a norm (R) in some system (L) which does not in fact satisfy the very criteria which their official practice and acceptance have established. In such a case, there is a sense in which the norm exists, since it is officially practiced and accepted, yet it is not valid, since it actually fails to satisfy the officially practiced and accepted criteria of validity. As Waluchow puts it, '[l]aw can go wrong in any number of ways, not the least of which is its failure to observe its very own conditions for systemic validity'.[25] Waluchow points to a well-known Canadian constitutional reference case to illustrate this sort of failure:

> One particularly striking example is to be found in the *Manitoba Language Case*, where the Supreme Court of Canada determined that over a century's worth of Manitoba legislation was legally invalid because the legislature had failed to meet a constitutionally recognized condition of legal validity – passage of laws in both official languages. Though the court had ruled that Manitoba legislation was legally invalid, it drew on rule of law values to justify a temporary suspension of invalidity. The purpose of the suspension was to give the legislature enough time to translate all existing statutes into French. What this case illustrates . . . is that rules can be accepted and practiced as valid law, and *yet fail actually to be valid* because they fail to comport with relevant tests of validity.[26]

24 Ibid., p. 140. 25 Ibid., p. 143.
26 Ibid., p. 139. The case to which Waluchow is referring is *Reference Re Manitoba Language Rights* [1985] 1 S.C.R. 721.

While the plausibility of Waluchow's account of this particular case might be doubted,[27] we should not be distracted from the broader merits of the approach by which he deploys a notion of legal system, with criteria of validity, which can serve as an objective factual test for use in assessing the true validity of norms which are (correctly or incorrectly) actually practiced and accepted by officials. This distinction enables an analytical approach which can hold simultaneously that the ultimate criteria of validity of a legal system rest on official practice and acceptance, yet in the event of a failure of such practice, validity rests with the legal system's criteria. Legal system, on this view, transcends the actual or current practice and acceptance of legal officials. Detailed explanation of the nature of this transcendence remains to be set out, as, for example, more must be said regarding the scope of official acceptance and its relation to a supervening legal system, whether official acceptance attaches to a constitutional arrangement, or to individual legal norms, or something else. However that further specification goes, its core commitment to the separability of official practice from legal system is set, in a manner which extends and preserves much of the system-centric views of legality offered by at least Hart and Raz and in some ways by Kelsen. The remainder of this chapter is devoted to exploration of this distinction of legal system qua ontological entity from the social reality of life under law, especially in contexts of varying degrees of stability in law-states.

FINDING TRANSCENDENCE: CAN SYSTEMIC VALIDITY BE INDEPENDENT OF PRACTICE?

We shall advance two related arguments to show the limits of the 'transcendent' view of legal system, particularly as advanced by Waluchow from underpinnings provided by Hart and Raz and their reactions to Kelsen. We shall argue first against the transcendence argument in general terms by contrasting the transcendence view with actual legal practice, to the detriment of transcendence. Second, extending that argument, we shall provide conceptual and empirical evidence undermining the transcendence view's presumption of a kind of unity of practice amongst officials sufficient to give rise to a transcendent conception of legal system.[28]

[27] E.g., we might talk instead of unconstitutionality instead of invalidity to emphasize the kind of failure at play in cases such as the Manitoba case. See, e.g., M. Giudice, 'Unconstitutionality, invalidity, and Charter challenges', *Canadian Journal of Law and Jurisprudence*, 15 (2002), p. 69.

[28] A note on terms: here we use 'system', 'unity', 'systemic unity' and 'systemic validity' as roughly interchangeable, deploying one expression rather than another on each occasion in a way

The first argument requires us to return to an earlier observation regarding Kelsen's rooting the unity of a given legal system in a basic norm with the status of a postulate or presumption of reason, and Hart's grounding the same sort of unity in officials' practice of a rule of recognition. Hart explains his disagreement with Kelsen in the following way:

> Suppose the British Parliament (or *mutatis mutandis*, Congress) passes an Act (the Soviet Laws Validity Act, 1970) which purports to validate the law of the Soviet Union by providing that the laws currently effective in Soviet territory, including those relating to the competence of legislative and judicial authorities, shall be valid. The enactment of this Act of Parliament or Congress would not be a reason for saying that English (or American) law together with Soviet law formed one legal system, or for using *sans phrase* any of the Kelsenian expressions such as that Soviet law 'derives its validity' from English law or that English law was 'the reason for the validity' of Soviet law. The reason for refusing to assent to these propositions is surely clear and compelling: it is that the courts and other law-enforcing agencies in Soviet territory do not, save in certain special circumstances, recognize the operations of the British (or American) legislature as criteria for identifying the laws that they are to enforce, and so they do not recognize the Soviet Laws Validity Act, though a valid English (or American) statute, as in any way determining or otherwise affecting the validity of Soviet law in Soviet territory. It is true indeed that the relationship of validating purport holds between that Act and the laws made by the Soviet legislature, which the Soviet courts do recognize; but the division of laws into distinct legal systems cuts across the relationship of validating purport, for that relationship, like the completion relationship examined above, may hold either between laws of different systems or between laws of the same system.[29]

Hart's thought experiment is meant to show that whatever merit we might find in the idea of a presumption of validity in explanation of how legal systems are unified, it plainly fails as an account of the social reality of the existence of legal systems. Without actual practice and acceptance of some source of law or validity, norms and institutions do not form part of the same legal system.

which depends on the particular emphasis of that occasion. The ideas are of course related: in the analytical legal theories of Hart, Raz and Kelsen, 'system' and 'unity' refer to the web and hierarchies of relations between norms, institutions, and officials, in a way which gives rise to the idea of validity as a type of membership relation. 'Systemic unity' and 'systemic validity' are meant to emphasize the systemic character of these relations, and also to distinguish the kind of system and unity we have in mind from the idea of a system of values or moral unity (such as one might find in the work of Ronald Dworkin).

[29] H. L. A. Hart, *Essays in Jurisprudence and Philosophy* (Oxford: Clarendon Press, 1983), p. 319.

It might be thought that Hart's thought experiment is little more than that, an experiment illustrating a principle yet bearing no relation to experience. Yet examples of states making presumptions of validity contrary to or in the absence of actual practice and acceptance are readily found. Moldova, for example, declared itself a sovereign state in 1990 upon the dissolution of the Soviet Union. In 1992, the region of Transnistria, which occupies a narrow strip of once-indisputably Moldovan territory on Moldova's border with the Ukraine, itself unilaterally declared independence from Moldova, amidst fears that Moldova might reunite with Romania, which borders Moldova along its eastern frontier. The current constitution of Moldova, the Constitution of the Republic of Moldova,[30] contains a familiar supremacy clause,[31] as well as explicit statement that the state of Moldova is indivisible.[32] The constitution also purports to grant Transnistria special autonomy, while continuing to assert that Transnistria is part of Moldova and subordinate to the Moldovan state.[33] The relevant social facts, however, cast doubt on the plausibility of such a claim of authority, or presumption that Transnistria is part of Moldova. While Transnistria, despite its wishes, lacks general international recognition under international law, it has remained effectively free from the control of Moldova since 1992, largely through the support of Russia.

The situation of Transnistria, where a presumption of validity is contrary to practice, is not unique. A further example may be seen in the history of Mexican law, in Article 136 of the Mexican Constitution of 1917.[34] This article, entitled 'The Inviolability of the Constitution' reads: 'This Constitution shall not lose its force and effect, even if its observance is interrupted by rebellion'. What Hart might call the 'validating purport' of this provision is clear: the Constitution claims continuous authority even in the event of its loss of effective power during a period of insurrection, such that conduct of the interregnum period is eligible to be judged by the restored legal system as if the constitution had remained effective all along. With Hart, however, we

30 Available at www.presedinte.md/eng/constitution.

31 Title I, Article 7, 'Constitution – the Supreme Law': 'The Constitution of the Republic of Moldova shall be the Supreme Law of the State. No law or any other legal act, which contravenes the provisions of the Constitution, shall have legal force'.

32 Title I, Article 1(1): 'The Republic of Moldova is a sovereign, independent, unitary and indivisible state'. And Title I, Article 2(2): 'Neither an individual person or a group of people, nor a social group, a political party or any other public organization may exercise the State power on their own behalf. The usurpation of the State power shall constitute the gravest crime against the people'.

33 See www.bbc.com/news/world-europe-17601580.

34 Available at www.oas.org/juridico/mla/en/mex/en_mex-int-text-const.pdf. The Constitution of 1917 is also the constitution currently in force in Mexico.

would certainly question whether such a presumption of continuing validity can form part of an accurate explanation of the social reality of life under law during a rebellion which effectively displaces the officials and institutions of the preceding legal order. For the duration of a successful rebellion, if the prior government and its laws (including its constitution) are no longer observed or recognized, then they are norms best understood as aspects of the legal history of the social system, and the preceding legal system ought to be characterized as having been replaced, even if history shows the replacement to have been temporary. Reflection on the gap between claim and practice helps to demonstrate the importance of viewing the interregnum as just as demanding of phenomena-appropriate explanation as the restoration. For consider: if the interregnum period were to stretch on indefinitely, then understanding the constitution as valid *in perpetuam* as restoration of its officials is awaited (and regarding competitors as having no force or effect) would require us to suppose that in the situation of the Mexican Constitution of 1917, the emergence of a successor to the Mexican legal system envisaged in 1917 is impossible by *fiat* of that constitution. There can, in other words, only be an interregnum period in that legal system, and can never be an end to it. Yet as a matter of social and legal practice and history, legal orders are in fact supplanted by successors, who are recognized as legal authorities by their norm-subjects and by observers and other legal orders, all while the preceding legal order is viewed in a historical sense only, notwithstanding similarities in content between preceding and succeeding legal orders. Assertions of enduring validity or presumptions of validity can only be accepted as adequate explanations at the price of what we suggest is implausible omission of consideration of the complex social facts found in a history of many varieties of continuity, interregnum and succession.

The lesson drawn from Hart's criticism of Kelsen's presumption of validity has a still more important role in the context of international legality. Consider recent debate regarding international constitutionalism, a topically aligned set of descriptive and normative arguments about the existence and desirability of an international constitution.[35] In a series of articles and a book, Bardo Fassbender, for example, suggests that it is misguided and indeed redundant to pursue establishment of a general international constitution to bring legal order to what many suppose is a disorganized and disunited international legal

[35] Two useful collections on international constitutionalism are J. L. Dunoff and J. P. Trachtman (eds), *Ruling the World? Constitutionalism, International Law, and Global Governance* (Cambridge: Cambridge University Press, 2009), and J. Klabbers, A. Peters and G. Ulfstein, *The Constitutionalization of International Law* (Oxford: Oxford University Press, 2009).

community.[36] Fassbender argues that the international community already has just such a constitution: the UN Charter in its entirety. In Fassbender's view, the UN Charter has all the marks of a truly international constitution:

> it establishes a horizontal and vertical system of governance, it defines the members of the constitutional community, it claims supremacy over 'ordinary' international law (art. 103), and it aspires to eternity. The Charter was the result of a 'constitutional moment', it was intentionally given a name denoting an especially elevated class of legal instruments, and it is universal in the sense that it applies without exception to all members of the community.[37]

Independent of other evidence, this statement of the content and character of the UN Charter is of course insufficient to demonstrate that it is in fact the constitution of international law, assuming *arguendo* the existence of such a thing. Without evidence of recognition by relevant states and international organizations such a claim falls prey to Hart's argument against the sufficiency of a relationship of validating purport to establish unity, or in this instance, constitutional unification. Fassbender supposes he can supply such evidence, offering examples of 'rules' he advances as instances of recognition of an international constitution:

> By way of example, I mention article 102 of the Charter of the Organization of American States (OAS) of 1948: 'None of the provisions of this Charter shall be construed as impairing the rights and obligations of the Member States under the Charter of the United Nations'. According to article 1, paragraph c, of the Statute of the Council of Europe of 1949, 'Participation in the Council of Europe shall not affect the collaboration of its members in the work of the United Nations'. Article 7 of the North Atlantic Treaty (NATO) of 1949 provides that '[t]he Treaty does not affect, and shall not be interpreted as affecting, in any way the rights and obligations under the [UN] Charter . . . , or the primary responsibility of the Security Council for the maintenance of international peace and security'.[38]

Fassbender notes that there are similar examples of references to be found in the International Law Commission's codification of the law of state

[36] See B. Fassbender, 'The United Nations Charter as constitution of the international community', *Columbia Journal of Transnational Law*, 36 (1998), pp. 529–619; Fassbender, 'Sovereignty and constitutionalism in international law', in N. Walker (ed.), *Sovereignty in transition* (Oxford: Hart, 2003), pp. 115–143; Fassbender, 'Rediscovering a forgotten constitution: notes on the place of the UN Charter in the international legal order', in Dunoff and Trachtman, *Ruling the World*, pp. 133–147; Fassbender, *The United Nations Charter as the Constitution of the International Community* (Boston: Martinus Nijhoff, 2009).

[37] Fassbender, 'Rediscovering', p. 140.

[38] Ibid., pp. 141–142.

responsibility, the Rome Statute of 1998 which created the International Criminal Court, and the 2007 Treaty on the European Union.[39]

The trouble, however, is that even a loose web of references to the UN Charter are insufficient to demonstrate that the Charter in fact serves the role of constitution for all of international law. Fassbender's reference to NATO is particularly instructive: despite NATO's reference to the UN Charter in its originating treaty of 1949, NATO sometimes acts without the authorization of the UN Security Council and without subsequent reference to the UN Charter. Nor have NATO's actions ever been judged by a court or tribunal for consistency (or lack of) with provisions in the UN Charter.[40] NATO might act according to principles of international peace and security, but as Hart shows, a match in the content of legal norms is insufficient to show the unity of legal orders and legal institutions.

Two other features of the evidence supplied by Fassbender tend to weigh against its supporting his assertion of the existence of what the title of his article explicitly acknowledged is at best a presently tacit international constitution – as his title indicates, he is 'Rediscovering a Forgotten Constitution: Notes on the Place of the UN Charter in the International Legal Order'. First, demonstration that international organizations refer to the UN Charter is not evidence for Fassbender's view that the UN Charter's claim to *supremacy* is recognized by international organizations. At most, international organizations such as NATO, the OAS, the EU, etc., state that they will aim to act consistently with rights, obligations and principles of the UN Charter. Such relations are better characterized as attempts to coordinate efforts of international instruments including the UN Charter, and not as subjection to supreme constitutional law. Even the examples bearing the strongest indication of deference to a UN body, such as NATO's above-cited recognition of 'the primary responsibility of the Security Council for the maintenance of international peace and security' are not most plausibly read as acknowledgement of subordination to a constitutional authority. Rather, they are more plausibly understood as commitments to a specified variety of coordination of efforts at international scale, and as public assertion by states who are members of both NATO and UN that they conceive their commitments to be part of a consistent set of non-competing voluntarily undertaken obligations. In summary terms, not

39 Ibid., p. 142.

40 Although the Former Yugoslavia and Serbia and Montenegro did try, unsuccessfully, to bring cases against various NATO member states before the International Court of Justice. See R. M. M. Wallace and O. Martin-Ortega, *International Law*, 6th edn (London: Sweet and Maxwell, 2009), p. 305.

all acts of recognition are acts which recognize a supreme law or source of law.[41]

A second troubling feature of Fassbender's evidence is apparent once we look beyond the relations between the UN and international organizations, and on to the more diverse and varied relations between the UN Charter and state practices. Here the facts of recognition are even more uneven and precarious across states, though only a large-scale empirical investigation would confirm this.[42] Just as recognition is not always simultaneously acknowledgement of a hierarchical relation of superiority or subordination, recognition may also carry varying degrees of force or commitment. It is disappointingly common, for example, for states or state institutions to refer to international humanitarian law without subsequently demonstrating fidelity to that law. Instead, such reference or recognition may be better characterized as political – misleadingly presented as obedience or compliance with international law. The most sustained defence of this view in the context of legal theory is provided in early work by Martti Kokenniemi.[43] In rich and extensive argument, Koskenniemi maintains that since international law is radically indeterminate, so fails to live up to the ideal of the rule of law, the creation and use of international law is always either apologetic, in which case states are creating or making reference to international law which coincides with what they were going to do anyway, or utopian, in which case states create or refer to international law which is so abstract and idealistic that they could never be held responsible for failing to abide by it. Koskenniemi's account of international law is meant to be universal: everywhere and always the creation and use of international law is political. As such, it is a conceptual thesis asserting that international law is inherently political. We might question this aspect of Koskenniemi's

[41] The diverse kinds of non-hierarchical relations of recognition between legal orders are theorized in almost innumerable ways. Consider the following small sample of new theoretical concepts that have been introduced: 'contrapunctual law', in M. P. Maduro, 'Contrapunctual law: Europe's constitutional pluralism in action', in Walker, *Sovereignty*, pp. 501–537; 'rules of engagement', in M. Kumm, 'The cosmopolitan turn in constitutionalism: on the relationship between constitutionalism in and beyond the state', in Dunoff and Trachtman, *Ruling the World*, p. 289; 'sympathetic consideration', in N. Walker, 'Beyond boundary disputes and basic grids: mapping the global disorder of normative orders', *International Journal of Constitutional Law*, 6 (2008), pp. 373–396; 'intervalidity', in S. Besson, 'How international is the European legal order?', *No Foundations: The Journal of Extreme Legal Positivism*, 5 (2008), available at www.helsinki.fi/nofo; and 'interlegality', in B. Santos, *Towards a New Legal Common Sense* (London: Butterworths, 2002).

[42] For further criticism of Fassbender's view that the UN Charter is the constitution of international law, see A. L. Paulus, 'The international legal system as a constitution', in Dunoff and Trachtman, *Ruling the World*, pp. 75–81.

[43] M. Koskenniemi, *From Apology to Utopia* (Cambridge: Cambridge University Press, 1989).

thesis.[44] Are *all* creations and uses of international law political? If not, how can we distinguish political from non-political appeals to international law? An answer to this question would require an approach to characterization of recognition of international law, sufficiently sensitive to distinguish well-intentioned from disingenuous recognition. Such an approach is beyond the scope of our investigation and present purposes, for which the most salient part of Koskenniemi's argument is his contribution to demonstration that while presumptions of validity are easily found, whether they are accurate guides to understanding various instances of prima facie unified legal systems and legal orders depends on further investigation into the actual practice and acceptance on the part of relevant officials and institutions.

FINDING TRANSCENDENCE: THE EXPLANATORY LIMITS OF THE TACIT PRESUMPTION OF OFFICIALS' UNITY

Presumptions of unity and systematicity tend to be coupled with another presumption whose presence in the transcendence view often appears without any explanation of its origin and foundations. The transcendence view often presumes that the officials present in some legal system are unified in a systematic and stable way very strongly correlated with the unity and stability of the legal system, such that officials' conduct is typically a simultaneous constitution and reflection of the larger presumption of the unity and identity of the legal order to which they belong. For advocates of this view, situations like that evident in *Manitoba Language Rights* stand as exceptions which prove the rule, a rare instance where officials did not constitute and represent systemic unity, requiring a kind of normative backfill of reference to rule of law values providing for the unity of the system even in the face of contrary practice, where legal officials were in a regular and sustained way wrong about what they regarded as valid law. But better, transcendence advocates might say, to see an appellate court's identification and surfacing of principles of systemic unity than continue adherence to a practice-based account of legal validity, which would compel acceptance of the absurd view that legal officials were applying legally valid laws, although mistaken, until some sort of transformative moment where valid laws would become invalid laws yet actions undertaken beneath the invalid laws are given fresh life by injection of rule of law life-support.

44 We might also reasonably question Koskenniemi's thesis that all matters of international law are radically indeterminate.

It seems to us, however, that the transcendence view is mistaken in at least two respects, both of which tend to underscore the importance of observation of actual practice of legal officials, and the comparative explanatory weakness of a presumption of unity whose existence is typically demonstrated by legal officials whose conduct may nonetheless be at variance with the presumption. As a first, indicative rather than conclusive response, let us note that it is familiar enough that legal officials' practice and acceptance of a given norm can vary over time and according to context, even amongst an otherwise unified body of officials. At time *t* officials might practice and accept norm *n*, but as time passes their practice and acceptance might change such that at time *t1* they have come to settle on norm *n1* – a familiar feature of adjudication regarding the content of open-textured terms such as 'free speech' or 'community standards'. In contrast with adherents of transcendence views, Hart's account of the rule of recognition as a dynamic social practice clearly attempted to ensure its analytical capacity to track this sort of change. To Hart's observations we should add notice of the possibility that official practice and acceptance might come full circle, such that at time *t2* officials might practice and accept again the original norm *n*. And, finally, we might notice that in common law systems, many official assertions of legal validity are explicitly or tacitly subject to being overturned by a superior legal official on grounds of interpretive or other error, leaving many assertions of legal validity effectively contingent, and the unity of the system most plausibly understood in a way which accounts for the dynamic processes by which superior validators interact with contingently valid norms.

The second observation is likely more important. Even within a stable municipal legal system taken by many analytical theorists to be the basic unit of legality, constitutional arrangements or other factors may give rise to overlap or coordination relations amongst various groups of officials and the legal institutions they inhabit. So, for example, we might say of the situation treated in *Manitoba Language Rights*, a period in which Manitoba legislation was only passed in English, that the officials in Manitoba constituted a distinct sub-group or subculture relative to the remainder of Canadian legal officials, to the extent that Manitoban legal officials did not recognize or practice a clear provision of the constitution. To be sure, the degree of remaining overlap and coordination in Canada was much greater than we might currently find in, e.g., Moldova. This should not blind us, however, to the fact that the two contexts are similar in an important respect: the actual degree of unity of the officials and their legal system is contingent upon actual practice and acceptance, not presumption.

We are certainly not the first to observe that the kind of unity presumed to be constitutive of legal systems in even relatively stable states may not actually, or always exist. A recent account exploring the relations between official (and non-official) acceptance and the existence of a single legal system points to a similar conclusion. Matthew Adler argues that given the diversity of conceptions of constitutional law held amongst different groups in the United States,[45] of both official and non-official types, we ought to adopt a group-relative view of constitutional law. And since a unitary, written constitutional law is foundational in the United States, as it is in many other legal systems, we may need to conclude that the US does not have one single, unified and comprehensive legal system, but several, referred to as a single legal system only as a matter of rhetorical ease or political expediency.[46] Whether Adler's characterization of the particular situation of the United States is accurate is a matter of reasonable debate; but what is more important, we suggest, is Adler's methodological commitment to subjecting theoretical presumptions about the rule of recognition, legal systems and legal officials to assessment against observationally available evidence. At the very least, it is intuitively unsurprising that examination of the actual acceptance and practice of fundamental norms in a federal, multi-state union such as the United States generates a picture of plural, varied legal systems, to which a presumption of unity may be implausible and misleading.[47]

As our preceding discussion of Adler shows, we are not suggesting that there is no sense left in speaking of 'systemic validity' or indeed 'legal systems'. Despite the demonstrated contingency of connection between a presumption of systemic validity and actual legal order holding in a social situation, we recognize the explanatory value of understanding, for example, the legality of Transnistria's declaration of independence in terms of the Moldova constitution. In the same way, it is useful to understand the constitutionality of Manitoba's laws in terms set out in the Canadian constitution during the period in which Manitoba's legislation was only published in English. And just as the laws of Manitoba came to be challenged, successfully, before the Supreme Court of Canada, so might, one day, Transnistria's independence come to be challenged under Moldovan constitutional law in some court.[48] In such instances a presumption of validity might be meaningful as an instruction, or at least a norm, to which a court could appeal in rendering a decision

45 See M. D. Adler, 'Popular constitutionalism and the rule of recognition: whose practices ground U.S. law?', *Northwestern University Law Review*, 100 (2006), p. 719.

46 Ibid.

47 See also R. H. Fallon, 'Precedent-based constitutional adjudication, acceptance, and the rule of recognition', in Adler and Himma, *Rule of Recognition*, pp. 47–67.

48 Much like Kosovo's unilateral declaration of independence was decided by the International Court of Justice.

(grounded, perhaps, in something like the rule of law values found by Canadian courts to occupy a vacuum created by legal invalidity). Nor do we mean to deny the feasibility or desirability of judging the laws and conduct of states and international organizations in terms of their conformity with the rights and obligations set out in the UN Charter. What we do mean to suggest, however, is that talk of systemic validity, or presumptions of validity, do not serve very well in explanation of the character of legal system as a primary unit of jurisprudential analysis, largely because the presumption of unity takes too little account of the actual conditions of social life where legal systems are partly constituted and partly enacted by the actual practice and acceptance of officials and institutions. An analytical jurisprudence which reaches beyond being morally neutral and on to being a thoroughly social explanation of the nature of law cannot be satisfied with presumption where direct descriptive-explanatory approaches are more faithful to the range of official practices under investigation. Moreover, such an investigation cannot presume along with advocates of transcendence so close a relation between official practice and transcendent identity of the legal system that cases such as *Manitoba Language Rights* are odd instances of system self-correction. Deeper explanation is called for, with greater regard for the variations of officials' conduct and group identity, and the variety of legal orders in which they are found.

PRESUMPTIONS OF VALIDITY AS NORMS FOR COURTS

We suggested above that while presumptions of validity and systematicity do not serve as reliable guides to understanding legal systems and the officials who operate them, these presumptions and the consequent transcendent identity-content of legal systems may still have a useful function in explanation of how courts might settle particular kinds of legal issues. Let us begin to go more deeply into this possibility by turning again to *Manitoba Language Rights*. The *Manitoba Act*, 1870, is a part of the Canadian constitution, and Section 23 of that act provides that all Acts in Manitoba be published in both English and French. Between roughly 1890 and 1985 the letter of Section 23 visibly set out a criterion of validity[49] for all laws in Manitoba; but the criterion failed to function as such since by all accounts officials ignored it during that time.

[49] For an account of why it could not set out an ultimate criterion of validity, see J. Gardner, 'Can there be a written constitution?', in L. Green and B. Leiter (eds), *Oxford Studies in Philosophy of Law*, vol. I (Oxford: Oxford University Press, 2011), pp. 173–174. See also F. Schauer, 'Amending the presuppositions of a constitution', in S. Levinson (ed.), *Responding to Imperfection* (Princeton, NJ: Princeton University Press, 1995), pp. 145–161; and Hart, *Concept*, p. 111.

The *Manitoba Language Rights* reference then renewed the functional life of the criterion. That renewal is owed largely to the then-recent 1982 Canadian constitutional renewal including entrenchment of a Charter of Rights, whose arrival heralded a new power of judicial review enabling courts to strike down or by other means alter legislation determined to be in violation of the constitution. By virtue of s. 52(1): 'The Constitution of Canada is the supreme law of Canada, and any law that is inconsistent with the provisions of the Constitution is, to the extent of the inconsistency, of no force or effect'.[50] Read without accompanying knowledge of the role of the courts as interpreters of the Constitution's requirements, this section reads very much like a presumption of systemic validity, a kind of transcendent legality identifying a unified body of norms whether presently identified and practiced or otherwise. Yet as we have tried to show in this chapter, at most such an assertion and reading can express an aspiration whose correspondence to social life depends upon actual practice and acceptance. S. 52(1) of the Canadian Constitution, while invoked more often, is in effect no different from Article 136 of the Mexican Constitution of 1917: both adopt explicit language to attempt to control the existence of law by their very terms, but both are best understood as directives to officials charged with providing a systemic response to challenges to its constitutional order, whether arising in an appellate court as is typical, or in some other venue.

The view just sketched, taking constitutionally asserted presumptions of systemic validity as directives and resources addressed to officials such as judges in specific situations, is continuous with other analytical theorists' reflections on how to characterize what can and does happen in systemic gap periods, typically more severe than the peaceful period of confusion in Manitoba. Hart, for one, appears to accept the view that presumptions of validity might be best characterized as norms addressed to courts in situations where they must decide on the validity of actions and laws in contexts of disruptions of constitutional order – interregnum periods, as we have framed them above. Writing about the possibility of a government returning from exile, in which occupying forces or a rebel government is expelled after some time of effective rule, Hart analyses how we might go about deciding questions of legality during the period of interruption:

> Here what is most important is to understand that this question may *not* be one of fact. If it were one of fact it would have to be settled by asking whether the interruption was so protracted and complete that the situation

[50] Available at http://laws-lois.justice.gc.ca/eng/const/page-16.html.

> must be described as one in which the original system had ceased to exist and a new one was set up similar to the old, on the return from exile. Instead the question may be raised as one of international law, or it may, somewhat paradoxically, arise as a question of law within the very system of law existing since the restoration. In the latter case it might well be that the restored system included a retrospective law declaring the system to have been (or, more candidly, to be 'deemed' to have been) continuously the law of the territory. This might be done even if the interruption were so long as to make such a declaration seem quite at variance with the conclusion that might have been reached had the question been treated as a question of fact. In such a case there is no reason why the declaration should not stand as a rule of the restored system, determining the law which its courts must apply to incidents and transactions occurring during the period of interruption.[51]

In commenting on this passage Michael Green explains that 'the statement that the laws were valid during the interregnum amounts to the claim that courts *after the restoration* should apply these laws when adjudicating disputes during the interregnum'.[52] Green adds, correctly in our view, that

> It does not appear that Hart thought one could say, even from the internal perspective, that the laws were valid *during the interregnum*. For that would mean that officials during the interregnum were justified in making the [internal legal statement] that the laws were valid. And given that the rule of recognition facts presupposed by such an [internal legal statement] were not in place at the time, one cannot say that they would be so justified.[53]

Green's and Hart's observations underscore still further the general observation we have developed here regarding the connection between law's claims to authority in an implicitly continuous and unified system (especially vivid in constitutional law), and the social reality of law. The connection is entirely contingent, both with respect to the momentary unity and continuity of a legal system over time, and with respect to the system-constituting practices of legal officials. Presumptions of unity and systemic validity have little use as analytical tools when deployed to explain the social nature of legality, and instead seem to be of greatest use for practical purposes, containing the background assumptions giving contextual meaning to constitutional aspirations enshrined in particular asserted constitutional legal norms, or practical creation of certain kinds of facts of legal continuity using special normative

51 Hart, *Concept*, p. 119.

52 M. Green, 'Kelsen, quietism, and the rule of recognition', in Adler and Himma, *Rule of Recognition*, p. 364.

53 Ibid.

tools such as retrospective laws. Pressing on beyond the conceptual reasoning of Hart, Green and Adler, further support for this understanding of the explanatory use of presumptions of systemic validity can be found in reasoning regarding the authority of the US Constitution. Consider a recent example provided by Larry Alexander and Frederick Schauer in the course of a defence of their view that judicial supremacy, despite its lack of appearance in the US Constitution, best describes the Supreme Court's role in interpreting constitutional law. Critics of their view charge that it has neither a textual basis in the Constitution, nor any support via a historical account of the origins of the Constitution. Alexander and Schauer respond:

> The Constitution's authority – its status as fundamental law – ultimately rests not on facts about the past, but on the Constitution's acceptance as authoritative in the present. This is a logical and not a historical point, and it is a logical point that undergirds our entire approach. To explain this point, which has eluded our more historically oriented critics, let us suppose, counterfactually, that the Constitution did purport to answer the question of interpretive supremacy. That is, suppose that Article VI's Supremacy Clause did not say simply and inscrutably that 'This Constitution . . . shall be the Supreme Law of the Land; and the Judges in Every State shall be bound thereby . . . ', but instead provided that 'This Constitution shall be the Supreme Law of the Land, and the interpretations of this Constitution by the Supreme Court of the United States shall be final and binding on all other judges of the United States, on all Judges in the several States, on all Officials of the Executive and Legislative Branches of this Government, and on all Officials of each of the several States'. Even were this to be the actual text of the Constitution, the question of judicial supremacy would still remain open. Even were this the constitutional text, there would still be the question of who would interpret *this* provision, and whether that interpretation would be binding on others. Whether one puts this in terms of the Wittgensteinian commonplace that rules do not determine their own application, or instead in terms of a Kelsenian *grundnorm* or H.L.A. Hart's ultimate rule of recognition, the central point is that the status of a legal text cannot ultimately, and cannot without infinite regress, be determined by that text itself. In order to determine a text's status we must go outside it. And because the text cannot answer the question of whether the text is authoritative, neither can it answer the question whether someone's interpretation of that text, including that part of the text that purports to designate an authoritative interpreter, is authoritative.[54]

[54] L. Alexander and F. Schauer, 'Defending judicial supremacy: a reply', *Constitutional Commentary*, 17 (2000), pp. 460–461.

Alexander and Schauer's identification of a need for 'outside' determination of a legal text's status is more than an observation that a legal text is not self-interpreting. It is a reminder of the social nature of legal phenomena, a fact which is ill at ease with unanchored presumptions of systemic validity tacitly aligned with presumption of officials' unified mirroring and public presentation of the content of those presumptions. As Alexander and Schauer show, even explicitly asserted presumptions of systemic validity and unity are only given meaning in practice. This insight lends fresh credibility to Hart's insistence that secondary rules of recognition are practice-based, leading Jeremy Waldron to observe that this commitment 'gives [Hart's] jurisprudence an earthy empirical, even sociological, flavor that is lacking in the positivist jurisprudence of someone like Hans Kelsen'.[55] Hart then, on our view, seems to be closer than Kelsen to holding the methodological means to characterization of legal system, as part of a demonstration of the purported centrality of a tripartite unity of legal system, legal validity and official action. Even while we are sceptical regarding Hart's acceptance of the centrality of legal system to explanation of the nature of law, he at least possesses methodological means capable of tracking various kinds of legality, and avoids the demonstrated perils inherent in recourse to a transcendence view of legality grounded on presumptions significantly at odds with the social reality of law.

LEGAL SYSTEMS AS EPIPHENOMENA

What else might we say, given that the use to which the concept of legal system is put in analytical jurisprudence is, despite our cautionary analysis so far, likely to be much broader than as a conceptual resource for officials charged with practical implementation of norms in trying circumstances of the sort presented in *Manitoba Language Rights*? Here we should return to the main question of the chapter: what is the precise relation between official or institutional practices and the existence of a legal system? As we have tried to show, the relation is constitutive, but no more. Where there exist official or institutional practices of the relevant sorts, a legal system can be said to exist. The asserted existence of a legal system, and likewise the asserted existence of a Hartian rule of recognition, is then best understood as an observational statement about the epiphenomena of official or institutional practices, in other words, as a shorthand or notional summary of a complex and highly various set of relations between officials and institutions in their

[55] J. Waldron, 'Who needs rules of recognition?', in Adler and Himma, *Rule of Recognition*, p. 332, internal notes omitted.

use of legal norms and powers.[56] Much like Gilbert Ryle famously explained that it would be a category mistake to ask to be shown Oxford University after having been shown the colleges, lecture halls, admissions office, etc.,[57] it would be a mistake to suppose there is, as a matter of social fact, a legal system or rule of recognition, transcendent and waiting to be discovered above and beyond the practices of officials and institutions. This realization has important consequences for understanding law, not least of which is a renewed recognition of the importance of thorough characterization of the official and institutional practices at the foundation of legality, first given substantial treatment by Hart, albeit, we think, seriously incomplete treatment.

IMPLICATIONS FOR CLAIMS TO AUTHORITY AND ANALYTICAL LEGAL THEORY

The concept of legal system has a particularly strong hold in analytical legal theory, so dislodging its central role will likely require much more than we have offered here. Still, we believe we have done enough to show that its centrality can no longer be presumed, but must be defended, and with greater sensitivity to its varied social contexts in which it is embedded. That will not be our project. Instead, we wish to emphasize just how liberating it is to proceed as analytical legal theorists without the transcendence conception of legal system and legal validity, and in turn to explore the implications for thinking about claims to authority, made by states, international organizations and others.

While the main aim of this chapter has been to raise doubts about the capacity of the transcendence conception of legal system to adequately describe and explain intriguing instances of life under law, we have done so mainly to

56 Brian Tamanaha makes a similar observation in a general discussion of the relation between a social theory of law and legal positivism: 'Although we regularly refer to state law as a hierarchically structured *institution*, when broken down into its constituent elements it becomes apparent that state law is more closely described as a collection of institutions, each with their own internal hierarchy of authority, often located in separate buildings with their own material and financial resources, often with conflicting interests and concerns, loosely connected to one another at certain points of intersection or co-ordination. Each institution itself consists of distinct, co-ordinated complexes of activities. To see how the whole comes together – or fails to come together, or works at cross purposes – two different angles must be examined: the inner functioning of each constituent institution and the specific points of linkage (where, how, under what circumstances participants from each interact with others). . . . While it is correct to say that the activities of these institutions, taken as a whole, constitutes the *state legal system*, in actual operation the 'wholeness' of law is more a projection than a reality'. B. Tamanaha, *Realistic Socio-Legal Theory* (Oxford: Oxford University Press, 1997), pp. 146–147.

57 G. Ryle, *The Concept of Mind*, intro. D. C. Dennett (Chicago: University of Chicago Press, 2002), p. 16.

show the importance for understanding the associated costs of taking claims to authority (primarily, but not exclusively, those made by states and international organizations) themselves as reliable guides to understanding the borders and reality of authority. Here is the connection. The claims of authority to govern made by states (and others) typically if not uniformly presume the transcendence conception of legal system. This we saw was true of Canada in *Manitoba Language Rights*, article 136 of the Mexican Constitution, the Constitution of Moldova and, even if somewhat more speculatively, Fassbender's account of the UN Charter. However, as we also saw in each instance, whether in fact there is corresponding legal order (corresponding to the claims of authority or presumptions of systemic unity) depends on subsequent investigation of observationally available evidence. Such evidence, we noted, often revealed dynamic, shifting practices of acceptance and divergence, rather than smooth, uniform recognition. To the extent then that claims of authority made by states (and others) presume or rely on the transcendence conception of legal system, such claims themselves are vulnerable to the limited and contingent success of presumptions of systemic unity. In a globalized world, such limitations and adverse contingencies are rather pervasive. This observation, while quite disruptive for mainstream analytical legal theory, should not come as a surprise, but once made opens up new avenues of exploration for legal theory. In particular, it shows the many ways in which authority shifts, and most importantly, how the borders of authority overlap, cross and often ignore the borders of states.[58] Where states' and international organizations' claims to authority fail, spaces and opportunities emerge for transnational, non-state agents' and institutions' claims to authority to succeed (which may or may not take the form of or look like typical state authority).

CONCLUSION

This chapter has been devoted to a search for firm foundations for legal system as a conceptual tool capable of explaining the nature of legality. Our search has found that the conceptual tool, apparently fashioned from justifiable generalizations regarding the phenomena it seeks to characterize, is in fact seriously underdetermined by the evidence from which it is built. Legal system, we have shown, is likely underdetermined by empirical evidence so far identified in its favour, to the extent that counter-examples weighing against examples drawn

[58] On the dynamic nature of authority and issues arising when authorities overlap and must coordinate, see the many contributions in R. Cotterrell and M. Del Mar (eds), *Authority in Transnational Legal Theory* (Cheltenham, UK: Edward Elgar, 2016).

from law-states and international law are available. Just as importantly, the idea of legal system seems to be conceptually underdetermined by its constituent concepts which are themselves typically supposed to be grounded ultimately in practice. Raz, for example, as we have seen in Chapter 2, does not say how we are to examine the social situation he claims undergirds the law-state, and when we search beneath the general law-state to society relation, and look more closely at the relation between official action and its constitution of a given legal system, we are given no methodological hints regarding the nature and scope of official action to be found as evidence of legal system constitution. We uncover instead presumption of links between legal officials, the law-state and legal system, and deepened explanation of the nature of the presumption is sometimes offered as though it is in effect the required evidence for the presumption or a method for seeking that evidence. Seen in this light, analytical legal theory is perhaps best read as being descriptive-explanatory in a negatively contrastive sense, measured against evaluatively committed legal theory. It is much less clearly descriptive-explanatory in relation to social phenomena, as is evident in its lack of epistemic precision regarding the social data it takes itself to be concerned to characterize, and the tools by which such data can be reliably obtained.

Assuming our analysis is persuasive, or even simply plausible, it seems necessary to ask how this situation could have arisen. Perhaps analytical legal theory has been a victim of its own success: the picture of legal system emerging from the investigation of the relations between law and morality, coercion and social rules perhaps so struck inquirers as intriguingly satisfying that the bulk of further effort has been devoted to deepening understanding of the idea of legal system in terms of its constituent concepts and their interrelation. Here, unfortunately, too much analytical legal theory has devolved into what Brian Simpson called 'writings about what other people have said about what other people have written about law and legal institutions'.[59] Were analytical legal theorists to have paid more attention to phenomena, perhaps those relations we aim to investigate in later chapters, those theorists might have paid greater attention to the need for analytical tools other than legal system or centralized authority, as demanded by pluralists, and might have better specified the observable grounds on which claims about the existence of a legal system are based. This course could have shown simultaneously the merits of legal system as an explanatory concept, and put it in historic context appropriate to an approach to law whose commitment to description should lead it to provide

[59] B. Simpson, 'Herbert Hart elucidated', *Michigan Law Review*, 104 (2006), p. 1455.

conceptually rich explanations depicting pluralism in its many historic variations, rather than trying to subsume it beneath concepts presented as though they are univocal and universal across cultures and history when demonstrably they are not. Puzzlingly, this insight is not foreign to analytical legal theory. Raz, for example, has argued persuasively that an attempt to depict the nature of law in universal terms must be itself composed of shifting concepts such that local and temporary perspectives and inquirer interests are always present, so '[t]here is no uniquely correct explanation of a concept, nothing which could qualify as the explanation of the concept of law'.[60] Where Raz and other analytical legal theorists go seriously astray, we believe we have shown, is in supposing that the idea of legal system is not amongst the shifting concepts, and is instead an indissoluble part of the nature of law. Once legal system occupies this place, its proper place, in an analytical jurisprudence, the resulting descriptive-explanatory account of legality is much better able, we believe, to respond to the interests of contemporary inquirers, 'citizens who travel', as we framed them in *Legality's Borders* – and for that matter, Italian Prime Ministers and others who rely on conceptual explanations as part of their understanding of the world in which they take action for practical purposes. Armed now with our conclusion that legal system cannot bear the explanatory burden previous analytical theorists have given it, we turn in the next chapter to further explore the range of conceptual tools needed to satisfactorily explore diverse forms of legality faced by contemporary inquirers. This exploration will take us onward to make good on our promise to modernize the relational approach by Hart, reaching beyond law's relation to social rules, morality and coercion, towards environment, security and technology.

[60] J. Raz, *Between Authority and Interpretation* (Oxford: Oxford University Press, 2009), p. 57.

4

The Elements of Legal Order

Much of the preceding chapter's discussion of legal system has proceeded in a manner simultaneously internal and external to analytical legal theory. We have explored the interior of arguments regarding legal system, and at the same time we have questioned the purposes and reach of analytical legal theory, most specifically in questioning the value of the concept of legal system itself. In taking this approach we are attempting to be sensitive to the merits of specific arguments, while recognizing at the same time that they are embedded in a set of presumptions, purposes and enthusiasms which must also be taken into account. This approach is neither new to analytical legal theory, nor to reflection on the nature and state of an academic discipline. In questioning the value of the concept of legal system while investigating analytical accounts of the concept, we depart from within analytical legal theory, and in particular Joseph Raz's observation that legal system is a 'conceptual tool' useful to inquirers holding specific interests and purposes.

We find additional inspiration in a celebrated one-line characterization of the discipline of philosophy: Alfred North Whitehead's assertion that 'The safest general characterization of the European philosophical tradition is that it consists of a series of footnotes to Plato'.[1] Amongst the lessons which might be drawn from this characterization, it is worth drawing out Whitehead's observations regarding the way philosophy is situated culturally and in relation to its own history. Whitehead's cautious limitation of his observation to the European philosophical tradition reminds readers that there is more to philosophy than what is dreamt of in European-derived views. Whitehead's wonderfully ambiguous description of the European tradition as a series of footnotes to Plato is also instructive. Contributors of footnotes may be supportive of the Platonic line, or they may be critical, but they are still commentators within

[1] A. N. Whitehead, *Process and Reality*, corrected edn (New York: Free Press, 1979), p. 39.

the European tradition and oriented around the Platonic line. And while Whitehead leaves room for exceptions to the 'safest general characterization', even the most honourable exceptions are no great threat to the plausibility of the generalization.

Whitehead's quip of course demands to be read as a purposeful exaggeration, yet it can be inspiring to analytical legal theorists nonetheless. It is well worth being reminded that notwithstanding the typically broad and general, sometimes universal explanatory aspirations of analytical legal theory, its questions, examples and practitioners are largely drawn from a European tradition, and indeed, more narrowly, an Anglo-American tradition. A further reminder of the limitations of a particular tradition and dialogue may be gathered from Whitehead's pointing to Plato's vast influence. While it would be an exaggeration to say that the last fifty years of analytical legal theory addressing the nature of law is simply a footnote to Hart, the suggestion has probative value. Hart's influence as an expositor of the modern municipal legal system has framed much of the dialogue of the last half-century within analytical legal theory, and contributors to that dialogue have tended to raise fresh insights or questions in terms reflecting the history of that dialogue. The potential benefits and dangers of this situation for analytical legal theory are roughly analogous to the benefits and dangers facing any discipline whose cultural embeddedness and central dialogues parallel the situation Whitehead saw in philosophy. To the extent that the culture in which the dialogue is embedded is broadly representative of all cultures, the dialogue may range from surprisingly universal to undesirably parochial; and to the extent that a dialogue's framing is dominated by a particular approach and succession of critical extension and variation, the dialogue may penetrate its subject matter deeply and comprehensively. Alternatively, a dialogue might fall prey to a kind of narrow scholasticism whose adherents reach higher and high levels of precision in examination of questions of diminishing interest as changing circumstances reduce their significance to the wider career of an academic discipline and associated social practices. Cultural embeddedness is evidently not in and of itself inevitably a problem, and is probably in any case unavoidable as we are all people of our times. Lack of self-consciousness of the nature and fact of cultural embeddedness and closure to novel insights and threads of dialogue is, however, very likely to be problematic. Genuinely novel phenomena arising might fail to receive the analysis they deserve, for example, or contributions to resolution of long-standing problems may go unrecognized because they are outside the scope of unduly narrow dialogue.

Our querying the centrality of the conceptual tool 'legal system' to analytical legal theory might seem at first encounter to amount to a call for revolutionary departure from a profitable line of footnotes to Hart and an analytical legal theory tradition needing, as Leslie Green has urged, more and better work on the same questions.[2] Yet our aims are much less revolutionary than evolutionary, and are offered in a spirit of self-reflection motivated by recognition that such self-reflection is a means to guarding against our cultural embeddedness becoming intellectual narrowness. Indeed, we are much less revolutionaries than disappointed advocates of a necessary evolution in analytical legal theory's attempts to develop a general account of law. From preceding chapters we conclude that a general account of law using legal system as a central conceptual tool requires further tools to account for novel non-systemic phenomena. Further and more disappointingly, the conceptual tool 'legal system' requires internal renovation, since it does not seem fit to bear the explanatory weight its proponents wish it to carry with respect to legal phenomena it accepts as within its descriptive-explanatory scope. We do not propose to conduct that renovation here, in large part because we think there are more pressing tasks for analytical approaches to legal theory – in particular, expansion of the relational approach initiated by Hart. Yet as we approach that expansion of relations we owe some explanation of what an account of legality might look like with much-reduced reliance on legal system as a central conceptual tool. In this chapter we offer the outlines of that account, already substantially developed in *Legality's Borders*, and renewed here with the aid of helpful critics who have motivated us to clarify and extend our views in various ways. This reconstructed analytical approach to legality, re-imagining analytical legal theory with greatly reduced reliance on legal system as a central conceptual tool, will then underwrite subsequent chapters' explorations of law's relations to freshly important social phenomena corresponding to our modernized analogue to Hart's 'ordinary citizen': the 'ordinary citizen who travels', emblematic of the twenty-first century as a century of unprecedented interconnectedness and inter-reliance of peoples and their environments.

In *Legality's Borders* we set out at length what we call an inter-institutional account of legality. The inter-institutional view attempts to characterize legality not in the familiar 'top down' descriptive-explanation of the constituent parts of a particularly salient form of legal order such as a legal system, but from the 'bottom up', observing the nature and interaction of elements of legality found in various forms of legal order including but not limited to legal system. Our exploration of the bottom-up approach is motivated by our knowledge of the history and consequences of a system-centred top down approach, and

[2] See L. Green, 'General jurisprudence: a 25th anniversary essay', *Oxford Journal of Legal Studies*, 25 (2005), p. 565.

we owe a very large conceptual debt to the analytical theorists who identified the elements of legality which we absorb into the inter-institutional account with little modification. The inter-institutional account's originality lies in the way it understands combinations of elements of legality as constituting legal orders including but not limited to legal system.[3] Our approach is thus culturally embedded in system-centred approaches while aspiring to innovation in the sense of demonstrating how a novel deployment of existing insights can amount to a superior approach to characterization of legality, displacing as less explanatorily powerful and so less desirable the preceding system-centred approach.

THE INTER-INSTITUTIONAL APPROACH TO CHARACTERIZATION OF LEGALITY

A key but not exclusively key element of our approach is continued reliance on the analysis of legal norms as *content-independent, peremptory reasons for action*. As elaborated by Hart, such norms are identifiable and serve as reasons for action without further consideration of their underlying purposes or justification.[4] These logically isolable content-independent peremptory norms are typically found in habitat with further core elements of legality, such as *legal-normative powers* of various types and force. Joseph Raz[5] usefully distinguishes powers to *determine*,[6] *alter*[7] or *enforce*[8] legal-normative situations. Such powers are most familiarly used by legal officials, but their use is not limited to legal officials. Each exercise of a legal power exhibits a second dimension of such powers: force. Continuing to follow Raz, we observe three

[3] We shall explain in further detail below just what we mean by 'legal order'.

[4] See H. L. A. Hart, *Essays on Bentham* (Oxford: Clarendon Press, 1982), pp. 243–268. For developments of Hart's view, see J. Raz, *Practical Reason and Norms*, rev. edn (Oxford: Oxford University Press, 1990); Raz, *The Authority of Law*, 2nd edn (Oxford: Oxford University Press, 2009); and Raz, *Ethics in the Public Domain*, rev. edn (Oxford: Oxford University Press, 1995), pp. 210–237.

[5] See Raz, *Authority*, pp. 105–111.

[6] These powers enable authoritative findings of law and legally relevant facts, and enable resolution of disputes. Powers of this kind include the powers of courts, tribunals, arbitration (both voluntary and mandatory) and mediation boards, police officers and university petitions committees.

[7] These are powers to introduce, repeal, modify, debate, etc., legal norms or legal arrangements which form part of a legal situation. Powers of this kind include the powers wielded by legislatures, public servants, courts and citizens in, e.g., assertion of constitutional rights contra infringing legislation.

[8] These are powers to compel compliance with laws or alert others to the need to enforce laws. Powers of this kind are exercised by, among others, state security services, private security services, police officers and citizens.

aspects summarized as the total force of an assertion of a given legal power. An exercised legal power expresses implicitly or explicitly a certain *scope* over social states of affairs such as norm-subjects or varieties of transactions, and varies additionally with respect to assertion of *duration* of the effects of the exercise of the power. Finally, legal powers vary in their embodiment of an assertion of *institutional force*,[9] a measure of the magnitude of a legal power in a given social situation, whether influence over hierarchically subordinate legal norms and norm-subjects, or at junctures between sub-systems of a given legal system, or overlaps between legal orders such as state and international law.[10]

Legal-normative powers wielding peremptory, content-independent legal norms may evidently be combined in various ways with various consequences for norm-subjects and legal-normative social situations. These powers and norms may additionally affect and be affected by the larger normative world they inhabit, which includes non-legal norms emerging from at least ethical, aesthetic and religious reasoning, conducted and applied to social life by officials and non-officials. Certain patterns of combination of powers and norms are typically more significant to inquirers than others. We follow much of Neil MacCormick's approach to characterizing the home of particularly significant norm-power combinations in *institutions*. MacCormick identifies a special, jurisprudentially and analytically purposed sense of 'institution' to capture a cluster of related norms functionally united to serve a single or purpose-circumscribed limited range of purposes.[11] This characterization of 'institution of law' as a functional unit of legal norms is contrasted with the terminologically close yet functionally distinct notion of a *legal institution*, an entity which operates institutions of law, sometimes to the extent of generating or varying those institutions of law, as, for example, a ministry of education can serve as a legal institution operating institutions of law requiring children of a certain age to attend school.

The picture of legality emerging from the combination of these elements, in many ways culminating in MacCormick's view, is compelling to the extent that it provides an account of legality which is not intrinsically wed to the system-centred or state-centred approach. The distinguished elements can be used as

[9] On the idea of 'institutional force', see W. Waluchow, *Inclusive Legal Positivism* (Oxford: Clarendon Press, 1994), Chapter 3.

[10] The elements discussed in the following sections are an abbreviated and adapted version of the discussion presented in K. Culver and M. Giudice, *Legality's Borders* (Oxford: Oxford University Press, 2010), pp. 114–129.

[11] N. MacCormick and O. Weinberger, *An Institutional Theory of Law* (Dordrecht, Netherlands: Kluwer, 1986), and N. MacCormick, *Institutions of Law* (Oxford: Oxford University Press, 2007).

guides or 'radar' as we have said, for detection and characterization of legality in any legal order and not just legal system. MacCormick's view is, however, incomplete and insufficient as an explanation of legality. It is incomplete insofar as it does not explain fully the overlap between legal institutions and 'social institutions which exist to carry out legal functions'.[12] More importantly, it is insufficient insofar as its explanation of legal institutions presumes the idea of legal system as an organizing concept or reference to social fact, and the basis for identification and distinction of legal from other social institutions.

Our extension of MacCormick's insights introduces the inter-institutional view as a device intended to explain systemic legality where it occurs, while remaining open to the possibility that there are non-systemic arrangements of legality which may arise outside the context of the state. Our view aims to respond to questions of identity and continuity by attempting to track legality-associated characteristics of legal institutions over time, and finds legal order in agglomerations of inter-dependent legal institutions. We urge attention to interactions of *mutual reference* amongst legal institutions, occurring at some level of *intensity*. We intend to capture both Hart's celebrated 'chains of validity' in hierarchical legal systems typical of modern municipal legal order, and equally the emergence and operation of institutions in interstitial situations such as the relations between roughly conventional law-states and so-called break-away entities such as Transnistria.[13] Transnistria's lack of international legal recognition qua state does not prevent its constituting a sort of legal perturbation warranting the neighbouring Presidents of Moldova and Ukraine asking for European assistance in addressing their irregular relations with the region, provided by a legal device, EU Border Assistance Mission to Moldova and Ukraine, whose omission of explicit inclusion of Transnistria in its name and mission belies its specific focus on the Transnistria.[14]

Before turning to the advantages of our account of law, it is important at this point to be clear about the precise role that the idea of legal order plays,

[12] MacCormick and Weinberger, *Institutional Theory*, p. 56.

[13] See www.bbc.co.uk/news/world-europe-18284837.

[14] See generally http://eubam.org/what-we-do/. The Mission tends to identify Transnistria in terms most readily understood as a manner of geographical reference and refers to its *de facto* capital Tiraspol in a metaphorical manner, identifying a source of commitments or actions without explanation of the nature of that source. The *EUBAM Annual Report 2015* summarizes the EUBAM mission in state-facing terms relative to Moldova and Ukraine, together with re-iteration of frequently used terms 'Transnistrian conflict' and 'Transnistrian segment of the Moldova-Ukraine Border'. EUBAM's mission is said at p. 9 to 'contribute to the peaceful settlement of the Transnistrian conflict through confidence-building measures and a monitoring presence at the Transnistrian segment of the Moldova-Ukraine border'. Available at http://eubam.org/publications/ and http://eubam.org/wp-content/uploads/2015/12/Report_2015_ENGL.pdf.

to ward off the view that we have simply introduced a new expression for the old idea of legal system, or alternatively that we have introduced a new, less familiar concept which plays the same role in an account of law as the concept of legal system. Let us emphasize that the idea of legal order is not amongst the explanatory elements of law we have set out above. Only the elements of law we have identified, including content-independent peremptory norms, institutions of law, and legal institutions and their relations, serve as explanatory tools.[15] This is important since it assists the observation that there is no single pattern or combination of elements of law which must exist for a legal order to exist. Legal orders take the form of, and so are the products of, whatever variegation of the elements of law emerge within, outside and across state contexts.

Two further remarks may help to explain the contrast we draw between legal system and legal order. First, we acknowledge that both 'legal system' and 'legal order' serve in part to determine the borders of law in a given social situation, yet we wish to draw attention to the quite different consequence of application of each idea. As we noted in Chapters 2 and 3, if one employs the concept of legal system one will look for the borders of law by looking for comprehensive, supreme and open normative systems, which arrange the norms and sources of law in a distinct hierarchy with formal officials and institutions. If, however, one employs the elements of legal order identified above, one will identify legality's borders in a given instance by observing combinations of content-independent peremptory norms, institutions of norm-applying, norm-creating and norm-enforcing kinds, and relations of mutual reference between some or all of these institutions. On the view presented here, one will not, in other words, look for and find law only where there are overarching claims of comprehensiveness, supremacy and openness, with formal sources, officials

[15] We anticipate that this reply will satisfy Wil Waluchow's concern that our idea of legal order is undefined and so of limited use in explanation of legality. See W. Waluchow, 'Legality's frontier', *Transnational Legal Theory*, 1 (2010), pp. 575–585. Waluchow also claims that the standard, legal system–based picture of law is perfectly able to explain the diverse forms of law, both state and non-state, since hierarchy among the sources of law is not a necessary feature of legal systems. Waluchow is here defending Hart against our criticisms of Hart's reliance on the concept of legal system. But while Hart never says that a hierarchy or ranking of sources of law is a necessary condition of legal system in which there are multiple sources of law – the most he says is that in 'familiar' instances of legal systems – he never provides an example of a legal system in which there are multiple sources of law which are not ranked by means of some hierarchy. International law might seem to be a candidate in which there are multiple sources of law (e.g., customs, general principles, treaties and conventions) which are not ranked, but it is well known that in Hart's view, international law only amounts to a set of laws and not a system. This is good evidence, we think, of Hart's core reluctance to extend the idea of legal system beyond its familiar context of use.

and institutions of the kind typically associated with states. Such phenomena are of course often associated with the concept of law, and can be seen to be present in some social situations; but on our view, these state-centred phenomena are best understood as only contingently connected to the nature of law, so should not be central in the best contextualized concept of law developed for use in explaining law in a globalized world.

Our second remark is related to the first. Some have worried that if we remove the concept of legal system from our theoretical explanation of law, we then become unable (and so should not try) to distinguish amongst 'our law', 'your law', 'their law', etc., and so end up with a kind of 'global normative soup' with no basis for articulation of its varied ingredients.[16] This would be problematic for a number of reasons, not least because distinct legal systems or legal orders, such as EU law, UK law, German law, Scots law, US law, First Nations law, etc., often serve as objects of long-standing and firm allegiance of particular communities. An adequate contextualized conceptual explanation of law must account for such social facts. We believe our view does just that, recognizing the possibility of distinguishing amongst legal orders yet claiming that borders amongst 'our law', 'your law' and so on are not always or necessarily best understood in terms of legal systems of the kind which claim comprehensiveness, supremacy and openness, with formal hierarchies, officials and institutions. This is so even if such claims form part of the self-understandings of those who adopt views of 'our law', 'your law', 'their law', etc. We maintain that application of the concept of elements of legal order offers a better approach to location and characterization of the borders of law. On our view, comprehensive, supreme and open legal systems are one possible kind of legal order; but the concept of legal order also includes all sorts of other combinations of norms and institutions and relations of interaction (hierarchical and non-hierarchical alike). We therefore agree that law is always law of some social group, but insist that both 'law' and 'social group' might vary significantly in structure and content. So while EU law, UK law, German law, Scots law, First Nations law, US law, etc., might all be regarded by their norm-subjects as distinct objects of allegiance, loyalty and value, not all are best understood as comprehensive, supreme and open legal systems, even if the relevant participants understand them as such. On this last matter, the question of explanation of participant perspectives, whether use of the theorist's term 'legal system' by participants in such contexts is a matter of

16 See generally J. Dickson, 'The idea of a legal system: between the real and the ideal', in N. Walker (ed.), *MacCormick's Scotland* (Edinburgh: Edinburgh University Press 2012), pp. 145–159.

habit, reflective choice or perhaps simply aspiration, a descriptive-explanatory approach to those contexts must take participant perspectives seriously but not uncritically. It is a commonplace that both more and less accurate participant understandings of social facts may be equally capable of guiding conduct in a manner sufficiently successful as to permit continued reliance on even inaccurate understandings. Our use of the idea of legal order captures all that is captured by legal system, permits attention to manifestations of legality beyond legal systems, and in recognizing this last possibility is a standing reminder of the importance of critical examination of participant perspectives in descriptive-explanatory approaches.

INDIVIDUALLY SUFFICIENT CONDITIONS

The preceding section's discussion of the relative merits of system- and order-based approaches to legality have prepared the way for further explanation of the concept of law produced by identifying elements of legal order and applying them in a given social context. It might be thought that the elements identified above constitute necessary and sufficient conditions of legal order, such that if any were missing in some social context law would not exist. Yet, while the elements are meant to be basic, and constitute some characteristic features of law, they are not meant to be individually necessary and jointly sufficient conditions of law. It would nonetheless not be a mistake to suppose that each is individually sufficient for law to exist (with the exception of relations of mutual reference, which logically require institutions to engage in mutual reference). On our account, there is legal order even in the very simple and short-lived games which young children might make for themselves on the playground. So, for example, a group of boys might decide that, for an afternoon, no girls are permitted to use the swings, based simply on their say so. Here we have a single, content-independent peremptory norm which let us assume is effectively accepted (by the boys at least), practiced and enforced for an afternoon. But is this really law? Most intuitions would likely suggest that it is not law, for it enjoys nothing of the complexity, institutionalization and supremacy which we typically associate with state law. Nor is it, let us plausibly assume, supported in any way by state law or its institutions. Such a line of reasoning – looking for an ultimate chain of validity on which to pull – is what too often leads legal theorists to rely on the notion of legal system to locate the key identifying characteristics of law.[17]

[17] For discussion, see Culver and Giudice, *Legality's Borders*, Chapters 1 and 2.

On our view, however, legal order is present in this situation, since the presence of a content-independent peremptory norm is sufficient to indicate the presence of legal order. Notice, though, that it is not a sophisticated, let alone fair, legitimate, etc., legal order. It has only one explicit norm, and perhaps a few implicit others depending on whether we would consider the group of boys to have normative powers of creation, application and enforcement which exist by mere assertion. The legal order, its norms and powers, have very little, if any, institutional force (we can assume that a single teacher on duty on the playground could end the legal order in an instant), and its scope and duration are also extremely limited. The boys have not made a law for other playgrounds, and our assumption is that the practice only lasts for the afternoon. Here, then, we have a very clear and easy way of explaining the similarities and differences between such a legal order and state law, without the need to exclude such an order from the realm of law.[18] State law includes content-independent peremptory norms, but is much more sophisticated, and typically enjoys much greater scope, institutional force and duration.

We should also explain that our focus on institutions in *Legality's Borders*, driven mainly by the examples of intra-, trans-, supra- and super-state law we wished to identify and explain, should not foster the impression that types of law with no distinct institutions or any institutions at all do not count as law on our view. For example, we do not want to exclude forms of indigenous and customary law which are not institutionalized, since these often exist as accepted social norms. Nor do we want to exclude the various versions of natural law as these are accepted and practiced in diverse places. In our view, these types of law, where they are not institutionalized, possess one of the elements of legal order – content-independent peremptory norms – which for us is enough to include them within the subject matter of general analytical jurisprudence. We did not say much about these types of law in *Legality's Borders* since our particular focus there was on the various forms of emerging legality (trans-state, intra-state, etc.), which have other core elements of legality, including institutions (in the sense of interconnected norms and normative powers) and social institutions (in the sense of organized actors). Still, just as our example of the playground norm is meant to illustrate, we hold a view which supposes that legal order can be found 'all the way down' to un-institutionalized norms.

[18] In fact, the need for exclusion disappears. An account which identifies and explains the similarities and differences between related phenomena is likely always superior to a strategy of exclusion.

We can also respond here to Andrew Halpin's charge that we did not adequately explain the difference between law and morality, religion and traditional norms. Referring to *Legality's Borders*, Halpin writes:

> Nevertheless, in the authors' view, there is a distinction to be drawn between legal normative orders and 'the other diverse orders informing daily life – moral, aesthetic, religious, and traditional' (149). Their immediately preceding reference to legal orders being 'joined to other legal orders' is intriguingly suggestive of closed membership of a club of legality, but it is far from clear what has to be done to gain entry. Religious or traditional norms might be treated as religious or customary law, but just might be left standing outside as merely informing daily life.[19]

Halpin is quite right to note that we did not say very much in *Legality's Borders* about how to distinguish between law, on the one hand, and morality, aesthetics, religion and tradition, on the other. But to do so was not our aim, which was primarily to explore the adequacy of state-based theories of law in explanation of non-state forms of law. We agree with Halpin, however, that religious and traditional norms might very well be treated as kinds of peremptory norms, and even (and in the case of religion, often) develop into highly institutionalized social practices. If so, then to the extent that religious norms and traditional norms, and religion and tradition more generally, exhibit the elements of law we have identified above, they are law and manifest types of legal order. But only to the extent, it is crucial to emphasize, *that they exhibit the elements of law*. It would be a mistake to suppose that religion and tradition, and morality and aesthetics as well, are always and everywhere reducible to socially practiced peremptory norms around which institutionalized practices might (or might not) grow. Religion, morality, tradition and aesthetics are important concepts which help organize understanding of social and personal life, each with their own set of distinctive characteristics. They also certainly deserve to be studied just as much as the concept of law.[20] But conceptual individuation, and conceptual differences more generally, do not lead to any presumption that in practice their manifestations, uses, functions, norms, etc., will not overlap. Our account of legal order is meant to capture the similarities *and* differences between law and related social phenomena, not to draw clean lines between inherently interconnected social spheres where such clean lines do not exist.

19 A. Halpin, 'Conceptual collisions', *Jurisprudence*, 2 (2011), pp. 507, 516.

20 We are of course not addressing here the view that law might be best explained in terms of tradition. See, e.g., P. Glenn, *Legal Traditions of the World*, 3rd edn (Oxford: Oxford University Press, 2007), Chapter 1.

Consistent with preceding argument, our account does not aim to track all linguistic usage of 'law' or 'legal'. Nor does it attempt to reproduce without remainder or addition prevalent intuitions about what counts as law and what does not, which typically rely on some undefined group to which 'our' refers in 'our concept of law'.[21] We do, however, think our view captures most familiar sorts of law, especially state law and international law. Such forms of law are typically institutionally complex, with greater institutional force, duration, and scope of application (when conditions of stability and continuity are satisfied). We also suggested elsewhere that in explanation of state law, for example, we might very well need to add supremacy and a minimum content of natural law amongst its typical characteristics.[22] This seems to us the best way of explaining distinctive kinds of law and legal order. If state law has distinctive features, as it surely does, then it will share some of the elements of law with other kinds of law. It may additionally have some features not shared with other law, though again this is contingent. For example, it might be the case now that international law contains the minimum content of natural law. What is most important for an account of the elements of law, we maintain, is that it be flexible and responsive enough to provide the tools to explain diverse forms of law and legal order.

In this way our view has certain affinities with the law-and-society approach adopted by Denis Galligan. In explanation of the difference between Hart and Kelsen on the methodology of legal theory, Galligan writes:

> The conclusion we may draw is that legal theory, in providing concepts, categories, and ideas, is a good starting point for an analysis of law in society; at the same time, it is only a starting point, which must be supplemented by considering how law works when it encounters social situations in all their variety. Before developing this idea further, there remains a minor puzzle: how can legal theory be a generalization from social practices and then be used to classify social data and explain its significance. If theory is based on social experiences, how can it help to understand those same experiences? The answer is plain: the student of law-and-society, faced with a mass of social data about how law is working in practice, takes advantage of the concepts developed in legal theory, which represent the accumulated practical experience on which the theory is based. The process is reflexive, for it may be that the particular case shows up something new that has not been accounted for in the general theory, or that aspects of the theory are

[21] See, e.g., K. Himma, 'Reconsidering a dogma: conceptual analysis, the naturalistic turn, and legal philosophy', in M. Freeman and R. Harrison (eds), *Current Legal Issues: Law and Philosophy*, vol. 10 (Oxford: Oxford University Press, 2007), pp. 11–12.

[22] See Culver and Giudice, *Legality's Borders*, pp. 129–138.

> based on mistakes or misunderstandings. Adjustments are then made to the theory to ensure that it continues to reflect social reality, while adding new concepts where necessary.[23]

In a similar vein, our concept of law offers what we called in Chapter 1 a contextualized conceptual explanation of legality in its diverse manifestations, which addresses but is not restricted to ordinary understandings. It might also be called a generalist view in that while its inspiration comes from a history of philosophers' approaches and interests, its potential utility is far more broad, and might be taken up in sociological theory just as usefully as in philosophy, or by a historian considering explanatory options for understanding of some set of historical events. It is a lens whose particular philosophical purpose is to assist in the social explanation of law in a variety of contexts within and beyond the state.

In proposing a contextualized concept of law we might be viewed as breaking ranks with the analytical tradition of legal theory. An objection might appeal to Raz's often quoted characterization of the nature of analytical legal theory: it is a mistake, Raz supposes, to assess

> the success of an analysis of the concept of law by its theoretical sociological fruitfulness. To do so is to miss the point that, unlike concepts like 'mass' or 'electron', 'the law' is a concept used by people to understand themselves. We are not free to pick on any fruitful concepts. It is a major task of legal theory to advance our understanding of society by helping us understand how people understand themselves.[24]

Raz is here responding to a view he attributes to David Lyons, which presumes that any concept of law can be proposed so long as it is useful for some sociological purpose. Such a view makes it seem as if the goals and purposes of analytical legal theory are in some way derivative and dependent upon the goals and purposes of a different and independent discipline, sociology. This dependency ought to be rejected, according to Raz, since it crowds out an

[23] D. Galligan, *Law in Modern Society* (Oxford: Clarendon Press, 2007), p. 12.

[24] Raz, *Ethics*, p. 237. As we noted in the last chapter, Raz's view about the task of explaining the concept of legal system is rather different from his view about the task of explaining the concept of law: 'The term "a legal system" is not a technical legal term.... Therefore, when trying to clarify the notion of a legal system, the legal theorist does not aim at defining clearly the sense in which the term is employed by legislators, judges, or lawyers. He is, rather, attempting to forge a useful conceptual tool, one which will help him to a better understanding of the nature of law'. Raz, *Authority*, pp. 78–79. Given the close association of the concepts of law and legal system in Raz's work, this difference is rather puzzling, or at least in need of further explanation.

important and defensible philosophical task. It is far from clear, however, that Raz has correctly characterized Lyons's view, and it will be useful to see why.

A ROLE FOR 'SOCIOLOGICAL FRUITFULNESS'

Raz's rejection of Lyons's view is not accompanied by direct quotation of Lyons – the term 'sociological fruitfulness' is Raz's, not Lyons's – so a fuller understanding of the disagreement will benefit from close attention to Lyons's views as he expresses them. Lyons writes:

> Traditional jurisprudence assumes, in effect, that what counts as law is to be determined by conceptual analysis – a careful explication of the idea of law, or rather the particular idea that is associated with the idea of a legal system, which draws appropriate distinctions between this idea of law and closely related ideas with which it might be confused. Philosophers of law sometimes seem to assume that the results of such conceptual analysis determine the proper boundaries of associated empirical studies. The anthropology of law, for example, may be conceived as having a subject-matter that is determined by the conceptual analysis of law.
>
> As it happens, social scientists do not approach their studies in this way, and this does not seem to be merely a matter of disciplinary insularity. Legal phenomena are identified not so much by reference to the familiar features of legal systems, such as courts and legislative authorities, but rather in terms of certain social functions, such as dispute resolution and the social control of behaviour. These social functions are performed by a variety of social arrangements outside as well as inside legal systems, even when legal systems exist. One who is trained in traditional jurisprudence might be tempted to regard such an approach as muddled, confusing legal phenomena ('properly so called', as Austin might put it) with other social phenomena from which they should be distinguished. But that reaction might be misguided. To see this, we must consider how our ideas about the world are affected by empirical studies in other spheres.[25]

To develop his argument Lyons draws on an analogy with the analysis of concepts which depict phenomena in the natural world:

> Throughout developed science, one finds that our prescientific ideas serve as only first approximations of the way the world is really organized. They are liable to be modified or displaced by conceptions that depend on the successful development of scientific theory. Our prescientific idea of water, for example, referred to readily identifiable properties of substances. Water

[25] D. Lyons, *Ethics and the Rule of Law* (Cambridge: Cambridge University Press, 1984), p. 57.

> was conceived of as a tasteless, colorless liquid (or something of that sort). But the development of physical theory has shown this to be, literally, crude and superficial, in the sense that it does not satisfactorily correspond to the underlying physical reality. Physical science enables us to understand that the same substance can exist in different states, because it identifies that substance in relation to significant regularities in nature which are rooted in microscopic structures and relations. As a consequence, some of the things that we might originally not have classified as water are now understood to be composed of other substances, and some of the things that we might originally not have classified with water we can now understand to be identical with it in physically important respects.[26]

Lyons continues:

> If we conceive of the world as having no natural 'joints' – as a collection of phenomena which are unregulated by natural law – then any arbitrary set of concepts, any manner of drawing distinctions, might be adequate for describing it. A set of concepts would simply serve as a way of systematizing thought about the world. But even to suppose that one way of thinking about the world has some practical advantages over other possible schemes is to suppose that there are causal regularities among natural phenomena, knowledge of which we can use in making things happen. And there is no reason to assume that natural laws are excluded from the social realm. Quite the contrary .... So, if we think of legal phenomena as amenable to empirical study, then we must entertain the possibility that increased understanding of the social realities which underlie legal phenomena will affect our very idea of what counts as law. The concept of law that we currently have may provide us with no more than a first approximation of the natural 'joints' within the social world.[27]

In Lyons's view, then, investigating or examining the concept of law is not an activity free from constraints. What we can know and say about the concept of law is subject to revision in light of responsiveness to the social realities of law. In other words, we are not simply at liberty to construct just any concept of law. The social world stands in the way. Yet at this point we might infer, on the basis of Raz's statement, that Lyons has simply failed to notice that there are key differences between analysis of concepts used to make sense of the natural world and analysis of concepts used to make sense of the social world. Here is how Lyons responds to such an objection:

> There are of course important differences between legal phenomena and the subject-matter of physical science, the most important of which seems

[26] Ibid., pp. 57–58. [27] Ibid., p. 58.

> to be the following. Much of social reality is not merely 'given' by nature but is a product of human activity and is *shaped* by human ideas. Like other social phenomena, legal phenomena *presuppose ideas* in ways that physical phenomena do not.... Furthermore, some of the relevant ideas vary: they are 'relative to culture'. This complicates enormously the study of legal phenomena. Thus, our idea of individual accountability for our acts and their consequences is not a cultural invariant. An ethic of guilt is different from an ethic of shame. Any study of legal phenomena must take variations like these into account.... It does not follow, however, that social reality is not regulated in significant ways by natural laws of cause and effect. Societies are organized in a variety of ways, but always within constraints of human psychology, social dynamics, and economic relations, which themselves are subjects for systematic study. How much of social reality is culturally variable and how much is invariant because of underlying natural laws remains to be seen. But we have good reason to believe there is much to be discovered by scientific study of social reality.[28]

From these observations Lyons reaches the following conclusion:

> We have no reason to assume that analytic studies of law have reached their limits. But an understanding of the relations between law and other social institutions may depend on the successful development of social theory. What distinguishes what we ordinarily call law from other social institutions, as well as what is common to them, and how important these similarities and differences really are is something that we cannot assume is discoverable merely by careful explication of our current concepts.[29]

There is much that is intriguing in Lyons's view, particularly the precise ways in which an analytical account of the concept of law is subject to revision in light of the social realities of law. Unfortunately it is not developed any further beyond the passages we have quoted.[30] Still, we have enough before us to see both that Lyons's view is more nuanced than Raz indicates, and further that Lyons raises concerns which Raz's own view seems unable to address. The core trouble with Raz's view, which seems to treat some undefined group of persons' understanding as a truth condition or fact against which theories of law must be tested, is that it is not easy to see how it allows analytical legal theory to progress beyond what Lyons calls a 'first approximation' of the concept of law. Specification of a means of progress is needed if it is possible – as

[28] Ibid., pp. 58–59. [29] Ibid., p. 59.

[30] For exploration of the ways in which concepts might be revised and re-constructed in light of social reality, see M. Giudice, *Understanding the Nature of Law* (Cheltenham, UK: Edward Elgar, 2015).

we think it is – for ordinary citizens' understanding to be flawed, confused or simply mistaken, which then requires theory and observation to provide a more accurate or illuminating understanding. If, on the other hand, no such room is needed, then we would expect analytical legal theories to simply report how people understand themselves, without any appraisal of the merits of such understanding. Brian Bix describes such a project as 'unambitious',[31] but it is likely much worse: it is the anti-philosophical abandonment of the pursuit of general jurisprudence.

Our resistance to giving ordinary understanding of law a dominant role in construction of a general account of law, favouring instead extension of the concept of law to include phenomena not traditionally included in the subject matter of analytical legal theory, is often treated as cause for worry that we will lose the ability to properly distinguish law from other kinds of social phenomena which are not law. Earlier in this chapter we addressed that concern by demonstrating the capacity of our view to include explanation of law in state systems, and to go beyond state systems, all with acknowledgement of overlap between normative orders and the consequent importance of resisting the temptation to draw hard distinctions where they may be unavailable because they are not present. Now, with the benefit of Lyons's insights into the importance of revisability for any descriptive-explanatory approach going beyond explanation of a particular group's concept, we may turn from demonstration of what our view includes, to examination of a methodological error it avoids by its inclusivity. What some have called a methodologically undesirable 'analytical imperialism'[32] is evident in system-centred views which presume both the centrality of legal system to the instances of legality worth theoretical attention, and further, the centrality of the state system in theoretical explanation of law. The cost of analytical imperialism arrives as a form of difference-seeking in aid of demarcation of state system of law from other forms of normative order, at the expense of attention to degrees of variation and relation amongst state systems and other forms of normative order – whether acknowledged as legal or not. When state law is compared with the rules of sports associations, corporations and voluntary groups, for example, a concern with similarities tends to fall out of the picture and only differences are highlighted. Galligan provides much of the needed analysis in his discussion of 'extended legal pluralism':

[31] B. Bix, *Jurisprudence*, 5th edn (Durham, NC: Carolina Academic Press, 2009), p. 25.

[32] B. Tamanaha, *A General Jurisprudence of Law and Society* (Oxford: Oxford University Press, 2001), p. 146.

> What is it that makes some rule-governed spheres *legal*? Several answers have been given: one describes law, in this case indigenous law, as *concrete patterns of social ordering*; another as *rules evolving spontaneously out of social life*; a third is in terms of *semi-autonomous social fields*. Each of these summons up the idea of a law as a sphere of conventions and understandings; but since many associations of people more-or-less fit that description, it cannot be the basis for distinguishing legal orders from non-legal. Legal pluralists sometimes add a second condition: a social sphere must not only be rule-based but also have officials and institutions to apply the rules. The institutional aspects, so central to Hart's description of a legal system, could then be the basis for eliminating the social spheres lacking them. Its promise soon peters out because many social spheres, such as sporting clubs or professional associations, are institutionalized, having officials and offices for making, interpreting, and enforcing rules, and yet are plainly not legal orders.[33]

Galligan's sensitivity to the costs and benefits of contrasting approaches and their proximity to ungrounded presumptions is helpful until the point of assertion without argument that sporting clubs and professional associations 'are plainly not legal orders'. This is a peculiar stopping point since such social institutions resemble much more closely state law than either of morality or coercion. Insisting on stark differences at the cost of identifying similarities seems to get things precisely backwards, succumbing to analytical imperialism in the midst of resisting it. What is needed instead, as we have argued above, is an account of law which does not attempt to draw bright lines or absolute differences between law and not law, where such lines or differences do not exist, and is instead committed to thin and specified presumptions regarding the possible generality of a concept of law while nonetheless retaining the capacity to assert and characterize difference amongst legal orders. On our view, it is quite easy to see what would make sporting clubs and professional associations legal orders, with their legal norms, legal-normative powers and institutions, *and at the same time*, what distinguishes them from state legal systems, namely their limited scope in subject matter and low degree of institutional force in relation to other institutions. Put simply, if related phenomena are both similar and different in important ways, what we need is an account or concept of law which is capable of identifying and explaining *both the similarities and differences*.

In the spirit of recognizing both similarities and differences, while our account differs both in terms of the elements of legality that it identifies and

[33] Galligan, *Law*, pp. 182–183, author's notes omitted, original emphasis.

the purposes to which such elements are used in explanation of law, there is nonetheless an important similarity of inclusion which our view shares with Lon Fuller's account of the inner morality of law. Writing nearly forty years before Galligan, Fuller provides in our view several sensible observations about the status of normative orders such as the rules of clubs, voluntary associations and universities. Fuller notes that if we are prepared to see law as 'the enterprise of subjecting human conduct to the governance of rules', then we ought to be prepared to see in countries such as the US '"systems of law" numbering in the hundreds of thousands'.[34] Commenting on a hypothetical example of a college that 'enacts and administers a set of parietal rules governing the conduct of students in its dormitories', Fuller explains

> If we extract from the word 'law' any connotation of the power or authority of the state, there is not the slightest difficulty in calling this a system of law. Furthermore, a sociologist or philosopher interested primarily in the law of the state, might study the rules, institutions, and problems of this body of parietal law for the insight he might thus obtain into the processes of law generally. However, so inveterate has become the association of the word 'law' with the law of the political state that to call a system of parietal rules in all seriousness a 'system of law' suggests an offense against the rules of linguistic propriety.[35]

Fuller notes, of course, that a quick and easy way to extend the meaning of the word 'law' is through stipulation, so that while we can note that ordinary language typically associates 'law' with the law of a political state, we might simply stipulate an extended use of the word 'law' which includes state law but also the sets and systems of rules we find in churches, sports leagues and universities. However, as he notes, such a strategy would be too quick and easy. Fortunately, it is not hard to find compelling reasons and arguments in favour of departing from the conventions of ordinary language. As Fuller maintains:

> A view that seeks to understand law in terms of the activity that sustains it, instead of considering only the formal sources of its authority, may sometimes suggest a use of words that violates the normal expectations of language. This inconvenience may, I suggest, be offset by the capacity of such a view to make us perceive essential similarities. It may help us to see that the imperfectly achieved systems of law within a labor union or a university may often cut more deeply into the life of a man than any court judgment ever likely to be

34 L. Fuller, *The Morality of Law* (Princeton, NJ: Princeton University Press, 1969), p. 125.
35 Ibid.

> rendered against him. On the other hand, it may also help us to realize that all systems of law, big and little, are subject to the same infirmities.[36]

We should emphasize again that we do not share Fuller's functionalist conception of law identifying the essence of law as the 'enterprise of subjecting human conduct to the governance of rules', and we do not aim to offer a conception of law of primary use for moral understanding and evaluation of the ways in which legal systems might achieve or fall short of the inner principles of legality. We do, however, share Fuller's general commitment that ordinary language or linguistic propriety should not serve as a decisive factor in explanation and construction of a concept of law, especially when such explanation and construction is limited to the idea of the law of a political state, so is unresponsive to reasons and evidence based in social reality which suggest revision is warranted.

It is worth returning at this juncture to Raz's view about the nature of conceptual explanation in legal theory, in which the theorist's task is not to develop concepts, but instead to explain existing ones. Some of the limitations of this view are helpfully expressed in Fuller's caution that explanation may sometimes require violation of the normal expectations of language, even while this caution arrives from a quite different account of law. In closer methodological proximity to Raz, Hart's methodological reasoning regarding his preference for a 'wide' concept of law reminds us of what is at stake.[37] As we noted in Chapter 2, in comparison between a 'wider' legal positivist concept of law, which includes morally iniquitous rules as possible legal rules, and a 'narrower' natural law concept of law, which excludes morally iniquitous rules from amongst the class of possible legal rules, Hart identifies a choice to be made:

> Plainly we cannot grapple adequately with this issue if we see it as one concerning the proprieties of linguistic usage. For what is really at stake is the comparative merit of a wider and a narrower concept or way of classifying rules, which belong to a system of rules generally effective in social life. If we are to make a reasoned choice between these concepts, it must be because one is superior to the other in the way in which it will assist our theoretical inquiries, or advance and clarify our moral deliberations, or both.[38]

[36] Ibid., p. 129.

[37] See, however, H. L. A. Hart's review of Fuller's *The Morality of Law* in the *Harvard Law Review* 78 (1964–1965), pp. 1281–1295.

[38] H. L. A. Hart, *The Concept of Law*, 3rd edn (Oxford: Clarendon Press, 2012), p. 209.

Hart's choice of the wider concept of law gave early notice of the cost of choosing the narrower:

> It seems clear that nothing is to be gained in the theoretical or scientific study of law as a social phenomenon by adopting the narrower concept: it would lead us to exclude certain rules even though they exhibit all the other complex characteristics of law. Nothing, surely, but confusion could follow from a proposal to leave the study of such rules to another discipline, and certainly no history or other form of legal study has found it profitable to do this.[39]

If we follow Hart in supposing that there is room for choice in selecting a philosophical concept of law, we should be particularly mindful that the choice is constrained in particular ways. We may follow Raz in rejecting sociological fruitfulness as a success criterion for a descriptive-explanatory account of law, while accepting at the same time that a descriptive-explanatory approach driven by inquirer interests must nonetheless be responsive to novel evidence. And in the same way, we may understand that the justification for commitment to inclusion of participant perspectives in development of an understanding of the concept of law is not at the same time justification for regarding those perspectives drawn from a particular time and place as basic data which as such cannot be confused, partial, mistaken or otherwise needing supplementation. Attention to novel phenomena arising, and to the possibility that participant perceptions are misguided, are part and parcel of capturing law in a manner less likely to simply repeat explanatory presumptions, and more likely to detect variations, similarities and change in human practice constitutive of law. If our general concept of law upsets participants' understanding of law or ignores them without showing their irrelevance, confusion or mistakes, then so much the worse for the general concept as a tool of social explanation of law, but that caution brings an obligation of comprehensibility, not faithful reflection of self-perception.

The preceding reflections on the purpose of a concept of law and its relation to social scientific evidence have enabled us to express what we view as a methodologically improved analytical approach to concept construction, retaining prior norm-level work in our account of the elements of legal order, and undertaking some of the work needed to extend that approach to legal phenomena beyond the state system. Much of that work is provided in *Legality's Borders*. Our inter-institutional view of legality as expressed there is free from the presumption of the centrality of the state legal system, so is better

[39] Ibid.

able to identify and explain a greater range of types of legality, from intra-state to trans-state, supra-state and super-state legality. Discussion in this chapter prepares the inter-institutional view for application to new phenomena by exploring in more detail precisely what we mean in seeking to address legal orders in addition to state systems of law, and how the inter-institutional view serves as a general tool for the detection and measurement of legal orders. In the last chapter we followed Hart in criticizing the use of presumptions of validity or systematicity as a means of determining the actual, social existence and borders of law. As we explained, such presumptions are unreliable guides in accounting for the social reality of law. Earlier in this chapter we introduced an alternative to presumptions of validity or systematicity. In our account of the elements of legal order, we suggested that legal institutions form into legal orders both when they practice content-independent peremptory norms, and exercise normative powers of various kinds, and when they mutually refer to each other at some level of frequency and intensity. The distinctive character of relations of mutual reference is such that by their very nature they invite the kind of social investigation which must be carried out over time. In this way they form part of a dynamic rather than static general concept of law, since if we want to know whether there is a legal order between institutions, which might exist within or across, or perhaps simply at the level of states, we must investigate the frequency and strength of their mutual reference. In stable state systems of law the frequency and intensity of relations of mutual reference between police institutions, courts, legislatures and border officials tends to be quite high, though even in stable, steady states the frequency and intensity of relations of mutual reference might still be uneven across various issues and across territory. This is perhaps the lesson of the *Manitoba Language Rights* case discussed in the last chapter. In failed, failing or weak states, the frequency and intensity of relations of mutual reference tend to be much lower, and might be non-existent on various issues and across territory, leaving order entirely in the hands of local groups. The capacity of our inter-institutional view to characterize these situations is of value in its own right, but we are of course aware that critics maintain the capacity of system-centred views to do the same. Where we part from our critics is in the capacity of our approach to find legality 'all the way down' to legal orders so simple and brief that they deservedly pass unnamed. In following legality to simple institutions, our approach is capable of characterizing situations where normative orders overlap, and in doing so to capture similarities and differences amongst legal and other orders. Most importantly, the heart of our approach is found in its orientation towards dynamic interchange amongst institutions of law and legal institutions, so an approach which need not construct a revised concept from observed momentary legal systems and is instead always and inherently phenomena-responsive.

FROM THE ELEMENTS OF LEGAL ORDER TO ITS PRECONDITIONS

We have reached a turning point in our argument as we move in the following chapters to contextualize our inter-institutional approach to the concept of law by examining law's relations to environment, security and technology. This examination is intended to enact the revised research agenda for analytical legal theory expressed in Chapter 1 as a continuation of the argument of *Legality's Borders*. We aim to provide the missing middle between analytical legal theory's narrow concern with questions regarding operations of law in state systems, and over-breadth driven by demands for comprehensive explanation of legality. The missing middle may be summarized as phenomena-responsiveness unburdened by the presumption of the centrality of the state system to experience of law, and further aware of the incompleteness of the state-centred descriptive-explanatory approach on its own terms. As we have seen in Chapters 2 and 3, the state-centred approach presumes rather than states an account of the relation between state, system, and society, and behind that presumption we found the fruits of an analytical imperialism which delimits its scope to the momentary state system. This approach eschews sociological fruitfulness as a matter of its commitment to investigation of the concept of law as a matter of self-understanding. Yet in preserving epistemic distance from mere reporting of linguistic use or autobiography, it omits to provide an account of the participant perspective it serves and how such a perspective incorporates novel evidence over time – whether from within the investigative limits of the state system, or from the experience of legality beyond the state and normative orders similar to yet distinguishable from legal order. Our exploration of law's relation to environment, security and technology begins to contextualize the concept of law we construct for our twenty-first-century travelling citizen, examining these phenomena within and beyond state systems of law and adjacent normative orders. The context in which these relations are found, at the social base of legal orders including but not limited to state systems of law, leaves this relational expansion of the concept of law especially well-prepared to take up the lessons of this chapter's focus on construction of a concept of law from elements of legal order equally ready for deployment in characterization of very simple and very complex legal orders. We have chosen to build our wider concept of law from elements of legal order, and a relational approach to social and physical phenomena most relevant to the interests of our inquirer. As we shall see in the following chapters, that inquirer is vitally concerned with continuity of legality within and amongst legal orders in a rapidly changing world, where the virtual overlaps with the terrestrial, the live with the artificial, and norms such as technological standards interact with and perhaps determine forms of legal order.

PART II

Law, Environment, Security and Technology

5

Globalization, the Preconditions of Legality and Law's Relation to Environment

INTRODUCTION: BEYOND COMPARISON

In a recent article contributed to a celebration of the work of William Twining, we observed that it is now beyond question that legal theory risks parochialism and diminished relevance if it fails to understand the implications of globalization for law.[1] What remains in question is just which theoretical approach or approaches are best able to respond to descriptive-explanatory and normative challenges arising from globalization. Some approaches may be rendered obsolete as their methods fail to respond to novel phenomena, or fail to take as their central focus matters judged by contemporary audiences to be relevant to their interests. Historically state-focussed analytical legal theory, once a dominant force in jurisprudential debate, is thought by some to be especially likely to fade into irrelevance. William Twining has been a particularly acute critic of analytical legal theory, offering arguments whose force is amplified by Twining's long history of work from within that approach. Twining argues that analytical legal theory is likely a spent force, doomed by its state-centred approach to be incapable of taking non-state legal phenomena seriously, so aspiring implausibly to a general theory of law on the back of a seriously incomplete descriptive account of law's habitat. Twining supports instead a renewed commitment to comparative law, gathering the data analytical legal theory cannot.[2]

[1] K. Culver and M. Giudice, 'Complementing comparison: renewing analytical legal theory to meet the explanatory challenge of globalisation', *Transnational Legal Theory*, 4 (2013), pp. 700–713. The first part of this article is reproduced here as the first part of the chapter.

[2] For a small sample of the literature already present where Twining suggests we go further, see, e.g., P. S. Berman, *Global Legal Pluralism* (Cambridge: Cambridge University Press, 2012); N. Krisch, *Beyond Constitutionalism* (Oxford: Oxford University Press, 2010); J. Klabbers, A. Peters and G. Ulfstein, *The Constitutionalization of International Law* (Oxford: Oxford University

This view of analytical legal theory is at once compelling and perplexing. The need for a viable theory of law to account for non-state forms of legality is compelling, and there are good reasons to hold a negative view regarding the potential of analytical legal theory to respond to this need. Yet questions remain regarding the capacity of a comparative approach to deliver both a broader descriptive picture of what is at least spoken of as legality within and beyond states, and an account of the concepts and categories most suitable to explanation of what is described. There is of course no disputing that comparative law advocates are engaged in much more than identification of similarities and differences across legal systems and their constituent legal norms, but it remains the case that comparative law is dedicated fundamentally to comparison rather than elucidation of the nature of law, and its insights into the nature of law emerge from comparison rather than a direct focus on the question of the nature of law. It also remains the case that while analytical legal theory is rightly criticized for failing to engage with novel prima facie legal phenomena, its authors have offered what have long been taken as plausible ways to frame state legal systems whose contents and history are core to comparative law and the social history giving rise to the new phenomena analytical legal theory has arguably failed to capture. Even while comparatists might justifiably look for complementary theoretical resources in venues other than analytical legal theory, analytical legal theorists might well take Twining's criticisms of them not as the end of their relevance, but as a challenge to be the complementary jurisprudential partner comparative law may need for cross-validation of its insights into the nature of legality emerging from its comparison across legal systems and cultures.

Our initial focus in this chapter is on Twining's challenge as described above and further detailed in the next section: the question of whether there is anything left in analytical legal theory worth saving and developing as an explanatory complement to comparative law. Our answer to this question is positive. We argue that the descriptive-explanatory tools of analytical legal theory may, with modifications enabling response to non-state phenomena, enable constructive explanation of the preconditions of legal order, understood as the social, physical, and technological conditions which make legal order possible and which fundamentally limit the normative claims states can make through their legal systems. Investigation of the preconditions of legal order

Press, 2009); G. P. Calliess and P. Zumbansen, *Rough Consensus and Running Code* (Oxford: Hart, 2010); H. P. Glenn, *The Cosmopolitan State* (Oxford: Oxford University Press, 2013); B. Santos, *Toward a New Legal Common Sense*, 2nd edn (London: Butterworths, 2004); A. Halpin and V. Roeben (eds), *Theorising the Global Legal Order* (Oxford: Hart, 2009); and C. Dauvergne, *Making People Illegal* (Cambridge: Cambridge University Press, 2009).

is our approach to deepening the analysis of the continuity of law begun in Chapter 2, where we arrived at the conclusion that the possibility, existence, and persistence of legality can only be fully understood once legality's relation to its social setting has been explained. In this and the final two chapters we broaden the idea of social setting to include both physical and technological preconditions of legality.

The importance of preconditions for a general theory of law was only dimly recognized by state-centred analytical legal theorists, and thanks to Twining and others is now visible as a fundamental problem of jurisprudence whose answer requires both greater attention to observationally available evidence and novel explanatory categories and concepts. Norm-level descriptive-explanatory tools at the core of the analytical account of state legality, we will begin to argue here, can be usefully repurposed to develop an explanatory account of the preconditions of legality which along the way grows analytical legal theory as a complement to comparative law, notwithstanding our recognition that comparative law has its own ways and means of understanding the nature of legality as part of its comparative purpose. We will attempt to show, however, that while renewed effort in comparative law approaches is certainly an important part of legal theory's response to globalization, it is not the only part and must therefore be situated within a larger agenda for legal theory and globalization work.

IMBALANCE IN ANALYTICAL LEGAL THEORY

In a recent lecture Twining usefully summarizes his train of ideas long under development as follows:

> From a global perspective a reasonably inclusive picture of law in the world would encompass various forms of *non-state law*, especially different kinds of religious and customary law that fall outside 'the Westphalian duo' of state (municipal) law and classical public international law dealing with relations between states. A map of law in the world that leaves out religious law, important forms of indigenous, customary or Chthonic law, emerging forms such as *lex mercatoria* and other examples of 'soft law' at sub-, supra- and international levels, just leaves out too much.[3]

As Twining argues, analytical legal theory is one approach which 'just leaves out too much'. Yet in Twining's gradual parting of ways with analytical legal

[3] W. Twining, *Globalisation and Legal Scholarship*, Tilburg Law Lectures Series, Montesquieu Seminars, vol. 4 (Nijmegen, Netherlands: Wolf Legal, 2009), p. 40.

theory in favour of his current advocacy of comparative law, more than just hints remain that an appropriately revived analytical approach might yet have a role in our understanding of law. In 2009 for example, Twining wrote in *General Jurisprudence: Understanding Law from a Global Perspective* that a call for increased sensitivity to evidence should not be confused with abandonment of the task of conceptual elucidation:

> The message for analytical jurisprudence is reasonably clear: *a priori*, intuitive analysis of concepts divorced from empirical knowledge of actual legal institutions, processes, rules, etc. will not add much to our understanding of law. However ... conceptual elucidation is still a necessary part of empirical and normative enquiries about law, but such analysis needs to be sensitive to advances in our empirical knowledge of the real world.[4]

Yet as matters stand, in Twining's long-held view,[5] analytical legal theory lacks the balance it needs to be a useful contributor to understanding of legality. Twining argues that Hart, Raz and others are largely to blame for the tendency of many analytical jurisprudes to turn away from observationally available phenomena and the issues they raise for legal theory:

> Hart treated philosophical questions as quite distinct from historical and sociological ones and rejected any idea of continuity between them. He was relatively unmoved by historical and sociological criticisms of *The Concept of Law* because he thought that these raised different questions from those that he had set out to answer. As a result, 'the social fact' dimensions of *The Concept of Law* were imperfectly realised. Joseph Raz and others followed Hart in trying to maintain a sharp distinction between philosophical and empirical questions. As a result they failed to resolve the tension between emphasising that law is a social phenomenon and refusing to consider it empirically.[6]

We take Twining's message to be relatively straightforward but no less important for that reason: even while advocacy of comparative law might be understood as implying abandonment of analytical legal theory as historically practiced, description and explanation are most valuable when each informs the other. While Twining is of course right that 'Law is a participant-oriented discipline largely concerned with the details of immediate, practical, local

[4] W. Twining, *General Jurisprudence* (Cambridge: Cambridge University Press), pp. 55–56.

[5] See W. Twining, *Globalization and Legal Theory* (London: Butterworths, 2000). See also B. Tamanaha, *A General Jurisprudence of Law and Society* (Oxford: Oxford University Press, 2001); and N. MacCormick, *Questioning Sovereignty* (Oxford: Oxford University Press, 1999).

[6] Twining, *General Jurisprudence*, pp. 57–58.

problems',[7] avoidance of parochialism requires generalization from local data, and even while Twining is right that 'as legal scholarship has generally become more transnational, the claim has been made that "we are all comparatists now"',[8] the simultaneous task of elucidation of concepts remains.

CONTEXTUALIZED CONCEPTUAL EXPLANATION

The contribution of this chapter is less a proof of the viability of a renewed version of analytical legal theory as a partner for comparative law, and more a kind of illustrated promise. We aim to explore the possibility illuminated in Twining's assessment of analytical legal theory, that its complementarity to comparative law has yet to be fully explored given the failure of Hart and Raz to take seriously the need for continuity with sources of 'social fact'. Our exploration begins from the problem of the preconditions of legality, attempting to understand the problem both at the level of theoretical explanation and in its social context as a problem for norm-subjects with a particular point of view to law. We will develop briefly a renewed version of the kind of perspective analytical legal theorists have sought to take to social facts, and we will use that perspective, that of the globally aware citizen in the twenty-first century, to guide choice of facts to which our contextualized conceptual explanation of law responds. We will attempt to show that the way in which these facts inform an account of the preconditions of legality illuminates the variety of legal orders and the thread of legality which links them even as they conflict, superimpose on others, are absorbed and change in other ways.

This argument is in sum a contextualized conceptual explanation of law.[9] It is important to note, even though we cannot fully explore the issue here, that by 'conceptual explanation' we do not intend to conduct *conceptual analysis* by making explicit what is implicit in some folk or lay concept of law. There might be much that is confused, mistaken or distorted by such a concept of law, requiring correction or revision in the form of what we have characterized in Chapter 1 as a *contextualized* conceptual explanation of law. A folk or lay concept might also be parochial and unwarrantedly state-centred, making it all the more important to construct new conceptual tools to better explain legal phenomena in a globalized world. Our approach is therefore better characterized as *contextualized conceptual explanation*, rather than conceptual analysis. Part of the activity of contextualization, we argue, is to develop a

[7] Twining, *Globalistion*, p. 31. [8] Ibid., p. 49.

[9] Contextualized conceptual explanation is, as we noted in the introduction, a form of 'constructive conceptual explanation' as developed in M. Giudice, *Understanding the Nature of Law* (Cheltenham: Edward Elgar Press, 2015).

conceptual account of law which takes law's relations to environment, security and technology as its focus in an exploration of the challenges globalization poses for legal theory, and in particular for understanding the preconditions of legality. Our approach to these relations and the preconditions of legality is contingent on inquirers' interests rather than an Archimedian attempt to find the perfect point from which to understand legality, and as an attempt of this sort, it is an attempt to deliver conceptual explanation of a *socialized* and therefore *contextualized* concept.

THE PRECONDITIONS OF LEGALITY: FROM MORALITY, COERCION AND SOCIAL RULES TO ENVIRONMENT, SECURITY AND TECHNOLOGY

The problem of the preconditions of legality arises in analytical legal theory almost as an afterthought. The presumption of the law-state's centrality to any viable account of the nature of law has enabled a curious blindness with respect to the theoretical interest of the diverse conditions which make legal order possible. This blindness in the face of social facts is made still more curious by the further fact that two of analytical legal theory's core tools are entirely separable from the shortcomings attributable to their historically state-centred application: the use of norm-level explanation to build a concept of law, and construction of that concept of law for the sake of a particular perspective and set of interests first identified by Hart as the 'ordinary citizen'. Hart, for example, certainly aimed at conceptual explanation of law as instantiated in state legal systems, but he did so using a descriptive-explanatory approach which departed from identification of the constituent parts of state legal systems. In what we have characterized elsewhere as a 'norm-level explanation' of legality,[10] Hart focussed on the character of legal norms in explaining the existence of law, famously arguing that the heart of law and indeed legal system lies in a special union of *rules* – primary rules of obligation and secondary rules of change, adjudication and recognition. Raz's later account of legal norms as types of exclusionary reasons for action deepens our understanding of law's place in practical reasoning, but remains strictly within a commitment to norm-level explanation of legality.[11] And while Raz's view of legal system introduces additional and corrective elements to Hart's account of legal system, his view that legal systems characteristically claim comprehensiveness, supremacy and openness identifies elements which are simply epiphenomenal of the claims

[10] See the introduction in K. Culver and M. Giudice, *Legality's Borders* (Oxford: Oxford University Press, 2010).

[11] See J. Raz, *Practical Reasons and Norms*, rev. edn (Oxford: Clarendon Press, 1990).

that emerge from viewing legal norms in their systematic context.[12] We might also notice that Twining's focus on comparative law, as well as his interest in the diffusion, transplantation, and reception of law[13] seems to leave intact the centrality of norm-level explanation. In these elements, there is the basis for a characterization of legality which is independent of state legal systems as one form of legal order, transferrable to other legal orders. In *Legality's Borders* and again in the preceding chapter we developed an extended account of this norm-level approach, arguing for an understanding of legality rooted in legal norms' operation in functional assemblies we called (following Neil MacCormick) 'institutions of law' whose operational homes are found in legal institutions which combine in various ways in distinctive legal orders. This understanding of legality is intended to provide the means of tracing the distinctively legal in various kinds of legal orders in various life-stages. We will return to the value of norm-level explanation below, but first we must detour into the question of the purpose of this explanation, how that purpose might be modernized in light of social facts arising, and how the features of Hart's, Raz's, and others' use of norm-level explanation in the context of state systems should alert analytical legal theorists to a further investigation likely to help response to the problem of the preconditions of legality.

A new reader of analytical legal theory could easily gain the impression that its use of a norm-level account in debates over the nature of law, the nature of adjudication, the nature of legal system, and so on, are part of an agenda aimed at disclosing what law 'really is' in a sort of social scientific aspiration to a scientific realist true description of things in the world. While such a goal might be present in the work of some analytical legal theorists, it is noteworthy that the basis of much current analytical legal thought is in Hart's work, which was explicitly interpretive. He departs from what at one point he called a 'hermeneutic'[14] approach to characterization of law, intended to respond to the interests of the 'ordinary citizen'.[15] Hart's starting point in the experience and concerns of the ordinary citizen is certainly a rhetorical device distancing his approach from the formal 'pure theory of law' approach of Kelsen. Yet much more importantly it represents adoption of an epistemic perspective expressed as explanation of the nature of law for the sake of particular interests

[12] J. Raz, *The Authority of Law*, 2nd edn (Oxford: Oxford University Press, 2009).

[13] See Twining, *General Jurisprudence*.

[14] See H. L. A. Hart, *Essays in Jurisprudence and Philosophy* (Oxford: Clarendon Press, 1983), p. 13.

[15] More accurately, Hart refers to 'any educated man' in introducing the perspective for which his account of the concept of law is offered. See H. L. A. Hart, *The Concept of Law*, 3rd edn (Oxford: Clarendon Press, 2012), p. 3.

or needs embedded in the practical reasoning of a particular kind of norm-subject. It happens that Hart's hermeneutic interpretation of law saw ordinary citizens of his era as concerned with the relation between law and morality, law and coercion and law and social rules, but these interests and corresponding salient social phenomena could well have been otherwise, and a different picture of law might have resulted, just as application of a norm-level approach to law's relation to contemporary social facts will certainly deliver a different picture of law now. How we might go about deploying this perspectival, norm-level approach to law's relation to the interests of the ordinary citizen in the twenty-first century may be illuminated by reflection on the results of Hart's application of the approach fifty years ago.

Explanation of law in light of its relations to morality, coercion and social rules has seemed normal, perhaps even obvious, to the generations of readers who have entered English-speaking jurisprudence through Hart's essays and seminal book *The Concept of Law*. In addition to the question of the nature of law embedded in Hart's investigation into the relation between law and social rules, the relations between law and coercion and law and morality have felt keenly important to citizens of societies undergoing rapid social change. The Hart–Devlin debate[16] serves as one crystallizing example of the salience of these particular relations in an understanding of law undertaken from the perspective of the ordinary citizen. As post-war England liberalized rapidly, the question of the proper limits of legalized morality loomed large as the Wolfenden Report of 1957 recommended repeal of a criminal law prohibiting homosexual behaviour between consenting adults in private. As Hart argued in favour of the report's recommendation, and Devlin against, the question of the proper limits of law's coercive enforcement of morality was probed with fresh clarity. Whatever position one takes with respect to the merits of the opposing arguments, what is clear is that the fact of the argument's occurrence is a reflection of the concerns of a society in a particular time in its history. Twining is no doubt correct that the contextualized conceptual explanation of law developed by Hart in *The Concept of Law* was unduly light in its reference to social facts and for a self-declared descriptive-explanatory account was too much concerned with the formal structure of law's claims to authority. Yet to some extent the proof of the pudding is in the eating, and at least analytical legal theorists have dined happily on Hart's offering, notwithstanding its empirical shortcomings.

What is more interesting for the moment than these likely remediable shortcomings is the setting in which these relations between law, morality,

16 See P. Devlin, *The Enforcement of Morals* (Oxford: Oxford University Press, 1965), and H. L. A. Hart, *Law, Liberty, and Morality* (Stanford, CA: Stanford University Press, 1972).

coercion and social rules were salient. That setting is one in which features of rapid social change of one kind were salient against a backdrop of stability in another dimension of social life, the relative political stability of post-war England. That stability permitted a social focus on those relations, as opposed to, e.g., continued focus on operation of the war-time state, or preparation for a war-time government to go into exile, etc. A further presumption of physical stability is evident – there is a presumption that the territory of the law-state is itself a constant, and is not in imminent danger of flood or irradiation or other situation changing fundamentally the context in which law's claim to authority is made.

It is quite intriguing, once these presumptions are surfaced, to observe how Hart and Raz were aware of the presumptions yet ultimately gave them very little attention, leaving their approaches to law ill-prepared for situations where those presumptions do not hold. Raz, for example, makes an explicit choice in early work to investigate 'momentary legal systems', to learn what we can about the relations between norms which constitute a legal system by viewing them in an abstracted snapshot of time, which clearly presumes stability and chooses to avoid the difficulties associated with explaining the continuity and identity of law over time.[17] This is not to say that Raz did not recognize this limitation, and indeed much later he observes that explanation of the identity and continuity of law over time remains amongst the 'unsolved puzzles' of legal theory.[18] In Hart's work, particularly *The Concept of Law*, it is somewhat easier to find recognition of the problem of continuity, and further recognition that continuity of legality might be other than succession of one legal system by another legal system. Hart discusses, for example, the state of affairs in South Africa in 1954 when the unity and interaction between judiciary and legislature broke down quite dramatically.[19] Yet for the most part, Hart presumes conditions of social and physical stability of state legal systems, treating only briefly the social preconditions of acceptance of law's authority which provides the social base for the existence of a functioning legal system. In contrasting Kelsen's notion of a presupposed basic norm against Hart's attempt to root a rule of recognition in social practice, Hart remarks that '[n]o doubt the practice of judges, officials, and others, in which the actual existence of a rule of recognition consists, is a complex matter'.[20] As Hart further explains,

> Even if [the rule of recognition] were enacted by statute, this would not reduce it to the level of a statute; for the legal status of such an enactment necessarily would depend on the fact that the rule existed antecedently to

[17] J. Raz, *The Concept of a Legal System*, 2nd edn (Oxford: Clarendon Press, 1980), pp. 189–197.
[18] J. Raz, *Between Authority and Interpretation* (Oxford: Oxford University Press, 2009), p. 58.
[19] Hart, *Concept*, p. 122. [20] Ibid., p. 109.

> and independently of the enactment. Moreover, as we have shown in the last section, its existence, unlike that of a statute, must consist in an actual practice.[21]

Anticipating critics, Hart continues:

> This aspect of things extracts from some a cry of despair: how can we show that the fundamental provisions of a constitution which are surely law are really law? Others reply with the insistence that at the base of legal systems there is something which is 'not law', which is 'pre-legal' 'meta-legal', or is just a 'political fact'. This uneasiness is a sure sign that the categories used for the description of this most important feature in any system of law are too crude.[22]

Of course, Hart's own view is that the rule of recognition is both law and fact; it depends simply on whether we are viewing it from an internal point of view (in which case it is law) or an external point of view (in which case it is fact). Yet, while important, the distinction between points of view still assumes much of what needs to be explained about the relation between social practice and law:

> A second set of questions arises out of the hidden complexity and vagueness of the assertion that a legal system *exists* in a given country or among a given social group. When we make this assertion we in fact refer in compressed, portmanteau form to a number of heterogeneous social facts, usually concomitant.[23]

We might, Hart suggests, simplify things in an Austinian way and simply refer to the class or whole world of officials as one person, but this would just put off the task of social explanation: 'this is either no more than a convenient shorthand for complex facts which still await description, or a disastrously confusing piece of mythology'.[24]

To Hart's credit, he resisted the temptation to regard 'a convenient shorthand' as sufficient for explanation of the usually concomitant, heterogeneous social facts at the heart of social use of law. Yet he did not reach beyond acknowledgement of the complexity of these facts. He closed his analysis with little more than 'convenient shorthand', asserting without historical or other evidential foundation that a legal system exists when officials accept the secondary rules of the system from an internal point of view, and

[21] Ibid., p. 111. [22] Ibid. [23] Ibid., p. 112. [24] Ibid., p. 113.

citizens or non-officials obey the primary rules of obligation for their part only.[25]

Beyond this particular shortcoming in Hart's account of the social bases of legality, it is of significant interest to us that Hart paid virtually no heed to the physical bases of legality, both in the presumption that states as principal manifestations of legality are fundamentally isomorphic in the relation of their legality to their territory, and in the presumption that their territory is fundamentally stable. Twining, by contrast, and with the benefit of fifty years of intervening history, recognizes the consequences of globalization for both social and physical presumptions regarding the stability of the law-state:

> A second obvious development is an increased recognition of the legal dimensions of issues and phenomena that are genuinely global, such as climate change, other environmental issues, radical poverty, the common heritage of mankind, migration, war, international crime, terrorism, pandemics, and the media.[26]

In this quick summary, Twining offers the beginnings of the elements of a new relational approach to legality under globalization, surfacing both social and physical factors needing investigation in their own right and reflection in a descriptive-explanatory theory of law. Where Hart's reflection of the concerns of the ordinary citizen led to investigation of law's relation to other social phenomena – morality, coercion and social rules – Twining adds physical phenomena. Climate change, environmental issues and pandemics are presented as 'dimensions' of legality's globalization requiring our attention.

Twining's inclusion of physical facts also opens the way to consideration of whether facts are all of the same ontological status in an ascription of legality to a given social situation. As Hart was well aware, some facts serve as preconditions for others, often reflected in rules regarding those facts. Recall Hart asking, in 'Positivism and the Separation of Law and Morals' that readers

> suppose that men were to become invulnerable to attack by each other, were clad perhaps like giant land crabs with an impenetrable carapace, and could extract the food they needed from the air by some internal chemical process. In such circumstances (the details of which can be left to science fiction) rules forbidding the free use of violence and rules constituting the minimum form of property – with its rights and duties sufficient to enable food to grow

[25] Ibid., p. 116. And earlier: 'Plainly, general acceptance is here a complex phenomenon, in a sense divided between official and ordinary citizens, who contribute to it and so to the *existence* of a legal system in different ways'. Ibid., pp. 60–61.

[26] Twining, *Globalisation*, p. 29.

> and be retained until eaten – would not have the necessary nonarbitrary status which they have for us, constituted as we are in a world like ours. At present, and until such radical changes supervene, such rules are so fundamental that if a legal system did not have them there would be no point in having any other rules at all.[27]

The availability of food is a precondition of continued human existence, and in reflection of the importance of continued existence, property rules safeguarding food production are enacted and maintained. Yet there is something quite different about the preconditions and conditions identified by Twining, leading us to wonder whether during a period of global prosperity and relative stability jurisprudes have inadvertently indulged in large-scale myopia. A great deal of effort has focussed on the identity conditions of legal systems and specific conditions under which individual norm-subjects operate within legal systems; yet very little attention has been given the problem of continuity of legality between legal systems, and the increasingly important question of the continuity of legality between legal orders which may be systems, or may be another form of legal order raising its own problem of identity. This set of problems offers an opportunity for analytical legal theory to combine its perspectival approach and norm-level approach to enable better mapping of the varieties of legal order, the preconditions of their existence, and interactions between legal orders driven by both officials within those orders, and exogenous changes to preconditions of their existence. To make good on this opportunity, however, analytical legal theory must do rather more than has been achieved by the founders of its modern form. Twining again deserves credit for showing the way. Where Hart resorts to 'science fiction' to illustrate the logical contingency of rules whose current factual context allows them to appear necessary, Twining's appeal to reality demands a more nuanced understanding of the way in which particular social facts are preconditions of legality, a demand tailor-made for a renewed analytical approach to legality at norm level and in institutions of law and legal institutions. Where Hart saw the problem of continuity and the preconditions of legality in blunt terms, imagining a radical leap to a then stable future in which humans have exchanged endoskeletons for exoskeletons, Twining lists social and physical facts whose interaction is far more complex. Climate change, pandemics and war, to name just three from Twining's list, involve potentially great threats to human existence, with great uncertainty associated with the time of their emergence,

[27] H. L. A. Hart, 'Positivism and the separation of law and morals', *Harvard Law Review*, 71 (1959), p. 623.

their force and their duration. Of the three exemplars just cited, only war is clearly within human control, and even with that feature, in its conduct and its effects it creates an unstable condition for the practice of legality – as made clear in Hart's reflections on retroactive law. The effects of both climate change and pandemics are arguably much less within human control, and bring consequences as serious or more serious than any war short of a global exchange of attacks using nuclear weapons. Most importantly, those consequences are highly variable in ways unrecognized by Hart's science fiction and its suddenly, yet stably different world. Where Hart illustrated the logical contingency of the content of apparently necessary rules, pointing to much different, yet stably different possible basic facts about the nature of humans, Twining opens the way to considering whether and how legality might exist under continually varying physical and social conditions following satisfaction of physical and social preconditions for legality.

Some preliminary remarks here regarding the relation between law and environment will begin our contextualized conceptual explanation of legality for our twenty-first-century travelling inquirer, and will set the context for following chapters' more extensive treatment of law's relation to security and to technology. We begin with law's relation to environment because it is at once most fundamental, and because its complexity beneath a prima facie simple surface demonstrates an insight we will encounter again in exploration of law's relation to security and technology – the insight that once analytical jurisprudes depart from the presumption of the centrality of the state system to explanation of legality and attend to preconditions of legality and problems overlooked in system-centred jurisprudence, the reward is a much richer contextualized conceptual explanation of legality. The relation between law and environment is fundamental and obvious in ways worth considering and setting aside. None deny, so far as we are aware, that a certain kind of environmental stability is presumed as a precondition by system-centred and other approaches to the nature of law, recognizing that humans are not carapace-clad and a minimal kind of environmental stability is an absolute precondition for social existence for more than a very short time absent extensive technological supports. The 'Westphalian duo' of state and international law, accompanied by what might be called the 'Montevideo presumption' of the typically territorial location of the state captures the legal theorist's acceptance that the central case of social life is a territorially located life, and territories are elements of environments composing weather affected by climate, ecosystems atop geological formations and so on. These dimensions of law's relations to environment are presumed yet easily stated, and are left unstated largely because they are uninteresting insofar as they are stable and not easily varied by the norm-subjects who live amongst these elements. At the same time, however, particular elements of this largely stable background to life under law can and do affect law in ways we shall suggest are underappreciated, warranting further consideration of law's relation to environment and inclusion of that consideration in a general contextualized conceptual explanation of law.

Two examples will help to make our case. The first example is one of what we shall characterize as environmentally mediated constitutional transition, seen in the province of Aceh, Indonesia in the wake of the physical and social catastrophe following 26 December 2004 landfall of a tsunami. In this example, we shall see that even familiar kinds of constitutional transition – in this case an unexpectedly rapid devolution of powers from a central government to a newly empowered provincial government – can involve environmental elements whose role requires inclusion in any adequate explanation of the identity and continuity of the form of legal order present, alerting us to the need to be open to the role of environment elsewhere. The second example is drawn from a more jurisprudentially complex situation driven by a still more decisive environmental event. Faced with rising sea levels likely to make its territory uninhabitable, the Pacific island state of Kiribati is developing a strategy of 'migration with dignity'[28] supporting orderly evacuation of its territory. Exploration of this example begins our querying the conceptual adequacy of accounts of system-centred legality which embody Westphalian and Montevideo presumptions to the exclusion of other forms of legal system and order.

The facts of the 2004 Indian Ocean earthquake and tsunami combine in a social and natural history of unprecedented catastrophe. At 7:58 on 26 December 2004 an earthquake of magnitude 9.1 occurred thirty kilometres beneath the earth's surface at a point off the coast of the Indonesian island of Sumatra, generating waves of up to ten metres in height striking the coast of Aceh Province and flooding as far as seven kilometres inland.[29] The number of dead in Indonesia alone were reliably estimated at over 160,000[30] of the 226,000

[28] www.climate.gov.ki/category/action/relocation/.

[29] International Federation of Red Cross and Red Crescent Societies, *Legal Issues from the International Response to the Tsunami in Indonesia: An International Disaster Response Laws, Rules and Principles (IDRL) Programme Case Study* (July 2006), p. 6. Available at www.ifrc.org/PageFiles/125717/indonesia-cs.pdf.

[30] S. Doocy, A. Rofi, C. Moodie, E. Spring, S. Bradley, G. Burnham and C. Robinson, 'Tsunami mortality in Aceh Province, Indonesia', *Bulletin of the World Health Organization*, 85 (2007), p. 276. Available at www.who.int/bulletin/volumes/85/4/06-033308.pdf.

deaths attributed to the tsunami as it reached twelve other countries including Sri Lanka, India and Thailand.[31] The earthquake was reported to be the '4th largest since 1900 and the world's biggest since a magnitude 9.2 earthquake struck Alaska's Prince William Sound in 1964'.[32] In addition to deaths immediately associated with the catastrophe in Indonesia, several hundred thousand persons were displaced, and remained displaced for an extended period. Citing UN and Indonesian government assessment work, Doocy et al. report that 'Approximately one year after the tsunami, Indonesian government estimates indicated 129 775 deaths, 38 786 missing and 504 518 tsunami-displaced in Aceh Province'.[33] The consequences of the disaster were profound, reaching across all aspects of social life. In 2006 The International Federation of Red Cross and Red Crescent Societies issued a case study examining legal issues arising in the context of their contribution to response. Their case study captures what humanitarian aid groups witnessed while awaiting Indonesian government permission to intervene, a catastrophe destroying many of the bases of social order:

> The tsunami also struck hard at Aceh's local economy, administration and infrastructure. Thirteen of Aceh's 21 districts were affected by the tsunami, six of them severely. Provincial government and administration was to a large extent paralysed by a substantial loss of personnel and expertise. Government records, voting lists, land title deeds and other personal records were washed away. Health services were incapacitated by destroyed and damaged hospitals, and a lack of skilled personnel. Economic activity, which had largely developed around traditional farming, forestry and fishing, was stunted. An estimate of preliminary damage and loss by the National Development Planning Agency, Bappenas PBP, for the province was US$ 4.5 billion. According to Asian Development Bank (ADB) estimates, reconstruction will cost up to US$5 billion over the next five years, with the cost of housing rehabilitation/reconstruction alone estimated at US$573 million.
>
> As the waters receded, the Acehnese people were faced with tens of thousands of corpses lining the streets and lying trapped under rubble, destroyed

[31] J. Pickrell, 'Facts and figures: Asian tsunami disaster', *New Scientist Daily News* (20 January 2005). Available at www.newscientist.com/article/dn9931-facts-and-figures-asian-tsunami-disaster/.

[32] Ibid.

[33] Doocy et al., 'Tsunami mortality', p. 273, citing United Nations Information Management Service (UNIMS) in collaboration with the Rehabilitation and Reconstruction Agency (BRR). *Tsunami Recovery Status Report* (8 December 2005), available at http://reliefweb.int/sites/reliefweb.int/files/resources/84D4D7659153EE79492570D800203196-unorc-idn-6dec.pdf. Figures for displaced persons are at p. 9.

families and livelihoods and many feared the outbreak of an epidemic due to a lack of safe drinking water.[34]

In this vividly described context, with many countries affected and many more responding in an outpouring of financial and in-kind aid, a prima facie familiar set of events played out: assistance was initially slow and even delayed by factors on the ground and political decision making, but it grew over time and addressed at least some of the results of the tsunami while catalysing efforts to develop better early warning and response systems in anticipation of the next similar natural event. There appears, at first glance, to be of little interest to legal theorists here, until in the context of reflection on a decade's progress since the tsunami, we observe puzzled media reports explaining a post-tsunami rise in Islamic religiosity and adoption of Shari'a law in Aceh. *Time* magazine[35] and the *Wall Street Journal*,[36] amongst others, focus with apparent surprise on the accompaniment of rebuilding efforts by Shari'a. Increases in religiosity following catastrophe are common enough as lack of piety is blamed as the cause of divine punishment, but an apparent transition to adoption of a new form of legal system seemed to capture commentators' attention to a degree not paralleled by otherwise pressing questions regarding other matters such as the ultimate effects of billions of dollars invested in recovery. As we shall explain, however, adoption of Shari'a was not so precipitous or extensive as might be inferred from media reports, and the consequences of the adoption which has occurred are far from a transition from one legal system to another. Rather, future investigation beyond the scope of our present work will need to observe and interpret signs of hybridity as Aceh continues its recovery from years of separatist violence, and the tsunami and subsequent renegotiation of Aceh's place within Indonesia as a province with a special status enabling adoption of elements of Shari'a.

However we eventually characterize the legal consequences of the tsunami, those consequences are of interest to our twenty-first-century inquirer on a number of grounds potentially including questions of personal conduct or stability of investment. That inquirer's interests go far beyond news of legal change, and on to understanding the bases and extent of those changes in Aceh, and perhaps further to whether those changes are likely to be seen in

34 International Federation of Red Cross and Red Crescent Societies, *Legal Issues*, p. 7, internal notes omitted.

35 P. Liljas, 'What the waves did to Aceh', *Time* (24 December 2014). Available at www.time.com/3641485/what-the-waves-did-to-aceh/.

36 R. C. Paddock, 'In Indonesia's Aceh, stricter Islam followed tsunami', *Wall Street Journal* (24 December 2014). Available at www.wsj.com/articles/in-indonesias-aceh-stricter-islam-followed-tsunami-1419453104.

neighbouring jurisdictions other than Aceh, particularly in the event of an environmental catastrophe. As we turn to satisfy those interests in inquiry, a much more complex situation with elements of considerable interest emerges.

Returning to the perspective of International Federation of Red Cross and Red Crescent Societies, the immediate context and interaction of natural change, social change, and legal change is reflected in the Federation's explanation of the reasons for a slow start to the flow of aid:

> At the time of the tsunami, Aceh had endured a long-running armed conflict for almost 30 years. Efforts to resolve the conflict had begun and produced two agreements and brief periods of calm. On 19 May 2003 Aceh was placed under martial law which was later modified to civil emergency rule. Consequently, foreign access to the province was restricted with limited outflow of information.[37]

The reasons for Indonesia's initial hesitation, subsequent terms of engagement with external aid, and the later emergence of Aceh under terms of 'special autonomy' as a province within Indonesia are bound up in a lengthy history. In this history, environmental catastrophe is arguably a precondition of a kind of jurisprudential turning point of a key yet poorly understood kind.

A detailed account of the history of Indonesia leading up to the pivotal tsunami event of 2004 is beyond the scope of our discussion, in part because a broad outline of surrounding events is sufficient to support our jurisprudential observations, and in part because the history is so complex and disputed that it defies concise characterization. In characterizing this history in summary fashion, we draw substantially on the recent work of R. Michael Feener in his 2013 *Shari'a and Social Engineering: The Implementation of Islamic Law in Contemporary Aceh, Indonesia*,[38] and a set of articles by Edward Aspinall. Their explanatory interests as historians of conflict and doctrinal change are not identical with our interests as explorers of the preconditions of legality as a contribution to understanding the problem of continuity. Their depiction of the events preceding and following the tsunami is nonetheless crucial to understanding the context in which a rapid and radical change to the environmental context of legality affected the continuity and identity of the Indonesian legal system.

What is of particular interest to us is the relation between the tsunami and what Feener characterizes as a rapid social transition in the role of Islam in Aceh. It is tempting, in light of attention to the rise of Shari'a in Aceh, to see

[37] International Federation of Red Cross and Red Crescent Societies, *Legal Issues*, p. 5.

[38] R. M. Feener, *Shari'a and Social Engineering* (Oxford: Oxford University Press, 2013).

the context as one in which Islamic values gained a new kind of institutional force in a transition. That transition might be viewed as a change from (1) Islam's pre-tsunami service as a social system atop which a secular constitution and legal system were operated by technocrats seeking national development in a manner inclusive of a province and using Islam as a basis of national social unity, to (2) post-tsunami service as a sometimes dominant source of legal norms (beginning with criminal norms) expressing widely if not universally shared social norms and tending to use technocratic approaches to law as a tool in order to advance those Islamic social convictions. Yet as Feener and others show, the situation is more complex and the change more gradual; and as we shall suggest, the role of the tsunami was not to create an opportunity for expression of pent-up demand for Shariʿa, but rather as a disruptor of a relationship between central government and autonomy-seeking Acehnese forces. That disruption created a new constitutional possibility as the prior relationship and terms of engagement became impossible. Three major forces are often cited in Aceh's rise to prominence culminating in post-tsunami special status enabling partial adoption of Shariʿa: a long-running insurgency seeking autonomous rule, gradual emergence of shared goals between autonomy-seekers and powerful Islamic social movements variably accommodated by the Indonesian government, and discovery of natural gas in Aceh. The nature and interaction of these factors is worth brief exploration as the context in which assessment of the effect of rapid environmental change is offered.

The thirty-year insurgency to which the International Federation of the Red Cross and Red Crescent refer was driven by the 'Free Acheh Movement', Gerakan Aceh Merdeka (GAM), the largest and most militarily effective of a number of autonomy-seeking groups.[39] Aspinall effectively summarizes the

[39] Bertrand explains the rise of GAM as follows: 'The Acehnese mobilization arose in reaction to a series of misguided integrationist, assimilationist, and repressive state policies that caused this basically strong community to turn away from the common Indonesian core. Initially, the Acehnese sided with the Islamist version of Indonesian nationalism, which was defeated by Soekarno's vision of Pancasila and secular nationalism. Participation by Acehnese elites in an Islamic rebellion in the 1950s was met with repression and integration with the North Sumatra province. This triggered, in turn, a regional resistance to the Indonesian state. Next, even though Aceh was restored to the status of a province in 1959, a Free Aceh Movement was created in the mid-1970s in response to other centralizing policies. During the 1970s, when oil and gas resources were discovered in Aceh, from which few benefits accrued locally, a new Acehnese elite, less Islamist and more regionalist, became disillusioned with the centralization of political and economic power. Initially, there was relatively little support for the movement in the 1970s, when it was swiftly crushed by the Indonesian armed forces. Its reappearance in the late 1980s likewise enjoyed minimal popular support until the armed forces designated the whole province a military zone and sweeping operations throughout the 1990s led to human rights abuses and the intense repression of civilians in order to "weed out" Free

scale and human cost of this insurgency and its significance to a central government seeking to foster national cohesion:

> The BRA (*Badan Reintegrasi Damai Aceh*, Aceh Reintegration Agency), the government agency charged with collecting data concerning conflict victims and providing them with economic assistance, indicated in June 2007 that 33,000 people were killed during the 29 years of the Aceh conflict, equivalent to approximately 0.75 per cent of the present population of approximately 4,350,000.[40]

The ongoing tension between autonomy-seeking movements in Aceh and the Indonesian central government in Jakarta was significantly complicated by Aceh's association with a relatively conservative expression of Islam, and the central government's approach to what appears variously to amount to attempts at limited inclusion or adoption of Aceh's Islamic movements, through to attempted co-option of those movements or at least their most popular values. Indonesia's political history from the close of the colonial era to the present is one in which central governments seeking to create unity in a diverse, archipelago state have sought to use largely non-religious values to do so, while simultaneously recognizing the power of religious values as a source of legitimacy. Once independence was achieved and international recognition won at the end of 1949, a nationalist and religiously non-preferential agenda was pursued under Suharto's 'guided democracy'. Following his succession in 1968 by Sukarno, a similarly religiously non-preferential 'New Order' guided Indonesia's development, officially rooted by 'Pancasila' principles advanced on an integrationist agenda as historically antecedent to and more deeply expressive of Indonesian national character than subsequently introduced religious values. Yet there have been points at which Islam has nearly become the dominant source of norms, leaving a residue of specific proposals and knowledge that the largely religiously non-preferential state could be otherwise oriented. Only a last moment change, for example, removed assertion of the Islamic

Aceh Movement supporters. It was this intransigence on the part of the Indonesian state, the failure to redistribute benefits of oil and gas exploitation, as well as the intense repression of the Acehnese population that fueled an ethnonationalist movement. Thus, Indonesian state policies of assimilation and repression ruptured the previously strong attachment of Acehnese to a unifying Indonesian nation'. J. Bertrand 'Indonesia's quasi-federalist approach: accommodation amid strong integrationist tendencies', *International Journal of Constitutional Law*, 5 (2007), p. 591.

[40] E. Aspinall, *Peace without Justice? The Helsinki Peace Process in Aceh* (Geneva, Switzerland: Henry Dunant Centre for Humanitarian Dialogue, 2007), p. 8. Available at https://www.hdcentre.org/wp-content/uploads/2016/08/56JusticeAcehfinalrevJUNE08-May-2008.pdf.

nature of a new Indonesian state proclaimed in the 1945 declaration of independence issued in the gap between Japanese collapse and Dutch attempts to reclaim their former colony; and just a few years later in 1953, the Acehnese contribution to a rebellion against the central government demanded fusion of Islamic identity and the state. Even once a nationalist agenda emerged under successive presidents, with Islam reduced to a means of change rather than the end of change, central governments took pains in accommodating Acehnese autonomy demands to provide state support for quasi-state Islamic social institutions. In the aftermath of the attempted coup in 1965 leading to the transition from Sukarno to Suharto, stabilization efforts included the formation of an Ulama Council by the government of the special region of Aceh. This council is characterized by Feener as 'a new institutional mechanism for the management of Aceh's Islamic religious leadership'[41] in ways enabling those leaders to articulate and promulgate Islamic values in a manner supporting particular policies and 'advancing a broader vision of Islam that could facilitate both social stability and economic development'.[42] Formal recognition and inclusion of a source of Islamic norms into a system of government was accompanied by central government's permission and sometimes sponsorship of increasingly sophisticated forms of Islamic education eventually capable of absorbing and repurposing insights from sometime legal realist Roscoe Pound in a 'development law theory' conceiving of law as a tool to advance social and economic development in accord with Islamic values. One frequently cited institutional development was the formation of the Faculty of Dakwah at the IAIN campus (State Institute of Islamic Studies) in Banda Aceh, a faculty studying and enabling proselytization and development of Islamic doctrine. While initially intended as accommodation of Aceh's demands for greater autonomy, the faculty's actual function led to creation of an Acehnese elite, some associated with GAM, and many capable of articulating precisely how Sharia might influence or take the place of existing law should greater autonomy be achieved, demonstrating a capacity for 'made in Aceh' alternatives to edicts from the capital in Jakarta.[43] The institutionalization and development of Islamic thought in this way created a social activity of value to both those such as GAM seeking autonomy and plans for the polity and legal system to follow rebellion, and to the Indonesian central government seeking to shape and in effect tame Islamic influence on the state.[44]

[41] Feener, *Shari'a*, p. 97. [42] Ibid., p. 98. [43] Ibid., p. 83.

[44] As Feener puts it aptly, 'in many ways, Aceh can be seen as a kind of social laboratory for New Order experiments with the state management of Islam'. Ibid., p. 44.

The discovery in the 1970s of natural gas reserves in Aceh gave autonomy-seekers yet another dimension of Aceh needing the protection of autonomy to enable best use of the new resource, while attracting the attention of central government officials keen to retain a previously relatively poor province as a source of national wealth. As these and other factors interacted in daily life in Aceh, decisive movement towards autonomy, towards an Islamizing political majority, or towards central government co-option and redirection of Islamic or autonomous impulses was very gradual, perhaps in part because the central government made concessions described above, and certainly in part because central government attention to autonomy-seeking movements focussed predominantly on the situation of East Timor then distributed attention to other autonomy-seekers. After the fall of Suharto in 1998 a *Reformasi* period involved response to problems of corruption, cronyism and other ills, and, under international pressure, orderly secession of East Timor. With the status of East Timor settled, under Habibie the Indonesian government turned to rein in Acehnese separatism by granting a status of special autonomy in 1999 via Law 44/1999 on Special Status for Aceh, with further supporting law in Law 18/2001 on Special Autonomy for Nanggroe Aceh Darussalam. Simultaneously, the Indonesian government sought to negotiate with GAM separatists leaders, ultimately to little effect,[45] as GAM leaders still aspired to independence and tensions continued, resulting in a declaration of martial law in 2003. As Aspinall observes,

> most analyses of the law and its implementation concluded that special autonomy was a failure (McGibbon 2004; Miller 2006). Continuing conditions of conflict in the province meant that many of the law's provisions simply could not be implemented. Moreover, the fact that the 'concessions were offered unilaterally' (McGibbon 2004: 16) rather than as a product of a bargain struck with GAM meant that the law had no appreciable effect in lessening the conflict. On the contrary, GAM leaders condemned the law as falling far short of Acehnese aspirations for full independence.[46]

Yet as Aspinall further reports, 'This situation changed dramatically after new negotiations began in Helsinki in early 2005, immediately after the massive Indian Ocean tsunami of 26 December 2004'. In the negotiations, GAM gave up on demands for independence in favour of autonomy, and the Indonesia

45 Ibid., pp. 136ff.

46 E. Aspinall, 'Special autonomy, predatory peace and the resolution of the Aceh conflict', in H. Hill (ed.), *Regional Dynamics in a Decentralized Indonesia* (Singapore: Institute of Southeast Asian Studies, 2014), p. 463.

government abandoned its 2003 aim to eliminate GAM in favour of permitting GAM to participate in political processes eventually including elected leadership roles, all expressed in Law 11/2006 articulating the terms of the Helsinki 2005 Memorandum of Understanding.[47] Subsequent political processes supported both enactment of new elements of Shariʿa, and application of elements of Shariʿa which had been enacted yet not effectively applied prior to the tsunami and Helsinki negotiations. The sense in which Aceh's post-tsunami legal world was continuous with the pre-tsunami legal world is usefully illustrated by following with Feener the career of general legislation and specific regulation regarding symbolically important criminal norms required by Shariʿa:

> The first regional regulation on Islam passed in Aceh during the post-Suharto period was Regional Regulation (I. *Peraturan Daerah*/Per Da) Number 5, issued in 2000. It begins with considerations stressing the need for Islamic values to be firmly established in Acehnese society. Those values were seen to be imperative as the religious life of its people was deemed essential to ensure justice and prosperity, as well as a means of preparing them to face the challenges of globalization. Pursuant to this, the law itself obliges all Muslims to observe Islamic law in its totality (I. *secara kaffah*) and outlines the broad areas to be covered by Shariʿa, including doctrine and religious practice, transactions, ethics, education, marriage law, inheritance, the regulation of religious property, criminal law, *daʿwa*, *syiar*, and 'enjoining good/forbidding wrong'. This list repeats verbatim what was found in the draft legislation of 1968.[48]

Feener identifies as especially significant subordinate 2003 *qanun* on consumption of alcohol, gambling, and association between unmarried men and women,[49] while observing that prosecution pre-tsunami was very rare, even while legal infrastructure to handle such prosecutions evolved to move Shariʿa courts from the supervision of the Department of Religious Affairs to the Supreme Court.[50] Post-tsunami, as the significantly more complex

47 *Memorandum of Understanding between the Government of Indonesia and the Free Aceh Movement*, Helsinki (15 August 2005). Available at www.ucdp.uu.se/gpdatabase/peace/Ind%20050815.pdf.

48 Feener, *Shariʿa*, p. 140, internal notes omitted.

49 Feener explains: 'In terms of defining offenses against the Shariʿa that could be more easily enforced and prosecuted under the legal system of a modern state, the most significant pieces of legislation in contemporary Aceh are three *qanun* passed in 2003: No. 12 on the consumption of alcohol, No. 13 on gambling, and No. 14 on *khalwat* ("improper covert association" between unmarried members of the opposite sex)'. Ibid., p. 144.

50 Feener, ibid., p. 145, observes that 'these three *qanun* have, to date, defined the only areas of Islamic penal law to supply cases to Aceh's Shariʿa Courts (Mahkamah Syariah/MS). Even

and specific Law 11[51] provided further means to create a hybrid system with effective Shari'a courts, debate regarding these specific 2003 *qanun* drove development of a new Islamic criminal code.[52] In 2009 the *Qanun Jinayat* was contentiously enacted by an outgoing government but enacted nonetheless, and variably effective implementation has followed,[53] sometimes giving rise to highly selective notice in the Western press of instances of action, e.g., caning,[54] seemingly at odds with the Helsinki memorandum's insistence on implementation of a legal order consistent with general norms of international humanitarian law.[55]

The career of these Shari'a criminal norms and their codification illustrates usefully the complexity of the situation in which the 2004 tsunami's arrival had a decisive force of a kind and weight we shall address momentarily. There is, it appears, no pivotal moment in which Shari'a took hold. Rather, a predominantly Muslim society in Aceh with a history of advocacy of Shari'a and long-standing use in limited matters such as family law was already on a path to greater inclusion of Shari'a at the time of the arrival of the tsunami. Progress on that path was very gradual, and Shari'a was as much a tool of central government accommodation of Acehnese society to

so, few arrests were made and no formal sentences were executed for violations of Islamic law for almost two full years after these laws were enacted. Indeed, it was only after the massive destruction of the 2004 earthquake and tsunami that the institutions of state Shari'a came to assert a more active role in attempt to manage the dramatic social and political transformations that swept over Aceh in the post- disaster/post-conflict period'. See ibid., p. 165, on changes to court structures.

51 As Bertrand observes, 'this text is a vast improvement over the 2001 Special Autonomy Law of Aceh. Even at a superficial level, it is quite clear that the new law pertaining to Aceh is superior. The 2001 Special Autonomy Law of Aceh has 34 articles; the Special Autonomy Law for Papua (2001) has 79 articles, while the Law on Aceh Government of 2006 has 210. The latter includes much more detailed elaboration of the rights and obligations of the governor and the Aceh legislature, the local electoral process, determinants of fiscal revenues, and control over the exploitation of natural resources. It also includes articles on such issues as human rights, security forces, and the obligations of the Aceh government to provide services in the social and health sectors. Clearly, the latest version covers a much broader range of issues and is more specific in its details than its previous incarnation'. Bertrand, 'Indonesia's quasi-federalist approach', p. 600.

52 Feener, *Shari'a*, p. 148.

53 See generally ibid., Chapter 6, 'The jurisdiction and jurisprudence of Shari'a courts'.

54 See, e.g., M. Jamaluddin, 'Indonesian couple caned for violating Sharia law, police official says', *Cable News Network* (30 December 2015). Available at www.cnn.com/2015/12/30/asia/indonesia-caning/?iid=ob_article_organicsidebar_expansion&iref=obnetwork.

55 See the *Memorandum of Understanding*, Section 1.4.2. The legislature of Aceh will redraft the legal code for Aceh on the basis of the universal principles of human rights as provided for in the United Nations International Covenants on Civil and Political Rights and on Economic, Social and Cultural Rights'. Available at www.ucdp.uu.se/gpdatabase/peace/Ind%20050815.pdf.

defuse separatist aspirations as it was a specific demand of the bulk of Achenese or GAM as an active political elite and military insurgency. Shari'a arrived with as much devolutionary as revolutionary force, following central government granting of limited autonomy in 1999, then reframing that autonomy in 2001. At last in 2006 post-tsunami and post-conflict, in still further devolved Aceh, earlier enactment of symbolically important Shari'a was at length matched by implementation, and then in 2009 by systematic expression of a much larger body of criminal norms. Even now the merit of inclusion of Shari'a is hotly debated in Aceh, and the future of the new hybrid legal order is uncertain. This gradual change was certainly punctuated by natural disaster, then shaped by international attention to the social situation of Aceh and participation in its reconstruction. So what exactly was the force of the tsunami and what role did environmental preconditions of legality play in the changing identity of legal order in Aceh? As we have cited Aspinall observing, 'This situation changed dramatically' after the Helsinki talks, in turn after the tsunami.

Feener, like Aspinall, and indeed all commentators on the rise of Shari'a, recognizes the importance of the tsunami, but gives it relatively little direct attention, as might be reasonably expected in the work of a scholar whose first concern is not with the relation of environment to continuity of legal orders of some identity. Feener's concerns are clearly different: 'The focus of this book is on the institutions and actors involved with this twenty-first-century project for the state implementation of Islamic law in pursuit of social transformation'.[56] Yet at the same time Feener is keenly aware of the importance of the tsunami in creating the conditions for the current rise of Shari'a in Aceh: 'The trauma of the natural disaster accelerated the peace process toward ending the conflict between GAM and the Indonesian government'.[57] It is of course understandable that a scholar focussed on how Shari'a has arrived at its present force in Aceh would write in these broad terms, which for us are both comprehensible yet incomplete for our purposes as 'trauma' and 'accelerated need further specification if we are to assign a precise scope and weight to the influence of the tsunami'. This becomes particularly important in light of the argument by Michael Buehler, reviewing Feener's *Shari'a and Social Engineering* title, that the prominence of Shari'a in Aceh is better explained by a purely political account, since increased adoption of Shari'a is evident throughout Indonesia even in jurisdictions unaffected by the tsunami:

[56] Feener, *Shari'a*, p. 4. [57] Ibid.

> Feener's argument that *shari'a* laws began to be adopted quickly and widely only *after* the devastation caused by the 2004 tsunami and in the context of a discourse on 'social engineering' and 'building back better' that ensued from an influx of foreign aid workers, is again undermined by the similar trajectory the adoption of *shari'a* laws has followed in other parts of Indonesia. While the legal framework to adopt Islamic law has been in place since 1999, there was an uptick in the adoption of *shari'a* regulations across the country in 2005, that is, soon after direct elections for local government heads were introduced that year. These direct elections increased the need for local politicians to be seen as innovative and visionary. It is difficult, in other words, to disentangle the effects that the late-2004 natural disaster had on the Islamization in Aceh from the effects changes in the political system had on the adoption of Islamic law throughout the province.[58]

This negative criticism is as difficult to evaluate as Feener's original positive claim: both attempt to 'disentangle' a complex set of causes and effects. The best news for our inquirer is that there are situations roughly analogous to Aceh providing comparative insight drawing attention to the question of the tsunami's role in rapid and unexpected political and legal change. As we address the question from our interest in identity and continuity of a legal order, the task of comprehensive disentanglement is less urgent for us than it is for scholars of Shari'a. Our concern is not with the particular content and form of Shari'a as a legal order, nor the content of the transitional justice truth and reconciliation commission following the Helsinki agreement. Rather, as inquirers into identity and continuity of legal order, we can advance understanding of the causal role of the tsunami by investigating it first at the more general level of the question of the difference made by the tsunami to the total constitution of Indonesian law pre- and post-tsunami, pre- and post- devolution as expressed in the 2006 Law on Aceh Government. Investigation at this level of organization necessarily involves consideration of the Indonesian state and the province of Aceh in international perspective, to the extent that post-tsunami aid arrived with European Union monitoring, and previously cited Helsinki agreement commitments to reform of the Acehnese legal system in a manner consistent with international humanitarian law. A system-centred approach limited to the interaction of the Indonesian state with the province of Aceh omits inclusion of not just sources of legal norms in the renovated Acehnese legal order, but the institutional force of their non-Indonesian advocates. Asking not a system-centred question regarding how the

[58] M. Buehler, 'Review of *Shari'a and social engineering* by R.M. Feener', *Indonesia*, 98 (October 2014), p. 151, internal notes omitted.

tsunami contributed to the rise of Shari'a, but more broadly what the tsunami did to legal order in Indonesia, we do not see an authority-claiming centre accommodating peripheral variation under a nationalist project and unitary constitution, and see instead a state-accepted devolution being driven in particular ways by a natural disaster to arrive at *de facto* renegotiation of Indonesia's constitution to include a provincial hybrid – recognizing of course that ongoing disputes regarding central control of appointment of judges in Shari'a courts, alongside similar issues in core-periphery legal relations, all contribute to uncertainty regarding the institutional force of the nascent hybrid legal order. In this view, explicitly aiming to explain both non-Indonesian legal sources and institutions and the further influence of the tsunami, a general yet reasonably precise assessment of the tsunami's effect prior to 'entanglement' can be offered. The tsunami's least controversial, least entangled effect seems to be its disruption of the preconditions of the central government's action as a legal authority-claiming exclusive jurisdiction such that accommodations or terms of negotiation of dispute are hierarchically assigned by the government to the dispute – most evident in legal-normative terms in the 2003 imposition of martial law and associated attempt to eliminate GAM.[59] Pre-tsunami, the central government's identity as expressed in the Indonesian legal system included simultaneously norms regarding conditions under which social services were to be provided, and conditions under which grievances were to be aired, with imposition of martial law as one response to the failure of GAM to use existing grievance procedures. Post-tsunami, the Indonesian legal system's claims to authority in Aceh became so distant from the system's implementation capacity in the interface between legal claims, officials, physical resources and supporting social sub-systems, that the Indonesian government could not provide basic guarantees with respect to application of its own standards. As reported by the Red Cross (cited above), there was a delay between the impact of the tsunami and the decision to permit non-Indonesian aid to contribute to disaster response. While the reasoning leading to permission of external intervention is not fully available, the delay is indicative of a gap or incompleteness in the government's total normative framing of the situation in legal rights, obligations, permissions, etc., supported by political decision making. The conduct of the Indonesian state in assertion of its legal system does not appear

59 According to Aspinall, 'GAM leaders did not budge from their goal of complete independence, and were dismissive of the special autonomy formulation. The continuing distance between the two sides on this fundamental issue meant that the ceasefires always broke down. Eventually, the government declared a state of 'military emergency' in the province in 2003 and declared it would eliminate GAM once and for all'. Aspinall, 'Special autonomy', p. 463, internal notes omitted.

to be in this instance anything like a borderline case where a state simply permits social states of affairs at variance from the requirements of applicable legal norms, as often occurs periodically and to varied extents in state-based legal systems whose identity and continuity are typically unquestioned. Whatever the reasoning leading to permission of external intervention, that intervention expresses admission of the incompleteness of internal response resources. No authority in such a circumstance is likely to be unaware of the range of possible consequences following external intervention, from simple debts of gratitude to invasion and replacement of political elites and legal systems, with intermediate options including adoption but not inclusion of externally sourced legal norms in disaster response. Even without speculating on the specific motivations of Indonesia's legal officials and the range of consequences they may have anticipated following permission of external intervention, it remains that the tsunami was the cause in whose absence it seems unlikely that international organizations' (and in particular, the European Union's) attention would have focussed on Aceh. It also seems unlikely that devolution of powers and *de facto* constitutional change would have gained a place on the agenda subsequent to international scrutiny motivating both the government of Indonesia and GAM to change their negotiating positions quite fundamentally from the prior stance of martial law and an exclusive state authority's capacity to set terms of engagement with bearers of grievances.

In this context, a focus on the place of Shariʿa in legal change in Indonesia has the potential to be quite misleading to our inquiry into the role of environmental preconditions in continuity and change of the Indonesian legal order, since the nature of the change in the relations between the Indonesian central government and Aceh is only contingently associated with Shariʿa. As we saw above, GAM was a separatist movement in an Islamic social context, not an Islamic separatist movement. It is easily imaginable that the dominant sources of the content of post-tsunami, post-conflict, post-devolution Aceh might be quite different. Acehnese law under devolution might have become secular in source, instantiating directly at provincial level norms of international humanitarian law together with a secular conception of development enabled by norms similarly imported from another system. There is no reason to suppose the fact of the tsunami would have any determining effect with respect to options for forms of legal order once devolution occurs following otherwise unexpected conflict resolution. After devastation including physical elimination of legal records, a legal tabula rasa of a limited form is created, where it perhaps remains easiest to use surrounding legal resources to both recreate and create applications of law resulting in something similar to the pre-existing social and legal situation. That is, however, only one option, and the absence of certain records, destruction of infrastructure and dislocation of persons equally offers an opportunity to introduce new legal norms and applications of those norms.

The combination of reasons supplied above supports our claim that the effect of the tsunami least liable to counter-claims of under-determination of that effect is the disruption of the hierarchical relation between state and grievance-bearing autonomy-seekers. Our interpretation is not the end of analysis, and while we believe our view is more persuasive than that offered by Feener as an explanation of the jurisprudential significance of the tsunami (and consequently the weight accorded the tsunami in a causal explanation of the emergence of Shari'a in an Acehnese hybrid legal system), we recognize that his expertise in the empirical dimension of the situation might easily bring fresh facts causing us to change our view. We are also conscious that further conceptual work remains to be done, perhaps in part because analytical legal theory's long holiday from the problem of continuity has left us without needed conceptual tools. But this much is of course ordinary in any jurisprudential context where experts in legal doctrine, historians, comparatists and others come together to engage what all recognize is a problem. Here, we suggest, lies the greater importance of any disagreement with Feener on characterization of the impact of the tsunami: no matter whether Feener's or our explanation is best, we believe we have demonstrated that an understanding of the environmental preconditions of legal order in Indonesia, and disruption via the tsunami, is an important dimension of a comprehensive account of legal change in this context, and an illustration of the importance of consideration of environmental preconditions in accounts of the nature of law capable of presenting a solution to the problem of continuity.

Our discussion above may be controversial in light of the complexity of the circumstances it examines and the tentative nature of the legal change which has occurred. It might be objected that it is too soon to tell whether the devolutionary actions surveyed are sufficiently durable to warrant assessing the situation as one in which identity and continuity have changed in ways usefully explained as a transition to a new hybrid legal order. It could be further objected that while we have supplied an intuitively compelling example of the relevance of environmental preconditions to continuity of a particular instantiation of a form of legal order, we too fall to the criticism we think troubles Feener: it is impossible to distinguish the effect of environmental change from the effects of other surrounding features in the causal story of legal change in Indonesia. Response to these objections may be constrained by the limited availability of relevant facts regarding a changing situation in Indonesia, but we hope we have shown enough evidence so far to warrant readers' asking for more evidence rather than rejecting the argument as a whole, and to ask for further examples for the conceptual claims we have shown to be plausible in the Indonesian context.

Our next example is drawn from a context within the familiar characteristics of state-based legal systems, yet unusual to the extent that it involves a very small state: the Republic of Kiribati. The unusual need not be unrepresentative however, and in this case, the nature of the state's territory as a group of islands makes it unusually vulnerable to a change in environmental conditions which might affect other, larger states less forcefully, but may affect them nonetheless. The experience of Kiribati may be regarded as a scalable version of what might occur elsewhere with respect to particular forms of environmental change. Kiribati's population of approximately 112,000 persons inhabits a territory composed of three island groups and smaller atolls totalling 810 square kilometres distributed over a little more than approximately one-third of a million square kilometres of the Pacific Ocean.[60] Following British colonial administration Kiribati achieved self-rule in 1971 and independence in 1979, under a constitution[61] continuing the prior common law-sourced legal system with incorporation of Kiribati customary law.[62] Notwithstanding its small size, Kiribati's status as an independent state is uncontroversial, as it is a member of the Commonwealth, the International Monetary Fund, the World Bank and, since 1999 the UN.[63]

Kiribati is of interest to us because its existence as a Montevideo-consistent state with a defined territory, populace and legal system is under threat from environmental change in a manner raising new questions about the continuity and identity of a legal system. None, we think, dispute that a sufficiently serious natural disaster can bring a legal system to an end, and all accept that law and environment are related in that basic way. But nothing about this possibility warrants re-thinking of our conceptual commitments regarding the nature of legal system or its centrality to contemporary jurisprudence – this is simply one more way in which a legal system can end, in addition to conquest, revolution and so on. Kiribati is different. The environmental change it faces may disrupt the foundations of its identity and change the conditions under which it can continue, all without necessarily ending the system's existence. This situation, we suggest, is one in which environmental change does challenge the idea of legal system to the extent that it demonstrates one way in which a legal order

[60] See generally www.president.gov.ki/about-kiribati/.

[61] Kiribati Independence Order, 1979. Available at www.paclii.org/ki/constitution/Kiribati%20Independence%20Order%201979.pdf.

[62] See generally www.paclii.org/ki/sources.html.

[63] www.president.gov.ki/about-kiribati/.

is subject to external influences in ways yet to be thoroughly characterized, and further demonstrates the dependence of legality on a social and natural base much broader and more varied than the practices of officials.

Kiribati, like many small island states, is vulnerable to sea-level rise. Effects anticipated include storm surges damaging port and other infrastructure, immersion of some areas, increased flooding of other areas, erosion and saline water intrusion into fresh groundwater supplies.[64] Governments of small island states including Kiribati have long been aware of the challenge,[65] and equally aware of scientific developments regarding the complexity of the challenge. As a recent new feature in *Nature* reports, 'the latest assessment steered clear of the Intergovernmental Panel on Climate Change's previous assertion that an 80-centimetre rise would inundate two-thirds of Kiribati' while continuing to predict rises of fifty centimetres and acknowledging the variability of effects on island states of sea-level rise.[66] A reduction in the estimated level of sea-level rise may, however, be less good news than a change in the shape of a challenge which might still be insurmountable, as even a lower level of sea-level rise may still overwhelm island states with few natural resources, growing populations and low incomes. President Tong of Kiribati has responded to its current state and future predictions by developing a plan for 'migration with dignity', writing in stark terms in the forward to the 2013 National Framework for Climate Change and Climate Change Adaptation that

> Kiribati has known for some time that the impacts of climate change will no doubt render it uninhabitable in the future. The science has been quite clear for some time now and new and emerging science is only confirming that the unthinkable is going to happen – while it is both a poignant and difficult issue – all the more so because of the emotional implications attached to it, it is also a call for us as a nation to be most diligent in our effort to be prepared for the unthinkable and for what lies ahead of us in the face of climate change.[67]

The Framework's plan for migration is set out as a matter of seeking a willing host nation, establishing a Kiribati community, and preparing for eventual final evacuation:

[64] L. A. Nurse et al., 'Small islands', in V. R. Barros et al. (eds), *Climate Change 2014* (Cambridge: Cambridge University Press, 2014), p. 1616.

[65] See, e.g., two reports of the Commonwealth Secretariat's Expert Group on Climate Change and Sea Level Rise: Lewis et al., *Sea Level Rise* (London: Commonwealth Secretariat, 1988), and Holdgate et al., *Climate Change* (London: Commonwealth Secretariat, 1989).

[66] K. R. Weiss, 'Before we drown we may die of thirst', *Nature*, vol. 526 (2015), p. 627.

[67] Office of Te Beretitenti, *National Framework for Climate Change and Climate Change Adaptation* (Kiribati, 2013). Available at www.president.gov.ki/wp-content/uploads/2014/08/National-Framework-for-Climate-Change-Climate-Change-Adaptation.pdf.

> The need to reduce the vulnerability of Kiribati to increasing physical risks caused by climate change forms an important part of the case for host country agreement to government-sponsored and self-sponsored emigration to resettle I-Kiribati overseas so as to establish a community which can then sponsor and assist the inevitable migration of the whole population, due to CC, as and when this eventually arrives.[68]

As *Nature* reported in November 2015, the Framework is more than political posturing:

> Last year, his government completed an US$8-million purchase of 22 square kilometres of hilly land in Fiji, to grow food and provide possible refuge for some of his people – although it will not accommodate all of them. He does not know when people will need to migrate, but he wants to purchase more land in Australia and New Zealand, saying that it is much cheaper than trying to build sea walls and other defences. 'If we build up these lands, it's going to cost billions of dollars', he says. 'We might as well be buying land for millions of dollars elsewhere'.[69]

This practical step is accompanied by reflection in the Framework on the legal status and power of Kiribati in the near-term, and in the longer term, raising issues at the side of most debates in system-centred legal theory. In reflections on 'Survivability and Self-Reliance' the Framework questions near-term matters such as jurisdiction over diminishing maritime spaces, and property rights after inundation. Greater jurisprudential interest arrives with a set of questions asked regarding the nature of statehood and 'options for a "disappearing state"' including the question 'Should "deterritorialized statehood" be a permanent or a transitional status?' and how such an ongoing status might be managed via 'reservations where displaced states can be reconstituted'.[70] Kiribati asks these questions without supplying answers, deploying possible descriptions of present and future states in cautious terms yet to have determinate legal meaning. It remains possible, as demonstrated in the emerging literature, to approach these questions via standard strategies for apparently novel phenomena, finding room for those phenomena within the open texture of broad concepts already used. Or we might deploy existing concepts in a manner which in combination captures and responds to the phenomena albeit at the risk of addressing it piecemeal and non-comprehensively – an amalgam, for example of the Law of the Sea, international refugee law, international humanitarian law, etc. Since our purpose here is not to resolve Kiribati's future legal status, but to demonstrate the importance of

68 Ibid., p. 21. 69 Weiss, 'Before we drown', p. 626.
70 Office of Te Beretitenti, *National Framework*, p. 26.

environmental preconditions of legal order in an account of legality, we shall leave to others the doctrinal questions arising regarding possibilities for application of existing law and legal categories to Kiribati citizens in a post-territorial era. We suggest, however, that the way Kiribati frames its concerns in terms not of refuge and assimilation but reservations and state reconstitution that these aspirations weigh in favour of conducting jurisprudential investigations finding new concepts and categories better capable of expressing and framing legal developments beyond accommodation in ill-fitting concepts. We share, then, the assessment of Jenny Grote Stoutenberg, that once analogies between deterritorialized states and special sovereign entities such as the Sovereign Order of Malta are set aside as incomplete, a much greater transformation, yet to be given its conceptual structure, remains to be developed: 'The ascription of full status and participation rights usually reserved for "traditional states" to genuinely non-territorial entities would require the greatest structural transformation international law has seen since the establishment of the so-called "Westphalian order"'.[71]

As helpful as these examples are to illustrate the importance of attention to the complexity of the preconditions of legality, and particularly environmental preconditions, they are in another sense misleading. The bases of challenges to continuity of legality may be much more mundane, yet still complex, as dramatic changes in social life may be few, and changes invisible to the ordinary citizen may nonetheless have far-reaching consequences. It is nonetheless necessary for a contextualized conceptual exploration of the nature of law to select certain families of social and physical facts to which it will be responsive, both because some facts are more relevant to legality than others, and more particularly, because some facts are more relevant than others to developing an epistemic stance from which to address the problem of continuity of legality as a theoretical and practical problem. This choice is just that, a choice reflecting investigators' sense of the concerns of ordinary citizens who might be readers of a contextualized conceptual explanation of legality. Demonstration that we have articulated 'correctly' or 'reliably' the concerns of an era is of course difficult in the absence of a global survey, and in any case the value of the contextualized conceptual explanation rests not in the population of a potential audience but in the explanatory value gained by an actual audience. We propose extension of Hart's relational method from his concern with law, morality and coercion, to consideration of law's relation to environment, security and technology, visible in the life world of the twenty-first-century

[71] J. G. Stoutenburg, *Disappearing Island States in International Law* (Leiden, Netherlands: Brill, 2015), p. 387.

citizen who travels and sees in these relations, considered individually and together, the grounds of troubling potential for lack of continuity of legality threatening law's capacity to protect our ordinary citizens' normative expectations. To return to an expression introduced in the first chapter, investigation of these new relations might enable the twenty-first-century citizen to pull off the mask of law which has for a long time shown itself in state legal systems' claims to comprehensive and supreme authority over the lives of their territorially defined norm-subjects.

THE PRECONDITIONS OF LEGALITY: SUMMING UP

The above discussion is admittedly incomplete and inconclusive. It is best viewed as an attempt to build from Twining's remarks on globalization to offer a glimpse of part of a renewed agenda for analytical legal theory, an agenda which takes seriously the logical contingency of dimensions of the natural world typically regarded as stable givens in the context of analytical legal theory. As our examples begin to show, however, profound change is not merely possible but evident in changing facts beyond the 'heterogeneous social facts' Hart saw at the root of legal order. Profound change is evident in both social *and* physical phenomena which serve as both the preconditions of legal order as seen historically in the law-state and its authorship of a continuous albeit evolving legal system. Investigation of law's relations to environment, security and technology is one means by which we can analyse such preconditions.

The sources of profound change we identify and explore are important for reasons rooted in their salience to the twenty-first-century citizen experiencing rapid globalization, and additionally important insofar as they give rise to fresh questions regarding the form legality might take in circumstances where the preconditions of legality as historically found in state-based legal systems no longer prevail. Hart's and Raz's preoccupation with the conditions under which a legal system may exist may become outmoded, as it is no longer clear that legality occurs exclusively under the authority or sponsorship of state legal systems. Those entities are revealed to be much less closed systems with occasional interface with others via, e.g., treaties, and much more nodes in networks of legality, or perhaps even national legal narratives passing through phases of identity as, e.g., sovereign state, to protectorate, to member of a supra-state legal order, through failed state status and on to some other status. It might well be enduringly the case that the norm-level approach to legality fostered by Hart, Raz and others remains viable in a world where law's relations to environment, security and technology give rise to novel arrangements of legal institutions. It is increasingly clear, however, that we cannot presume the centrality of the law-state in the way past theorists have done, so must open our investigations to addition of further central objects of study, and attempts to deepen our reflection on legality's nature by reflecting on its relation to newly important, emerging social and natural phenomena. In doing so, we complement the comparatists and their lateral view across legal cultures, providing in our three relational foci opportunities to go deeply into how particular legal cultures experience institutions of law characterized by comparative legal analysis.

6

Legality, Security and Leviathan's Ghost

The preceding chapter's focus on law's relation to environment was just the first step in contextualized construction of a concept of law via consideration of its relation to other phenomena visible to our ordinary citizen of the twenty-first century. This chapter's task is to complement and extend the relational view. Where law's relation to environment revealed what might be called fundamental preconditions of legality and touched relatively briefly on environment's role in continuity, here our examination of law's relation to security is mainly focussed on preconditions of various particular forms of continuous or discontinuous legal order, with relatively little attention to fundamental security preconditions of legality. This focus extends our exploration of law's relation to phenomena judged important from the point of view of the twenty-first-century citizen who travels and encounters varying degrees of security more often than its total absence, and it deepens our approach to characterization of both state-based and non-state-based legal phenomena to which an adequate general theory of law must be responsive.

Our investigation of law's relation to security arises in the context of globalization and increased recognition of the diversity of forms of political and legal order. In this context it is increasingly common for legal theorists to investigate whether features of legality previously presumed to be universally found in states are in fact so, or whether such features are found in greater degrees of variation than previously supposed, or perhaps found beyond states, as, e.g., investigation of the extent to which the rule of law as an ideal may be realized in international law as well as state law. Similarly motivated investigations are now inquiring into the link between sovereignty and security, in the context of state systems of law whose identity is at least partly characterized in terms of claims to or effective assertion of sovereignty as an ideal measured in terms of actual security. As we become increasingly well-acquainted with diverse forms of legal order performing functions previously presumed to accrue to states, there is less an air of paradox than a puzzling change needing better explanation when we read headlines such as the *Economist*'s recent examination of Iraq under the title 'Iraq without America: sovereignty without security'.[1] Is the old equation of sovereignty with security under threat as a theoretical explanation of the nature and locus of legality's principal manifestation? How ought analytical legal theorists to respond to the need claimed by Amitai Etzioni, amongst others, to explain the 'fading of the old world order of national borders and the evolution of a nascent global regime'?[2] Analytical legal theorists might yet need to take seriously the phenomena and possibility mooted by economist Peter Leeson in the title of his 'Better off stateless: Somalia before and after government collapse'.[3] However these questions are resolved, it is increasingly implausible to suppose that they are simply borderline cases, perhaps best viewed as twenty-first-century versions of the social situations John Stuart Mill once thought beyond consideration in certain forms of moral debate, arguing that 'we may leave out of consideration those backward states of society in which the race itself may be considered as in its nonage'.[4] Such an implausible division of the world's cultures receives little support today. Moreover, for the purposes of a theory of law aspiring to the greatest possible level of generality, an approach to legality which presumes that the wealthy, stable, liberal-democratic states of the Global North carry the mark and measure of legality risks parochial irrelevance in a world where, as Leeson reports, 'According to the 2007 Failed States Index, nearly 16 percent of the world's countries (32) have "failing states"'.[5] In this context, breaches of the identification of sovereignty with security are not simply borderline cases whose resolution into 'proper sovereignty' or 'total lawlessness' is just a development to be awaited. Rather, we have arrived at a new version of Hart's 'persistent question' about law's relation to coercion: what might analytical legal theory contribute to understanding the relation between state sovereignty and security in an era where even major powers such as the USA increasingly treat sovereignty as

1 'Iraq without America: sovereignty without security', *The Economist* (31 December 2011). Available at www.economist.com/node/21542200.

2 A. Etzioni, 'A liberal communitarian paradigm for counter terrorism', *Stanford Journal of International Law*, 9 (2013), p. 344.

3 P. Leeson, 'Better off stateless: Somalia before and after government collapse', *Journal of Comparative Economics*, 35 (2007), pp. 689–710.

4 J. S. Mill, *On Liberty*, 4th edn (London: Longman, Roberts and Green, 1869), Chapter 1, Section I.10.

5 Leeson, 'Better off stateless', p. 690. Current data are available at the Fragile States Index online: http://fsi.fundforpeace.org.

situational and defeasible[6] and a once paradoxical situation of sovereignty without security now seems to be reality?

This chapter proceeds in four parts. The first is an investigation of the concept of security, aiming to contextualize the concept in legal theory and in practice, to better understand the ways in which security matters to the emergence, continuation and extinction of a given legal order. The second part turns to the relation between security and law as understood via our inter-institutional approach. Our exploration of law's relation to security will benefit, we believe, from our previously argued view that explanation of legality proceeds best when not encumbered by the presumption that state-based law is the central phenomena to be explained by a theory of law, placing other examples of legality in hierarchical relation to the central, organizing experience of state-based law. In the third part we return to the question of the data to which a descriptive-explanatory account of law aims to be responsive, inquiring into the possibility of new insights into law arising from greater attention to social scientific investigations given comparatively little attention in state-centred investigations of the nature of law and legal order. The discussions in the first three parts contribute to the fourth part's return to a new persistent question, identifying a research agenda for analytical legal theory's engagement with the diverse phenomena of security, with particular attention to continuity of legality.

WHAT IS SECURITY?

Any investigation of law's relation to security must begin with the vagueness of the concept of security, and the diverse conceptions of the concept evident at present and in the history of its application. These features of the concept raise several challenges for analytical legal theorists exploring the law-security relation in the twenty-first century. Our analysis may be limited by the ineliminable vagueness of the concept of security, and even an epistemically modest analysis may be limited by the impracticality of surveying all applications of the concept to root out special uses or misappropriation of the concept in service of only loosely related purposes. These inevitable shortcomings are tempered, however, by our investigation's needing not a comprehensive conceptual analysis and social history of security, but an understanding of how the concept of security can inform understanding of legality. More particularly for our purposes, we need an understanding of the techniques and arguments

[6] E.g., extra-territorial drone attacks.

deployed by analytical legal theorists, in dynamic interaction with social phenomena prompting particular investigators' concern with particular aspects and applications of the concept of security. It may be helpful to examine a rough parallel between this analysis and Joseph Raz's investigation of the rule of law. In 'The rule of law and its virtue' Raz insists that the rule of law is one 'political ideal' amongst several virtues of a legal system, variably present, and potentially present in both admirable and deplorable legal systems:

> The rule of law is a political ideal which a legal system may lack or may possess to a greater or lesser degree. That much is common ground. It is also to be insisted that the rule of law is just one of the virtues which a legal system may possess and by which it is to be judged. It is not to be confused with democracy, justice, equality (before the law or otherwise), human rights of any kind or respect for persons or for the dignity of man. A non-democratic legal system, based on the denial of human rights, on extensive poverty, on racial segregation, sexual inequalities, and religious persecution may, in principle, conform to the requirements of the rule of law better than any of the legal systems of the more enlightened Western democracies. This does not mean that it will be better than those Western democracies. It will be an immeasurably worse legal system, but it will excel in one respect: in its conformity to the rule of law.[7]

Our analysis of security follows the spirit of Raz's distinction of censorial from expository tasks in understanding the rule of law, accepting the need for expository sensitivity to varying degrees of realization of security, and the role of security as one feature amongst others in life under law. We draw a further lesson from Raz's context-sensitive analysis noting the situation of Western democracies as just one locus of the rule of law: our analysis must at least eventually be thoroughly contextualized in relevant data, largely but not exclusively social scientific. In developing a relational approach relevant to the interests of our travelling citizen, the data on which we draw must be historically sensitive while reaching beyond history to consider contemporary facts bearing on security's relation to legality.

In this context, historical antecedents to contemporary applications of the concept of security are relatively few, associated chiefly with the rise of the modern nation-state and particular situations in the existence of such states. As Jeremy Waldron observes while addressing American legislative and executive response to terrorism,

[7] J. Raz, 'The rule of law and its virtue', in *The Authority of Law*, 2nd edn (Oxford: Clarendon Press, 1980), p. 211.

> when people talk in the literature or in court about 'the definition of security' what they usually produce is some view about what security requires at a particular time (in the way of legal or political measures). They say nothing about the meaning of the concept itself. Although we know that 'security' is a vague and ambiguous concept and though we should suspect that its vagueness is a source of danger when talk of trade-offs is in the air, still there has been little or no attempt in the literature of legal and political theory to bring any sort of clarity to the concept.[8]

To say that there has been 'little or no attempt' to clarify the concept of security is of course rhetorical overstatement – Waldron cites Hobbes and Bentham as using the idea of security, albeit with slim accompanying conceptual explanation. Hobbes famously argued that a sovereign's capacity to provide security to subjects is the central reason why subjects ought to reject the 'war of every man against every man' in the state of nature, in favour of binding themselves to the directives of their sovereign.[9] Bentham deployed a different conception of security, or perhaps simply deployed a similar conception in a different context. Bentham was centrally concerned, as Gerald Postema has demonstrated, with law's protection of norm-subjects' expectations, and the ways in which security of expectation could be threatened by retroactive or unclear legal directives.[10] So while Waldron is right that the nature of security has received relatively little attention, it is scarcely as though earlier theorists had nothing to say about security, or its relation to law.

A similar picture is evident in the work of contemporary analytical legal theorists writing in the context of the modern municipal state. Hart, for example, explained as a natural necessity the fact that all legal systems have rules regulating the use of violence, ownership of property and the protection of promises. Without such rules, Hart thought, there would be little merit in having a legal system at all. Given the way humans are and can be expected to behave in social contexts, rules governing violence, property and promises are necessary for social life. Hart did not indicate clearly, however, whether he supposed such rules could bring about the security they aimed at, or whether they

[8] J. Waldron, *Torture, Terror and Trade-offs* (Oxford: Oxford University Press 2010), pp. 111–112, internal notes omitted.

[9] T. Hobbes, *Leviathan*, ed. C. B. MacPherson (London: Penguin, 1968), Chapters 13 and 14. Larry May has recently put Hobbes's view of security to use in showing when sovereign states' claims to be free from outside intervention (when international crimes are alleged) is compromised. L. May, *Crimes against Humanity* (Cambridge: Cambridge University Press, 2005), Chapter 4. May presents the 'security principle' as a necessary condition of the justification of states' claims to be free from external intervention.

[10] See also G. Postema, *Bentham and the Common Law Tradition* (Oxford: Clarendon Press, 1986), p. 272.

depend on pre-existing respect for persons, property and promises. Moreover, Hart takes no steps, beyond asserting the 'minimum content of natural law' as a 'natural necessity' of legal systems, to investigate the precise nature or significance of security, or to identify its characteristic features. Here Waldron's view of the lack of attention to the concept of security is certainly correct, even while it remains unclear just why Hart's analysis did not extend further.

What, then, might a better account of security do to meet the challenge Waldron sets, having surveyed antecedent accounts and found them dedicated more to use than explanation of the concept of security? Waldron agrees with Hobbes that physical safety sits at the core of security. Hobbes was surely right that subjects can enjoy no security if their survival or physical well-being is unprotected and constantly at risk. Yet even Hobbes maintained that mere survival in any condition is insufficient. As Waldron notes, safety, for Hobbes, also includes a 'happy life so far as that is possible'.[11] This, however, is as much as we get from Hobbes.

Waldron's contribution to explanation of the concept of security follows a path glimpsed in Hobbes's view, rooted in the idea of physical safety, then supplemented with additional features which capture or identify elements which round out and explain our commitments displayed in using the concept of security. Immediately beyond physical safety, Waldron observes, we must distinguish the notion of personal or human security from notions of collective or national security. Collective security involves the type of peace and stability found in the absence of conflict or war between states, while national security refers to the type of power or endurance of state governments and institutions considered in relation to their own territories. As Waldron maintains, however, neither of these types of security are valuable for their own sake; rather, they are only valuable to the extent to which they serve such personal goods as personal security. Waldron thus limits his discussion of security to personal security, leaving aside issues of collective and national security (to which we return below).

Waldron's analysis of personal security suggests that at first glance it might be thought to be nearly synonymous with personal safety:

> Nobody wants to be blown up. So security might be understood simply as a function of individual safety. We might say, *I* am more secure against terrorist attack when the probability of *my* being killed or harmed as a result of such attack goes down; and *we* are more secure when this is true *of many of us*. I shall call this *the pure safety conception*.[12]

[11] Waldron, *Torture*, p. 114. [12] Ibid., p. 117.

Yet the pure safety conception of security is, Waldron argues, radically incomplete as an account of the nature, value and importance of personal security. In particular, he claims, it fails to consider seven issues:

1. The pure safety conception offers no explanation of why we fear death or injury in some guises and not others – why we orient the notion of safety which we are using to form our conception of security towards *violent* death or injury and perhaps particularly towards violent death or injury at the hands of a particular sort of assailant, namely terrorists.
2. The focus of the pure safety conception is bodily survival and bodily integrity. But what about material loss, such as loss of property or economic value? Is a notion of security adequate if it does not take these into account?
3. The pure safety conception focusses on the objective facts of death and injury and the actual probabilities of their occurrence. It says nothing about the subjective aspect – fear, for example, considered not just as an emotional response to a diminution in actual safety, but as a mental state that is itself partly *constitutive* of insecurity.
4. Similarly, the pure safety conception does not adequately highlight the element of assurance or guarantee that the word 'security' connotes. I am secure not just because I happen to be safe, but because I am *sure* of not being killed or harmed.
5. The shortcoming referred to in point (4) also means that the pure safety conception does not alert us to the relation between security and the possession of other values that the element of assurance may relate to. It may be inappropriate to think of security as a good in its own right; it may be more sensible to think of it as a mode in which other goods are enjoyed. I enjoy my property or my health securely. I may enjoy certain liberties, such as the practice of my religion or the freedom to express my political views, securely.
6. The pure safety conception focusses mainly on the individualized physical facts of death, injury, and loss rather than more diffuse harms to persons and people in general resulting from disruption of their way of life or the interruption of familiar routines. In that regard, it fails to capture the connection between the idea of security and the idea of a social order, which by definition, is something enjoyed by many.
7. Finally, being a purely individual measure, the pure safety conception does not yet provide a basis for talking critically about the security of the whole community. It does not adequately confront aggregative or distributive issues. In setting out the pure safety conception we discussed

> safety as a probabilistic measure of death or injury for individual persons and the most we could say about security for a whole society is that *we* are more secure when the probability of death or injury goes down for many of us. This is very imprecise. We need to consider ways of talking about situations in which one person's security is enhanced at the cost of another's. In these situations how are we to say whether the security of the whole society has gone up or down?[13]

Waldron's resulting account is a rich discussion of these issues, arriving at the conclusion that security is a complex, multi-dimensional personal and social good whose distribution raises important issues of justice, particularly when increasing the security of some by a marginal, and often unproven amount greatly diminishes the security of others in clear and unmistakable ways.

LEVIATHAN'S GHOST

Waldron's account of security is plausibly viewed as the most conceptually sophisticated account presently available. Yet it is seriously incomplete in ways relevant to the twenty-first-century ordinary citizen, and to an understanding of security's role in continuity of legality in and between state and non-state legal orders. It is most evidently incomplete in its dominant focus on the interests of the individual citizen, extending this focus to the interests of groups of citizens, yet omitting further extension to other social situations likely to inform the conceptual investigation of security Waldron advocates. Even if we accept Waldron's claim that personal security is experienced principally within the state, that claim regarding the locus of the bulk of available evidence needing explanation seems a weak reason for disregarding other evidence, including, for example, omission of substantial engagement with collective security at state or inter-state levels, particularly as various dimensions of globalization such as personal investment in international markets give even the experience of individual security connections beyond a particular state.

It might seem at this juncture that what is most needed is extension of Waldron's view to the inter-state phenomena he has omitted from his analysis. Yet to do so would be a mis-step, we suggest. This extension would further entrench a perspective haunted by what might be called 'Leviathan's ghost' – the presumptions and habits of an analytical perspective embodying a vision of security in life under law as a matter of negative freedoms wielded by an internal actor against an external force or actor, most typically the

[13] Ibid., pp. 117–118.

norm-subject in the state. This perspective, the residue of 'analytical imperialism' noted in Chapter 4, presumes the centrality of a subject-sovereign relation familiar from the Hobbesian vision of social contract in which the sovereign holds absolute authority but for certain regions of social affairs where the subject retains specified freedoms from sovereign intrusion. However familiar the approach might be, particularly in the subject-sovereign relation in the law-state, seeking to understand security through its lens is likely to distort rather than clarify our understanding of the phenomena of security in the world of the twenty-first-century citizen.

Two aspects of the focal relation embodied by Leviathan's ghost seem to us to be especially troublesome, particularly for those concerned to address the problem of continuity of legal order. First, focus on the subject- (or subject-group) sovereign dyad tends to presume an enduring hierarchical relation whose stability is primarily a function of the interactions between the subject and sovereign. This focus, a reflection of the perspective and priorities of an investigator, tends to leave certain contextual matters to one side, and draws into its analysis only those contextual matters of greatest relevance to the dyadic relation under investigation. It is unsurprising, then, given the American context Waldron investigates, that the resulting conception of security is closely related to the subject-sovereign dyad. That relation is one which focusses on human rights as one critical set of positive 'freedoms to' and negative 'freedoms from'. These freedoms are at the core of preservation and assertion of personal and group identity in the context of an overwhelmingly powerful American Leviathan, which might be tempted to infringe those freedoms in the absence of explicit and effective bars to infringement. Waldron's focus is certainly appropriate to his investigation of human rights in the context of the detention facility operated by the United States at its extra-territorial Guantanamo Bay Naval Base in Cuba. Yet close investigation of a subject-sovereign dyad in this context leaves a great deal left to be explained in a broader account of the law-security relation. One instructive dimension of Waldron's focus on the Guantanamo example may be seen in its depiction of a situation where subjects are stable and cannot change that stability, and the sovereign is equally stable.[14] Not all instances of this dyad raise the same security concerns, and this dyad is not the only form of relation between norm-subjects and authorities in which security is a concern. In dyads, for example, where external

[14] In such a situation, certain dimensions of security assume importance proportional to the likelihood that the underlying context is unchanging – the importance of bodily integrity as a form of personal security enabled by regular sleep, for example, increases as increasingly serious negative medical consequences follow continued sleep deprivation.

legal force may vary the positions of sovereign and subject, a sovereign may be compelled by peers to respect prior undertakings to respect bodily integrity, or to respect subjects' right of exit. The content of the subject's security interests and conception of security may change, and the reason for that change may be re-constitutive of the original subject-sovereign dyad into a triad, in which each party's legal claims have a particular institutional force.

Even a broader analysis of security taking into account variations to the presumed stability of subject and sovereign may be insufficient, however, leading to a second observation regarding the legacy of Leviathan's ghost. This dyad is not the only place in which security is found, in Waldron's terms, 'as a mode in which other goods are enjoyed'.[15] Waldron lists goods including property, health and freedom of religion and political expression; but what is more interesting is his explanation of security as a 'mode' – most charitably understood as a context, circumstance, or perhaps state of being which is the substrate condition in which specified goods are not just present in some minimal form, but capable of being meaningfully treated as substantive goods as agents plan future courses of action.

It would be uncharitable to ascribe much explanatory weight to Waldron's use of 'mode' in this context, as a supporting component of his central focus on private citizens' experience of security. Yet this explanation opens the way to an expanded investigation of whether the mode of security is always and everywhere the same, or whether as a complex precondition of enjoyment of goods, the summary term 'mode' is the tip of a metaphorical iceberg needing closer investigation. Where an investigation carrying the assumptions of Leviathan's ghost is preoccupied with state-authorized coercion to which a countering force is seen in ordinary citizens' specially protected freedoms, consideration of security as a 'mode' in relations beyond the subject-sovereign dyad in the situation of collectives, interstate interactions and others, soon requires greater attention to the concept of security and its multiple conceptions in various situations.

Once our twenty-first-century travelling inquirer's attention is turned to the concept and experience of security beyond the inquirer's modestly prosperous life in a stable state system of law, a diverse range of dimensions of security beyond the state become evident. Our inquirer's conception of financial security may be informed by her global investment portfolio, which she reviews on her tablet computer – carefully following security protocols to avoid becoming a victim of hackers operating in the 'cybersphere' long since beyond the control of any state, leaving no trace of their origins as they appropriate

[15] Waldron, *Torture*, p. 118.

identities and financial assets. Buoyed by investment success our inquirer might then use the communications standards of the 'internet of things' as she opens an application enabling her to monitor video-cameras and thermostats in her cottage on a far-off tropical island. While contemplating her next trip to her cottage she might mull a recent conversation with an official from the island, discussing the implications of a view expressed by Joel Klein and Condoleezza Rice, leaders of the Independent Task Force on US Education Reform and National Security. In a widely cited opinion piece for CNN summarizing themes of the Task Force report, Klein and Rice asserted that 'Today, globalization and the technological sophistication of our economy are widening already troubling socioeconomic disparities, rewarding those who acquire the right skills and punishing brutally those who do not. Much is at stake . . . . It is not hyperbole to say that the state of education in our country is a challenge to our national security'.[16] Our inquirer's friend might identify shortcomings in education as significant challenges to her state's and region's capacity to respond to the challenge of food security as it intersects with climate security and energy security,[17] and more pressingly, to take action on biosecurity at the population health scale to prepare for a possible outbreak of the Ebola virus.

Financial security, information security, education for national security, food security, climate security, energy security and biosecurity are each familiar dimensions of security in the twenty-first century, so familiar that there is no immediate need to delve into further social science evidence or deep conceptual analysis to recognize them as dimensions of security. Their familiarity does not, however, permit us to follow Waldron's lead in viewing them as usefully analysed solely in terms of their presence as modes of goods-enjoyment in which a subject wields specific legal protections against a sovereign or others who might otherwise coercively deprive the subject of enjoyment of goods. To understand these dimensions of security as counterparts or forms of opposition to coercion is implausible to the extent that the coercive relation between state and subject or subject-group is not present at the same scale or with the same degree of directed human agency, demanding explanation in terms of more than coercion and likely resulting in coercion being recognized as just one dimension of the multi-dimensional phenomena of security. Conceiving of

[16] C. Rice and J. Klein, 'Rice, Klein: education keeps America safe', *Cable News Network* (20 March 2012). Available at www.cnn.com/2012/03/20/opinion/rice-klein-education/.

[17] B. Weber, 'Changing rainfall common problem for entire globe, says UN-sponsored book', *Canadian Broadcasting Corporation News* (20 October 2014). Available at www.cbc.ca/news/canada/north/changing-rainfall-common-problem-for-entire-globe-says-un-sponsored-book-1.2805548.

food security or climate security in terms of individual enjoyment of goods, for example, simply misses the complex systemic, non-dyadic and whole-of-society way in which food and climate insecurity are experienced and faced. Viewing food security or climate security as a sort of mode of enjoyment of personally experienced goods which must be safeguarded against coercive interference may also misread the extent to which human agency and direction are involved. A state legal system's coercive apparatus may be operated by a number of officials in principle identifiable by investigation labelling as authors of coercion, yet where water insecurity and energy insecurity give rise to food insecurity, the complexity of interacting factors giving rise to the phenomenon weigh against regarding it by means of tracing the causal roots of these factors to coercive actions on the part of officials. Both humanly intended and natural factors beyond human prediction or control are implicated in the causal story of food security. Perhaps more importantly in the context of an inquiry into legality and security intended to have global reach, a concern with state coercion and citizens' wielding of rights against that coercion, often reported in appellate court decisions with respect to civil rights, seems to be a quite special concern particular to established and continuous state systems of law whose stability is often correlated with material wealth. Particular civil rights and associated security such as rights to freedom of expression or assembly may be a feature of flourishing state legal systems whose existence is over the historical long run exceptional rather than the norm. A great deal of our experience of the relation between law and security occurs in a different context. Consider, for example, monarchies such as Saudi Arabia, and single-party states such as China, some of the most prominent dimensions of security are not a feature of a layer or insulation between subjects and the coercive power of the sovereign, but are instead constitutive of the continuing identity of each, and perhaps surrounding others as well. Food security and biosecurity, for example, may be constitutive of norm-subjects' identity even while security of freedom of expression or assembly is limited or absent. Security may well be enduringly conceived as a mode in which other goods are enjoyed, but the relevant conception of 'goods' must be expanded beyond the civil rights discussed by Waldron, and extend to modes of being. Food security and biosecurity are pre-conditional to the kind of legal order in which individual norm-subjects or groups of norm-subjects might enact any form of cultural identity, never mind the style of existence established in certain sophisticated legal systems where institutions of law protecting private property and freedom of expression give rise to particular individually chosen ways of life.

AN INTER-INSTITUTIONAL VIEW OF THE RELATION BETWEEN LAW AND SECURITY

Our agenda-opening investigation of the relation between law and security is in a sense a renovated version of Hart's concern with the relation between law and coercion. As we have renovated we have been mindful of the presence of Leviathan's ghost, recognizing that concerns regarding the subject-sovereign relation and constraints against the sovereign's capacity to coerce are concerns whose prominence is permitted by presumption of the relatively untroubled continuity of the underlying legal order. The dimensions of security we have identified in discussion above tend to demonstrate that continuity in an underlying order is significantly contingent, subject to various forms of insecurity in what Leviathan's ghost regards as a nearly static backdrop of social and natural factors. In this context, our travelling inquirer is certainly concerned with legal authorities' capacity to coerce, but that is not all. Our inquirer is interested in the broader dimensions of security implicated in realization of a life-plan, less and less constrained by what economists call 'adaptive preferences' guided by what seems possible in a particular situation, and guided more by aspirations informed by possibilities seen around the globe.

If we guide our inquirer-satisfying investigation by detecting and characterizing legality by application of our inter-institutional approach, we uncover several instructive contrasts between stated-centred approaches to characterization of law, and an inter-institutional approach. To draw these contrasts we can return in this section to further consideration of the limitations of scope evident in Waldron's account of security. Two particular limitations are especially instructive. The first he explicitly recognizes and we have already identified: his concern is not with the coordinated efforts of multiple states to avoid conflict or war (collective security), or the stability or power of state institutions acting within their own borders (national or 'homeland' security). From a moral point of view, neither type of security is valuable for its own sake, but only to the extent to which it contributes to the value of personal security, which is enjoyed by individuals. The second limitation in Waldron's account is less explicitly set out, yet of greater importance for our purposes. Concern with personal security, while leaving issues of collective and national security to the side, makes the most sense against the backdrop, or under the presumption, of a stable, and typically liberal-democratic, state. In this context, collective and national security can be presumed, so the prominent aspect of the law and security relation to be investigated can be understood simply as the relation between liberal-democratic states with constitutional commitments to fundamental rights and freedoms on the one hand, and issues of personal security (and their aggregation) on the other.[18] But this is only one aspect of the relation between law and security. Just as it is with the relation between law and morality, the relation between law and security has many aspects or questions, not one.[19]

In contexts where states are not stable, i.e., where their institutions have limited and precarious control over their territory, or perhaps only control part of their territory, perhaps due to civil conflict, internal disorder or intrusions by external forces, issues of personal security tend to go hand in hand with issues of collective or national security. To take a straightforward example, if a particular state is unable to enjoy regional security in its relations with neighbouring states, it is for the same reason unable to guarantee the various dimensions of personal security Waldron identifies. In such cases, it is not difficult to see that while only personal security has non-instrumental value, collective or regional security is amongst the preconditions of personal security. The two dimensions of security are inextricably linked.

As a further step forward, while Waldron's account of personal security is already multi-dimensional, we likely need to add two further dimensions to capture the relations between personal security and collective and national security. Personal security, when understood as a multi-dimensional individual good (enjoyed individually and in groups) which can be affected by the various decisions, laws and policies of state institutions, is best characterized as personal security in an operational sense or dimension. That is, personal security might be increased (though unevenly across populations, as Waldron notes) or decreased (again, either evenly or unevenly) through the operations of state institutions. But personal security in its operational dimension is considered as an object of decision or consequence of state institutions' actions when the state and its institutions are stable and free from collective or national *in*security. Attention to the importance of collective and national security, however, highlights the second dimension of personal security that we need to add to Waldron's account. Personal security has a pre-conditional dimension, such that its status as an object of decision or consequent of state institutions' actions depends upon the stability and efficacy of institutions whose existence and practices are necessary or perhaps sufficient to make subjects' personal

[18] This is not to say that issues of personal security could not serve as the object of focus in stable states which are not liberal democratic, only that Waldron's particular focus is liberal democratic states such as the United States.

[19] See L. Green, 'General jurisprudence: a 25th anniversary essay', *Oxford Journal of Legal Studies*, 25 (2005), pp. 565–580.

security a meaningful object of consideration for political actors. If the preconditions of stability between states or of the institutions within states are not met, it is difficult to see how a state can focus upon, let alone plausibly purport to guarantee to some degree the personal security of its citizens.

Waldron is of course aware that the enjoyment of personal security requires not just the right laws and decisions from state institutions, but effective institutions in the first place:

> The routines of ordinary life whose security we value are not just first-order routines like shopping, schooling, and soccer; but also secondary routines that respond to what might be thought of as routine problems. There are fires, crimes, and accidents; there are threats from nature and sometimes threats from outsiders; there are disagreements about what ought to be done in response to these. Among our repertoire of mechanisms for dealing with danger, disorder, and dissensus, we have fire brigades, hospitals and police forces; we have a legal system, courts, and prisons; we have FEMA and the national guard; we have our political system, at municipal, state, and federal levels; and we have our Constitution, our fundamental rights, and our settled obligations under human rights law .... The existence and the effectiveness of these mechanisms is also crucial to the assurance that security in normal times involves. Disruption of them may enhance our anxiety and undermine our security; and sometimes the appropriate response may be to strengthen them or transform them so that they become more effective against the dangers they are supposed to protect us from even at the cost of other values they are supposed to embody.[20]

Notice, however, that Waldron is assuming a context of backdrop where 'we' (the 'we' of the United States) does in fact have fire brigades, police, courts, a constitution, etc. The only question within Waldron's attention is whether the state institutions of 'our' state are providing for our security at just the right level, striking the right balance with citizens' enjoyment of personal liberties. No attention is given in Waldron's view of these institutions to the nature or role of other states, or regional, international or global organizations whose existence and effectiveness matter to the personal security of subjects of particular states such as the United States. There is also no discussion in Waldron's account of what issues security might pose for states which are not stable, or how the promises of law might vary in contexts where the preconditions of state or collective security are not met. Waldron is of course entitled to focus on the questions which seem most important to him, so we can raise no objection to his choosing to focus on personal security; but there are dangers

[20] Waldron, *Torture*, p. 156.

to adequate explanation when such a focus masks certain presumptions as well as additional dimensions, and their interaction, of personal security. Let us take up one further presumption we have noted and revisit here as it marks a key difference between Waldron's view and our inter-institutional view. Waldron's view of security is state-centred, as we have seen; but what remains to be explored more fully is the distorting effect of this state-centred approach for the understanding of security which is apparently deepened by Waldron's focus on the state. Waldron conceives of collective security as the security which holds amongst states (or 'nations' in Waldron's words): 'it concerns security as among the nations of the world (or various subsets of them) determined by institutions, alliances and the balance of power'.[21] As a goal, collective security 'needs to be pursued by groups of nations either acting in concert or by sets of antagonists acting in ways that establish stable equilibria; or it needs to be pursued by the whole community of nations acting in concert'.[22] By national security, it will be recalled, Waldron has in mind the stability or integrity of national institutions: 'the phrase "national security" conveys ideas about *the integrity and power of the state itself* as an institutional apparatus'.[23] And finally, personal security, in all its dimensions, is understood as the security held by subjects of some state which can be protected or compromised in various ways by the state. This close association of state and security of course reaches back much further than Waldron. Hobbes, as we saw, linked the legitimacy of the state to how well it provided security to its subjects. Later, Vattel wrote: 'Nations or States are political bodies, societies of men who have united together and combined their forces, in order to procure their mutual welfare and security'.[24] And similarly, Rudolph von Jhering explains that '[t]he end of the State as well as of the law is the establishment and security of the conditions of social life'.[25] Such a picture seems to make the most sense when single states are viewed one at a time and in isolation. But, even within states, state-provided security is only contingently provided. In unsteady or failing states, security, at lower or more local levels, is sometimes provided by non-state groups or institutions. In a recent collection published in the Stanford Security Studies series, several authors reach the conclusion that in states popularly labelled as failed or failing, while state institutions are typically unable to provide for the security of state inhabitants, the resulting situation is not an absence of

[21] Ibid., p. 115. [22] Ibid., p. 158. [23] Ibid., p. 115.

[24] Vattel, *Le droit des gens*, quoted in J. Crawford, *The Creation of States in International Law*, 2nd edn (Oxford: Oxford University Press, 2006), p. 7.

[25] R. von Jhering, *Law as a Means to an End*, trans. Isaac Husik (Boston: Boston Book Co., 1913), p. 317.

social order, but social order secured by alternative, non-state authorities.[26] For example, in a study of non-state authority in various countries in the Middle East, Anne Marie Baylouny explains how 'alternative authorities' come to be:

> Alternative authorities generally start out as newcomers to the power game, concerned with obtaining a higher social status. They begin their claim to influence with either economic success or physical ability. These individuals made money and connections or obtained influence through the use of violence . . . . Militias can . . . impose their authority purely through force, but they usually also rely on political ideologies to justify their rule. Nevertheless, religion, political ideology, and reputation are not sufficient to cement a position of authority. To become an authority, one must furnish services and mediate with state authorities. Would-be authorities either intercede with state institutions on behalf of community members or replace the state entirely.[27]

Similarly, in a study of South African cities, Loren Landau and Tamlyn Monson observe that security and order are not necessarily missing simply because state governance is missing:

> The absence of state-centered, stable regulatory regimes does not reflect an *ungoverned* space, but a space that is *alternatively* governed. Such alternatives may take any number of predictable and unexpected forms, where even the regulation and territorial control undertaken by state actors does not necessarily promote principled, state-centric systems of rules and regulation. In almost all cases, authority and power are shared among actors in dynamic ways that are not necessarily state centered, state authored, or informed by clearly articulated and unified strategies of control.[28]

In her article devoted to investigation of illicit economies, Vanda Felbab-Brown notes how basic enforcement of contracts is necessary, and better explains how illicit economics function than the perception that it is simply such economies' ability to distribute illegal goods of various kinds:

> Although illicit economies thrive in ungoverned spaces where the official regulating entity's means of suppression are limited, they nonetheless frequently require some level of internal regulation. At a minimum, just like

[26] A. L. Clunan and H. A. Trinkunas (eds), *Ungoverned Spaces* (Stanford, CA: Stanford University Press, 2010).

[27] A. M. Baylouny, 'Authority outside the state: non-state actors and new institutions in the Middle East', in Clunan and Trinkunas, *Ungoverned Spaces*, pp. 140–141.

[28] L. B. Landau and T. Monson, 'Immigration and subterranean sovereignty in South African cities', ibid., p. 168.

> licit economies, the illicit ones greatly benefit from and frequently depend on some degree of predictability and the assurance of property rights. The 'wild' space is rarely fully wild; in the case of illicit economies, it is only differently governed.[29]

Often, as Felbab-Brown observes, it is mafias that can provide the basic protection and 'assurance' for economic transactions to take place.[30]

Even within steady or stable states, law's security is heavily dependent on a variety of norm-subjects, both official and non-official, respecting norms and institutions whose existence matters for the personal security of subjects. As we saw in Chapter 2, the existence of law depends upon the recognition of a diverse and large range of people, extending well beyond the class of appellate judges and other surrounding legal officials. Recognition, or at least acceptance, on the part of ordinary citizens and subjects also matters. These observations are crucial as a contribution to a broader picture of law's relation to security than Waldron offers. Here we can say that the preconditions of personal security often require a fairly diffuse social base of acceptance or efficacy, which may or may not map directly onto the existence and efficacy of state institutions.

So far we have seen that a focus on personal security in the context of a stable state makes it easy to overlook the preconditions of internal, regional, and international stability of institutions and their practices which matter to the possibility and enjoyment of personal security. We can also see that the presumptions of states with regard to security also mirror in important ways the presumptions of states with regard to their legal systems. We have seen that states typically claim supremacy for their legal systems, such that there are no legal norms (even international norms) which can claim authority within their borders if not authorized in some way by the state legal system itself. The notion of hierarchy in use here is readily seen as a reflection of the idea of recognition expressed in Hart's and Raz's theories of legal system. Unless a norm is recognized, primarily by the officials or norm-applying institutions of a legal system (i.e., its state institutions), it is not a valid legal norm, or indeed any kind of legal norm, operating in the state. Only those norms which can be traced back up some chain of validity, ultimately resting with a foundational or supreme institution or source of law, count as norms of the legal system or state.[31] The idea of recognition is thus closely associated to the idea of

[29] V. Felbab-Brown, 'Rules and regulations in ungoverned spaces: illicit economies, criminals, and belligerents', ibid., p. 179.

[30] Ibid.

[31] See H. L. A. Hart, *The Concept of Law*, 3rd edn (Oxford: Oxford University Press, 2012), p. 107.

hierarchy. An institution or official either binds lower institutions or officials with their directives, or an institution or official looks up the hierarchy by recognizing the authority of a higher institution or official (much like a lower court is bound by but cannot bind a higher appellate court). Here we can see how the prevailing understanding of personal security follows a similar line of reasoning. Security is understood, from the perspective of state institutions, as provided from above (i.e., by the state), and is similarly understood, from the perspective of subjects, as provided by state institutions. The two perspectives are simply two sides of the same coin. State-provided, or better, state-*claimed* security, on this view, is what we might call hierarchical security, which is similar in character to state law, which is also typically hierarchical.[32]

Yet as we saw in Chapter 2, the picture of law as fundamentally state-based and hierarchical invites us to overlook law's dependency on some social grouping or unit, which may or may not be a state. And as our examples discussed above have enabled us to demonstrate, the security enjoyed by subjects may or may not depend entirely on state institutions. The preconditions of personal security, which emerge when we reflect on the possibility of personal security in both contexts of stable and unstable states, include the stability of all sorts of institutions both within and outside particular states.

So we need an alternative to the hierarchy-based notion of recognition. Here we can rely on the inter-institutional theory presented in Chapter 4, and in particular the notion of mutual reference. By decoupling state and security, and the associated ideas of hierarchy and authority which go hand in hand with the idea and presumptions of states, we can see how various institutions might mutually refer to each other at some level of intensity in a way which creates stability and order. At the international level, e.g., states might mutually refer to each other in a way which creates both a non-hierarchical legal order (in a way which creates their borders but also establishes order between them) as well as security between them and for their subjects. Such mutual reference is amongst the preconditions as well as operation of security and law, but notice that it would not make sense to say each state recognizes or is somehow bound by the norms or institutions of the other. While in many instances the mutual reference between institutions might be hierarchical, in several others instances, such as those envisaged here, the mutual reference is non-hierarchical, and so productive of non-hierarchical legal order and non-hierarchical security between states.

[32] For discussion of the prevalence of hierarchy in theorizing about state legal systems, see K. Culver and M. Giudice, *Legality's Borders* (Oxford: Oxford University Press, 2010), Chapters 1 and 2.

So what kind of relation emerges? One particular conclusion seems safe to draw, and follows from our resistance to the temptation to suppose that the relation between law and security is a causal relation, with either law causing or providing for security or security causing or providing for law. Instead, by observing that at the foundations of both security and law, and again in both hierarchical and non-hierarchical forms, are relations of mutual reference between institutions, we are able to see that the relation between law and security is probably best characterized as mutually constitutive. This, however, does not mean that it is a simple constitutive relation, since security has many dimensions, and we have said nothing about the variety of inter-institutional relations of mutual reference which can constitute law and security. We will not carry out that task here, recognizing that our investigation of law and security requires integration into our larger relational account of law. In what follows we will trace some dimensions of law's constitution of security without immediately integrating them into our larger account, leaving that task for Chapter 8. We shall use these dimensions as demonstrations of the extent to which presumption of the centrality of the state-based legal system must be brought into question and better explanations of the phenomena of legality given greater attention. We shall also begin to demonstrate how an inter-institutional theory can identify appropriately compelling or desirable objects of explanation as the primacy of place once given the state is transformed into a broader view of legality's habitat.

LAW'S SUBJECTS AND THE ABSENCE OF THE HALLMARKS OF STATE-BASED LEGAL SYSTEM

As we have demonstrated, a Waldron-inspired 'safety' conception of security is rooted in the question of legitimate place of coercion in the relation between a subject-sovereign dyad. The continuity of the state-based legal system – home to that dyad – is largely presumed. Our broader view of security sees a different situation, one in which a subject-sovereign dyad may be just one of the relations present in a situation where there are overlapping claims of diversely sourced institutions of law and legal institutions. This situation may be seen and explored in a context discussed recently by Joseph Raz in 'Why the state?'[33] There he observes the emergence of overlapping claims to authority

[33] J. Raz, 'Why the state?', King's College London Law School Research Paper No. 2014–38, Columbia Public Law Research Paper No. 14–427, Oxford Legal Studies Research Paper No. 73/2014 (12 October 2013). Available at http://ssrn.com/abstract=2339522 or doi:10.2139/ssrn.2339522.

in the context of Ebola's threat not just to a state or states but to regional and global biosecurity. He writes:

> For a long time the Security Council had a modest interpretation of its authority under Chapter 7 [of the UN Charter]. Recently, however, the interpretation of that power became very inflationary. Yet it has not been challenged, with the result that the Security Council now has extensive power to override state governments over a range of issues. One significant extension is the decision to allow Chapter 7 resolutions based on the self-called responsibility to protect [observing in n. 16 the 'SC Resolution 1706 (31 August 2006), calling for the deployment of UN peacekeepers to Darfur, applied the R2P principle to a particular context for the first time . . . ']. But perhaps the most dramatic extension of the powers of the Security Council is the most recent one: in determining that the Ebola outbreak in Africa constituted a threat to international peace and security, it assumed Chapter 7 powers to interfere in the internal affairs of member states in matters affecting the Ebola outbreak [citing in n. 17 'Security Council resolution number 2177 (2014)'].[34]

There is much to be said about the force of this example for thinking about the centrality of state-based legal theory amongst the problems of jurisprudence, as Raz goes on to do. What is more interesting for present purposes is the fact that the relation between biosecurity and law involves a conception of security and set of actors reaching far beyond coercion and a subject-sovereign dyad. To understand biosecurity with respect to disease in terms of the individual citizen is at best a partial view, needing supplementation by consideration of biosecurity at the scale of population health, and the place of a population in an interconnected region which may or may not correspond tidily to state borders. As Raz makes clear in citing an 'outbreak in Africa' rather than an outbreak in specifically identified states, the locus of law's interaction with security is at least regional, possibly continental and possibly global. More importantly, as Raz justifiably describes the Security Council resolution as amounting to 'interference' in the affairs of states, the situation is not one in which a state-based legal system (or states and systems) authoritatively advances norms with respect to Ebola in a manner revealing the state system to operate as a comprehensive set of norms claiming supremacy over a given jurisdiction while open to use of legal norms imported from other systems. There is, notably, no simple trumping relation between the Security Council's use of R2P norms and state norms. Nor is there any state employment of Security Council norms via a process of open adoption. There is, rather, intense mutual

[34] Ibid., p. 15.

reference amongst overlapping legal institutions and institutions of law, in a legal order whose duration and continuity are impossible to predict. Just as importantly, understanding security in this situation as needing explanation in terms of a sovereign's exercise of coercive power simply misses the nature of the insecurity involved – while coercive orders are no doubt sometimes necessary in the context of population health protection, the legal norms framing collective response to a natural threat are best viewed as enabling increased security, not coercing increased security into existence.

LAW'S TERRITORY

Raz's deployment of the Ebola example arrives in the context of his asking 'Is the state likely to remain the most comprehensive legal social organisation within its domain?'[35] His answer is that 'Various developments give room for doubt',[36] amongst them the situation we explored above. The example of response to Ebola illustrates Raz's identification of 'three important lines of development' in legality beyond the state: 'First, the emergence of international organisations with independent law-making powers that are not conditional on consent by states subject to them. Second, changes in the way new international laws emerge. Third, the extended range of agents with powers of action in international law'.[37] Raz is undoubtedly right to assert the importance of these developments, yet their explanation remains significantly incomplete as an account of facts challenging the priority of state systems in practice and as objects of explanation. Theoretical characterization of states as bearers of comprehensive, supreme and open legal systems is destabilized not just by what might be regarded as international organizations' incursion into states' jurisdictions, but further, by features of law's relation to security in the context of the state legal system's occupation of territory. While it has long been recognized that state legal systems are not identical with some piece of territory, as it is familiar that states make extra-territorial claims regarding the conduct of their citizens abroad, and so on, it has long been accepted that state legal systems are fundamentally rooted in some territory.[38] This theoretical commitment can now be seen to be highly dubious to the extent that it supposes legality is the product of legal systems and legal systems are rooted in

[35] Ibid., p. 13 [36] Ibid. [37] Ibid., p. 14.

[38] Rare exceptional cases stand apart, e.g., the Sovereign Military Order of Malta, which exists as a sovereign order notwithstanding its loss of its historic territory of Malta, and is one of the 'intergovernmental organizations having received a standing invitation to participate as observers in the sessions and the work of the General Assembly and maintaining permanent offices at Headquarters'. See www.un.org/en/members/intergovorg.shtml.

territory, while some of the dimensions of law and security such as biosecurity are governed by legality which is clearly not the product of state-based systems on any account but the most tortuous and speculative tracing of state-based authorities authorizing the specific actions of international organizations such as the UN. As Raz's Ebola example and its context demonstrate, law's territory now seems to be in many respects global and its authoritative authors equally global, or at any rate untied to authorization by particular legal systems with which they are plausibly said not to subordinate or inform but with which they 'interfere'.

THE JOINTNESS OF SOVEREIGNTY AND SECURITY

An inter-institutional perspective on the relation between legality, security and territory opens the way to consideration of legality, security and sovereignty. Just as legal systems have long been held to refer to territories, so the claims of legal systems to sovereignty have been regarded as claims to *control* over states of affairs in a particular territory. Sovereignty's claims to control have of course never been considered to be necessarily absolute: the claims of a sovereign state have long been contextualized within human possibility. Common law systems have long invoked the idea of an 'act of God' as an occurrence beyond the control of sovereign or subject so neither is held liable or blameworthy for such uncontrollable occurrences, even while the notion of coercion is entirely tied to human agency such that the sovereign's coercion of a subject is easily distinguished from an act of God which advances the interests of the sovereign while harming those of a subject. Yet apart from a few familiar limitations on the sovereign's capacity to assure security, sovereignty and security have long been considered jointly necessary conditions for the existence of a legal system, so on some views, the presence of legality.

The expanded understanding of security we have developed seems to us to challenge directly the equation of sovereignty and security. As we reported in the introduction to this chapter, it seems entirely possible there may be claims of sovereignty and sovereign-like function in the absence of security, as the *Economist* suggests is the case of Iraq in the 2010s, and may be the case in Syria and its prolonged state of violence which appears to be less a civil war than a multi-party, multi-purpose rejection of the Syrian state. The structure of security-deficient sovereignty may be seen elsewhere in other dimensions of security, including, for example, African states affected by lack of food security, or drought-ridden states affected by climate insecurity, or their counterpart, flood-ridden states such as Kiribati affected by rising sea levels produced by climate change. Yet there seems to be no rush to suppose that such states' lack of capacity to ensure their security ought to count against the credibility of their claims to operate legal institutions and their constituent institutions of law.

As we also observed in this chapter's introduction, it also appears that the security historically supposed to be a co-product of the presence of legal system may not require a sovereign source of authority. Leeson's suggestion that Somalia might be 'better off stateless' contains more than an indictment of the moral depravity of the recent governments of the state. The suggestion opens the further possibility that response to various dimensions of insecurity enabling a legal order's continuity (and the protected expectations that brings to citizens) might be best delivered via institutions of law and legal institutions other than those of a state-based legal system. This insight can be found not just in the claims of legal and political theorists, but in the reflections of state-based officials. Joe Clark, former Canadian Prime Minister and former Secretary of State for External affairs, argued recently that states often lack critical flexibility in response to certain global challenges, yet 'By stark contrast, non-state actors can often respond to urgent need, or open and maintain lines of communication with significant leaders or groups who are "off limits" for governments. That difference in the freedom to act should cry out for partnership, for finding areas where state and non-state, working together can save lives, or moderate crisis or deadly tension'.[39] Following this recognition of the limits of state capacity for action, Clark offers a note of qualification, asserting that 'What these non-state actors do not have is the authority to change the rules. They bring the imagination the world needs, but only nation-states have the mandate and the power to change laws and regulations and treaty obligations'.[40] It is to be expected that a former senior official of a state insists on the continuing supremacy of state legal systems, but the immediately prior admission of the importance of partnership may be more important, as Clark's memories of state supremacy are not matched by the present state of affairs. Partnership amongst the easy division of state and non-state actors is, as Raz's discussion of Ebola indicates, not a clearly hierarchical situation wherein state-based systems delegate authority to Clark's 'non-state actors' or Raz's 'international organizations'. Rather, where there is 'interference' there is diminution of the credibility of the explanatory assertion of the supremacy of state legal systems and further support for viewing them as adjacent to other sources and forms of legality. 'Better off stateless' is in this context both an evaluative judgement of what is plausibly claimed as the fact of legality and security in Somalia over some period, and an intriguing practical

[39] J. Clark, *How We Lead* (Toronto, Canada: Random House, 2013), p. 72. [40] Ibid.

possibility for response to insecurity and provision of continuity of legality. It is far from just goading more desirable conduct by states or 'state-building' aid from other states, particularly in contexts where legal orders better suited to insecurity-response might sit ready for action, e.g., indigenous legal cultures, international organizations bearing both technical expertise and governance standards for water or agricultural systems.

LEGAL SYSTEM AS A POLITICAL IDEAL

The above consideration of legality and security points to several shortcomings in the explanatory reach of state-based accounts of legality. This assertion of shortcomings needs qualification, however, since state-based accounts of legality are evolving even while we have advanced our inter-institutional account in response to what we view as inadequacies of those accounts. Even Raz now admits the presence of 'other forms of law' adjacent to state-based legal system, writing recently that '[e]ven if state-law is in some ways the pre-eminent form of law we find in the course of inquiry, that by examining it alongside other forms of law, our understanding of state-law as well as of law in general changes. That itself could be an important outcome. It will inevitably change the way we see state-law and its relations to other kinds of laws'.[41] Raz's newly qualified identification of state law as 'in some ways the pre-eminent form of law' is far from his historic assertion that state-based legal systems are the home of all the legality worth analysis. This variation in Raz's view is nourishing fodder for critics supposing that a corpus of work must be straightforwardly consistent from end to end. In the case of at least Raz's work, this criticism must be rejected immediately. As a descriptive-explanatory theorist sensitive to developments in practice, what Raz sees today in, for example, the actions of the Security Council had no counterpart in the world Raz observed as the evidentiary basis for 1970 publication of his first book, *The concept of a legal system*. Raz has consistently modified his descriptive-explanatory view in response to emerging phenomena, rightly preferring responsiveness over a trivial kind of internal consistency in his views, while, as we have suggested in prior chapters, remaining unclear on the means by which he has modified his views. While considerable work remains to be done, beyond noting the existence of international organizations and investigating their nature and incorporating it into a view of law with a significantly different explanatory role assigned the concept of legal system, we welcome as advocates of an inter-institutional view

[41] Raz, 'Why the state', p. 1.

Raz's gradual acknowledgement of legal phenomena beyond the state needing explanation in a general account of legality.

Where Raz evidently advances, other views lag in ways instructive to those who join us in taking steps to integrate analysis of the law-security relation into a general account of law driven by an inter-institutional account of legality. In his magisterial *Legality*, Scott Shapiro, for example, simultaneously mischaracterizes Hart's foundational views while advancing the mischaracterization as a means to improving legal theory in a way which in fact leads it to ignore precisely the data which we and Raz think need more careful explanation. In a lengthy note to the introductory portion of *Legality* Shapiro argues that:

> Traditionally, legal philosophers have not treated the concept LAW like the concept WATER, namely, they have not supposed that discovering the nature of law requires deference to another outside a posteriori theory. Even though Hart claimed that *The Concept of Law* was 'an exercise in descriptive sociology' (CL vi), his analysis bears little resemblance to standard procedure in the social sciences – he didn't perform or examine any detailed case studies, engage in statistical analysis, etc. – nor did he consult findings in that field. He seemed to have assumed that the nature of law could be determined exclusively by conceptual analysis.... My own view is that Hart was right with respect to the concept of law. Social science cannot tell us what the law is because it studies *human* society. Its deliverances have no relevance for the legal philosopher because it is a truism that nonhumans have law. Science fiction, for example, is replete with stories involving alien civilizations with some form of legal system. These examples show that it is part of our concept of law that groups can have legal systems provided that they are more or less rational agents and have the ability to follow rules. Social scientific theories are limited in this respect, being able to study only human groups, and hence cannot provide an account about all possible instances of law.[42]

At least two parts of these claims seem to us to be seriously mistaken. The first error lies in the inference from Hart's limited citation of social scientific evidence however produced that he thought it irrelevant to understanding of the concept of law. Quite apart from his career as a practicing lawyer, Hart was in fact sensitive to social science evidence in his overall scholarship. For example, as the abstract for his Southey Lecture at Melbourne University reports, 'Professor Hart examines the achievements and failings of the recent legislation. In an analysis of the statistics available since the passing of the *Abortion Act* 1967, he indicates the various effects which the legislation appears to

42 S. J. Shapiro, *Legality* (Cambridge, MA: Harvard University Press, 2011), pp. 406–407n16.

have produced'.[43] This lecture was accompanied by further public intervention into debate, as Hart co-authored with political economist David Soskice an article 'After the Act' for the *Guardian* in 1972.[44] This sensitivity to social scientific evidence is not an isolated, or later-career matter: evidence contrary to Shapiro's characterization of Hart is visible in the locus classicus of many of Hart's views, in *The Concept of Law*. In his long-debated remarks on the minimum content of natural law Hart writes that

> it is both possible and important to inquire into quite different forms of connection between natural facts and legal or moral rules. Thus, the still young sciences of psychology and sociology may discover or may even have discovered that, unless certain physical, psychological, or economic conditions are satisfied, e.g., unless young children are fed and nurtured in certain ways within the family, no system of laws or code of morals can be established, or that only those laws can function successfully which conform to a certain type. Connections of this sort between natural conditions and systems of rules are not mediated by *reasons*; for they do not relate the existence of certain rules to the conscious aims or purpose of those whose rules they are.[45]

In this passage Hart is certainly not conducting or citing social science or natural science, yet he plainly accepts the need to integrate the conclusions of the sciences into understanding the way social and physical context shape what law is and can be. So much, then, for the notion that Shapiro's view of how to investigate the nature of legality is rooted in agreement with Hart or a Hartian approach.

What is more odd than Shapiro's misreading of Hart is his sense that the kinds of assertions usefully made by a theory of law must be so total and universal in their aspiration that they must include total accounts of experiences we lack and might always lack, such as experiences of alien life exhibiting legal systems. While there is little merit in denying that social science has little to tell us of aliens, it strikes us as seriously mistaken to take this shortcoming as a reason against giving attention to demonstrably relevant evidence we can gather from

43 H. L. A. Hart, 'Abortion law reform: the English experience', *Melbourne University Law Review*, 8 (1971–1972), p. 388.

44 H. L. A. Hart and D. Soskice, 'After the act', *The Guardian* (3 May 1972). See also Nicola Lacey's discussion of this period of Hart's life: 'The partial legalization of abortion in England and Wales, of which he had been a powerful advocate, had been effected by the Abortion Act 1967, and Herbert was now keen to trace the consequences of the legislation. He worked with David Soskice, a young economics colleague at University College, to trace the statistical evidence which might illuminate declining recourse to dangerous 'back-street' abortions and hence bolster the utilitarian case for maintaining and indeed extending legal access to abortion'. N. Lacey, *A Life of H. L. A. Hart* (Oxford: Oxford University Press, 2006), p. 302.

45 Hart, *Concept*, pp. 193–194.

social and often natural sciences. To do otherwise, following Shapiro's suggestion, is parallel to supposing that we ought to cease efforts in elucidation of the nature of legality because we have yet to possess all experience humans will ever have of law and so lack the needed totality of a form of evidence needed to warrant integrating it as evidence into an account of law. Yet this is an absurd ground on which to cease integration of a form of evidence into an account of law. Just as it is advisable to moderate the scope of our claims for the reliability of a view of law which has yet to benefit from observation of the totality of human experience of law, so it is advisable to moderate the scope of our claims for an account of law relying on incomplete social scientific evidence regarding alien experience of law. In neither case does incompleteness of a certain kind of evidence warrant setting it aside entirely; rather, its incompleteness is noted and carried through as a caveat with respect to the explanatory scope and strength of the account of law it informs. Shapiro's implausible denial of the relevance of social science seems to us to be crippling to his state-based approach to legality insofar as our investigation of the relation between law and security illuminates legal phenomena in need of explanation yet not detected if legality is viewed as exclusively state-based. His view commits him not just to a state-based explanation of those phenomena were they to be accessible, but to deny their accessibility to ripeness for consideration. That these phenomena are indeed ripe for consideration by analytical legal theory seems to be usefully demonstrated to the contrary (albeit incompletely) by Raz. He identifies yet leaves only partially examined the non-state legal phenomena to which his revised view will respond, examining 'possibilities of reaching different conclusions that will be sustained by the same building blocks' as used to construct the preceding state-focussed account of legality as found exclusively in legal systems.[46] The path forward for historically state-focussed theorists in the analytical vein surely lies along the course set by Raz, and not in the self-defeating insularity advocated by Shapiro.

While we await next steps from Raz and similarly minded analytical theorists, we are left with the question of what to do with legal system as an element of a general account of the nature of law, and where to seek greater insight into the empirical matters seen in the law-security relation and needing consideration in a renewed descriptive-explanatory account of legality. One view of the place of legal system in characterization of legality is that of an enduring explanatorily valuable concept reflecting a changing empirical situation where besieged legal systems see usurpation of their historic claims and scope

[46] Raz, 'Why the state?', p. 1.

by international organizations and others. That view is too close to Leviathan's ghost, we suggest. It recreates the errors of its unrevised commitments to a conception of law in terms of hierarchies of authorities evincing presumptions of comprehensiveness, supremacy and openness, but at a higher level of organization, perhaps the international or at some intersection point between the claims of international organizations and the organization of states. Our inter-institutional view takes a different departure point, seeking instances of institutions of law and the legal institutions by which they are wielded, observing frequent and intense mutual reference amongst legal institutions in a particular area of social life such as a situation of regional food insecurity or a crisis of biosecurity. This approach takes as its starting point for assessment of legal continuity the actual function of legal institutions and agglomerations of institutions emerging as legal orders. The claims or self-perception of particular legal orders such as legal system inform but do not determine the assessment of continuity of legality made from the point of view of an inquirer using an inter-institutional approach – as we have seen from the example offered by former Italian Prime Minister Mario Monti and cited in Chapter 3, the perceptions of a legal system's officials regarding the nature and scope of that system's authority may, on their own reflective account, be mistaken. Taking legal system as in 'some ways . . . pre-eminent' yet no longer the only 'form' of legal order, legal system has no particular presumptive place of importance as a descriptive-explanatory device. On our view, the place of the concept of legal system is under question even to the point of asking whether upon reconsideration of the concept in light of both changing legal phenomena and greater awareness of a wider range of legal phenomena needing explanation, it might be the case that legal system is no longer usefully viewed as a descriptive-explanatory concept. Instead, from a global inter-institutional perspective, legal system might be viewed as a kind of political ideal, variably realized in much the same way as the rule of law. The plausibility of this view is underwritten in part by Raz's characterization of international organizations as supplying 'interference' to some states in certain circumstances. This suggests that even on Raz's preliminary view, it is now credible to be sceptical of the notion of global legality as a set of structurally near-identical and limitedly operationally varied legal systems. Some are closer in word and action to the explanatory recipe ascribed to them by state-based analytical theories of law, and others are further away, such as those instances of continuous legality in which at best shared jurisdiction and perhaps more credibly overlapping jurisdiction are found. Familiar examples of cases needing to be reconsidered include the situation of First Nations in Canada, Greenland in relation to Denmark, Maori in New Zealand, American Indians in the United States,[47] and the Sami in Norway, Finland and Sweden. Contrasting yet no less instructive examples of the varying forms of legal order falling away from any credible claim to legal system may be found by review of the failed and failing states index to which we referred in the introduction to this chapter. What has changed, perhaps, since 1970, is the range and diversity of realizations of legal systems in states such that the diversity plus 'interference' leaves legality sufficiently pluriform that legal system is the possibly temporary badge of achievement of a relatively few states, whether eventually identified as some of the G8 or a broader set such as OECD member states, or some other organizing category.

LEGALITY'S TRACES

Our investigations of law's relation to environment and security have shown the incompleteness of state-based theorizing about law as a means to understanding the preconditions of legality and to resolution of the problem of continuity. Both the preceding chapter and this chapter have also shown the

[47] That state legal systems might not be anywhere but in a few limited exemplars truly comprehensive, supreme and open is underscored by historic evidence from one state system often considered to be amongst the clearest examples of that account: the United States. In *Cherokee Nation v Georgia*, 30 U.S. 1 (1831), Marshall, CJ, delivered the opinion of the court on matters including the question of the legal status of Indians not subject to the US nor plainly recognizable as a sovereign state of stature identical to a foreign nation, arriving eventually at the view that the United States is committed to viewing Indians as holding their own 'entirely distinct' status. As Marshall explains the jurisprudential challenge,

> . . . the peculiar relations between the United States and the Indians occupying our territory are such that we should feel much difficulty in considering them as designated by the term foreign state were there no other part of the Constitution which might shed light on the meaning of these words. But we think that, in construing them, considerable aid is furnished by that clause in the eighth section of the third article which empowers Congress to 'regulate commerce with foreign nations, and among the several States, and with the Indian tribes'.
>
> In this clause, they are as clearly contradistinguished by a name appropriate to themselves from foreign nations as from the several States composing the union. They are designated by a distinct appellation, and as this appellation can be applied to neither of the others, neither can the appellation distinguishing either of the others be in fair construction applied to them. The objects to which the power of regulating commerce might be directed are divided into three distinct classes – foreign nations, the several States, and Indian tribes. When forming this article, the convention considered them as entirely distinct. We cannot assume that the distinction was lost in framing a subsequent article unless there be something in its language to authorize the assumption.

Available at http://supreme.justia.com/cases/federal/us/30/1/case.html.

need for attention to novel sources of data, responsiveness to novel methods and the merits of openness to novel explanatory categories. Investigation of law's relation to security seems particularly promising as a means to identifying explanatory tools suited to characterization of forms of legality beyond the state and to response to the problem of continuity. Where once we may have followed Hart and Waldron in a focus on the dimensions of the subject-state dyad in the context of a stable, territorially fixed state, we must now do more, driven by our new awareness of the place of security in failing states, and dimensions of security beyond states in matters such as food security and biosecurity. We must identify particular instances of law's relation to security of greatest interest to our inquirer, and we must choose and apply particular investigative methods to better understand law's relation to security in the several dimensions it appears to an inquirer with individual interests, membership in collectives with interests, and concerns for others and their security.

Further investigation of law's relation to security, beyond the scope of our present work, might wish to take up methods well-suited to understanding what Raz calls 'interference' in presently stable and failing states, whether extending investigation of biosecurity as begun by Raz's remarks on Ebola, or taking up other facts associated with disruption of a given form of legal order. We note with particular interest a successor and outgrowth of what Hart called 'still young sciences of psychology and sociology',[48] in methods developed under the rubric of political ecology. Philippe LeBillon, for example, has applied political ecology methods to contexts of conflict regarding natural resources.[49] His investigation reveals fact patterns regarding resource wealth and legality which might seem counter-intuitive, yet for that very reason demand inclusion amongst the data we consider in developing a general account of law. In *Fuelling War: Natural Resources and Armed Conflicts*, LeBillon demonstrates that in at least some countries, including Angola and Iraq, continuity of legal system and increased fidelity to the ideal of the rule of law has not emerged from the presence of resource wealth assumed to be an enabler of national development. Rather, resource wealth has been a source of conflict inhibiting development of state systems expressing the rule of law as a virtue, as resources are sometimes the cause of conflict regarding their control and profit from their use, a situation quite different from historic struggles to obtain resources to support pursuit of political goals – resources are not sometimes the end of

48 Hart, *Concept*, p. 193.

49 See, e.g., P. LeBillon, 'The political ecology of war: natural resources and armed conflicts', *Political Geography*, 20 (2001), pp. 561–584.

conflict, not a means to support conflict.[50] Political ecology offers an approach to understanding some of the social facts germane to a legal theorist's assessment of the form of legality which is achieved in these situations in the absence of development of legal institutions combining to support a state system of law.

As a conceptual vocabulary is developed for legal theorists' investigation of such situations, our challenge as investigators of the problem of continuity is to identify what remains or arises, and to develop concepts and vocabulary appropriate to assessment where we seek not just the mark of legality at some static point in time, but legality's 'traces' as marks of legality over time, even when faint. This is difficult in the case of conflicts over resources giving rise to insecurity in personal, collective and territorial forms, with implications for understanding of the subject-state-territory relation. It is still more difficult in our next area of inquiry, in the relation between law and technology. Here the most prominent questions concern the security of information whose reliable circulation is increasingly implicated in the ordinary daily life of legal orders and their subjects. The connection between security and technology is not simply, however, one in which security supports information flow as a kind of optional extra in social life. Rather, technology has its own relation to life under law, as technologies associated with information flow are now firmly embedded in the familiar physical facts of daily social life, from traffic lights to security cameras to food traceability systems, all integrated into the internet of things, and governed by enabling and limiting laws. At the same time, information technology has given rise to an intangible virtual world whose relation to legality's traces remains largely unexplored as the pace of technological development easily outpaces legal theorists' attempts to follow. Law's relation to technology as mediator between real and virtual worlds, and law's use as a means to control and provide security of expectations in those worlds occupies our next chapter.

50 P. LeBillon, *Fuelling War*, Adelphi Paper No. 357 (Oxford: Oxford University Press for the International Institute for Strategic Studies, 2001). Available at http://blogs.ubc.ca/lebillon/files/2015/01/adelphi357.pdf.

7

Information Communication Technologies and Legal Theory

The preceding chapter's examination of the relation between law and security illustrates some of the ways in which new phenomena may demand new methodological debate and new methods. Some of the new alliances between legal theory and empirical methods amount to deepening of existing relationships, as may be seen in legal theory's increasing connection to comparative law in an era of rapid globalization. Other alliances involve new approaches in the social sciences, yet over familiar territory, as scholarship of the political ecology of violence addresses geographic territory and cultures with which legal theorists may have long acquaintance. This chapter turns to phenomena whose demand for new methodological debates, methods and alliances is accentuated by its operation in a less familiar spatial environment, the network environment created by the launch of the internet and the unprecedented speed and volume of information exchange it has enabled.

The structure of this chapter reflects the interests of our twenty-first-century citizen who travels, finding as she does a rapidly expanding and intensifying network of new communications technologies (ICTs).[1] In some, typically remote locales, the deployment of these technologies may be limited to wire-dependent voice telephones or satellite voice telephones with short text messages delivered via sms (small message system) protocol. In other, equally remote locales, technology in use may match familiar web-based integration of text, images and voice our traveller uses at her urban home for purposes as

[1] In using the term 'new ICTs', we aim to supply a working definition sufficient to motivate jurisprudential discussion. We aim by this term to capture electronically mediated communications technologies whose most familiar applications include the Internet, and wireless mobile voice telephony, recognizing at the same time that the terms 'new ICTs' is falling out of currency as the distinction between communications technologies and adjacent technologies is elided by increased integration of communications capacities into objects having some other primary function.

diverse as learning, commerce or entertainment. Our traveller might even see from time to time more advanced applications of the new information communications technologies, easily understood as extensions of those technologies yet no less intriguing in light of their promise, perhaps remote medical diagnostics, or 3D scanning of an object later reproduced elsewhere by 3D printing, or even use of hologram technologies enabling transmission of the actual words and actions of a performer to be seen in lifelike reproduction thousands of kilometres away. Our travelling citizen's reactions to the new ICTs may, on reflection, generate more confusion and questions than answers. While our citizen finds new communication technologies nearly everywhere she goes, she finds that their prevalence and use varies by place, as does the blend of more and less sophisticated technologies. The social effect of the new information communication technologies seems to vary similarly, from amplification of familiar communications practices, to transformation of commercial practices as our traveller finds, for example, little use for financial instruments such as traveller's cheques in a world where access to local currencies – if needed at all – is readily mediated by communications technologies available nearly everywhere. Our traveller knows that these communications practices are regulated in various ways, so she welcomes the way in which the world is opened to her by the rise of new ICTs. At the same time she sees headlines carrying news of hacking attacks on government databases holding defence data, and in her daily life worries that her personal health data gathered from her exercise bracelet might not be secure as she transmits it to her physician. In the short term, she thinks, the new ICTs and their effects have been easily treated by familiar legal concepts and tools, yet she wonders about the longer term. Might the new ICTs demand new legal concepts and practices, and perhaps new institutions to guide use of these new concepts and practices reaching across historic state and intra-state institutional boundaries?

In the first part of this chapter we will explore what our travelling citizen might regard as the way the new ICTs open new questions and possibilities for life under law, demanding revision of presumptions regarding the social ontology of life under law. The second part of this chapter turns to the operational context and questions raised by what our citizen might regard as closure or limits or borders in social life under law enabled by the new ICTs – and in some cases, the difficulty of creating such borders. As we explore the implications of the new ICTs for understanding of legality, and the problem of continuity we are examining as a means to understanding legality, it will be helpful to begin from some provisional distinctions relevant to our understanding of the new ICTs and their operation.

Since widespread use of the world wide web in the late 1990s, use of the internet has become woven into our daily activity in visible and invisible ways making it so ordinary that the proper noun phrase 'the Internet' is nearly obsolete. At the same time, we have become accustomed to referring quite casually to various aspects of 'cyberspace', the geography-independent world created by structured exchange of information by networked computing devices. We hear equally, for example, of cybersecurity, and cyberdefence, as we have noted in the preceding chapter. Unlike the internet, however, which can be demonstrated to refer to a physical assemblage of network technologies together with their use and the effects of their use, cyberspace was never intended to have so precise a reference, and is now at best a set of stipulative definitions departing from the deliberately inspecific meaning and exploratory use given it by the originator of the term, science fiction novelist William Gibson.[2] No purpose is served here by enumerating various uses of 'cyberspace'; rather, it is sufficient for our exploration to observe that it is generally used to refer to a separate world of communications existing apart from the workaday physical world. Other, parallel terms have arisen as we have sought to characterize the way the communications enabled by terrestrially rooted internet technologies appear to enable us to depart from our terrestrial habits and imagination in various ways. Talk of the 'virtual world' now holds much the same connotation as 'cyberspace', explored not just in speculative 'hard' science fiction but in popular films such as *The Matrix* series. These films depict a dystopia where what is perceived to be the real world is in fact virtual, and the real world is a post-conflict wasteland, giving rise to happily entertained filmgoers and a market

[2] The *Oxford Dictionary of Science Fiction* reports current usage of Gibson's neologism 'cyberspace' and his later elaboration ascription of meaning to it:

> cyberspace ***n***
> the entirety of the data stored in, and the communication that takes place within, a computer network, conceived of as having the properties of a physical realm; the environment of virtual reality. Compare matrix.
>
> 1982 W. Gibson *Burning Chrome Omni* (July) 72/2 I knew every chip in Bobby's simulator by heart; it looked like your workaday Ono-Sendai VII, the 'Cyberspace Seven'.
>
> 1984 W. Gibson *Neuromancer* (1989) 51 Cyberspace. A consensual hallucination experienced daily by billions of legitimate operators, in every nation, by children being taught mathematical concepts [. . .]. A graphic representation of data abstracted from the banks of every computer in the human system.

See www.oxfordreference.com/view/10.1093/acref/9780195305678.001.0001/acref-9780195305678-e-102?rskey=2r9Ulf&result=103.

For Gibson's original use of the term 'cyberspace', see his short story 'Burning chrome', *Omni* (July 1982), pp. 72–77, 102–104, where he explores his characters' devious operations in 'mankind's extended nervous system' (p. 74).

for philosophers' explanation of issues raised in the films.[3] Cyberspace, on this conception, is a real world, but it is a world apart. What happens in the virtual world is not simply a simulacrum of the real world, mapping back to it by firm links, however temporary or long-lasting. Rather, virtual worlds construct separate, often purposely self-contained realities, perhaps most vividly illustrated by the rise of web-accessed, user-constructed worlds such as Second Life (www.secondlife.com), and massively multi-player online role-playing games such as World of Warcraft (http://us.battle.net/wow/en/game/), set in an alternate universe of the kind long-explored by speculative science fiction. As Gibson has observed, a neologism developed to provide a setting for his science fiction has been given technological expression:

> I took my neologism and that vague chain of associations to a piece of prose fiction just to see what they could do. But I didn't have a concept of what it was to begin with. I still think the neologism and the vague general idea were the important things. I made up a whole bunch of things that happened in cyberspace, or what you could call cyberspace, and so I filled in my empty neologism. But because the world came along with its real cyberspace, very little of that stuff lasted. What lasted was the neologism.[4]

The 'real cyberspace' whose existence Gibson takes as a fact has enjoyed a cultural moment whose full analysis is beyond the scope of our inquiry, yet is nonetheless worth exploring in illustrative fashion. From the perspective and interests of our ordinary citizen gradually turning her attention to the relation between the new ICTs and law, the rise in awareness of cyberspace as a constructible alternative reality has provoked an opening of sometimes utopian thought re-imagining the relation of government and officials to citizens, and indeed, the nature of officials and citizens. The closing of the cultural moment of cyberspace as a place of possibility has been equally speculative and real in ways we explore in the second part of this chapter, focussing on the implications of the rise of the 'internet of things' for the presumption of the centrality of continuous, hierarchically organized law-states as the principal objects of explanation in a general theory of law. Cyberspace has at length been transformed from a notional space inhabited by possibilities detached from workaday life, emerging instead as a space capable of determining the course of

[3] See, e.g., W. Irwin (ed.), *The Matrix and Philosophy* (Chicago: Carus, 2002); C. Grau (ed.), *Philosophers Explore the Matrix* (Oxford: Oxford University Press, 2005).

[4] 'The art of fiction, no. 211, interview with William Gibson', *The Paris Review*, 53, no. 197 (Summer 2011), p. 133. Available at http://io9.com/5815019/william-gibson-says-cyberspace-was-inspired-by-8-bit-videogames.

workaday life as virtual and terrestrial worlds have been bridged by internet-based control of physical objects and processes. As use of the new ICTs to monitor and control terrestrial objects has grown, accompanied by algorithms enabling mutually responsive communications amongst controlled objects, the alternate, minimally terrestrially connected virtual world has breached its status as simulacrum and along the way breached the separateness of information flow from decision and action. The emergence of the internet of things, we shall suggest, is potentially highly disruptive to presumptions undergirding conceptions of legality's ontology as expressed in categories of officialdom, citizenship, borders and associated obligations, permissions, commands and so on.

In the next part of this chapter we take up the conceptual and historical 'opening' of systemic, state-based legality and associated social systems by the rapid emergence of the new ICTs. Since our purpose in doing so is to illustrate dimensions of the relation between law and technology, we shall emphasize presentation of conceptual claims supported by illustrative evidence, and do not propose or purport to provide a comprehensive survey or account of relevant information communication technologies. And, since we seek principally to illustrate the variety of the multiple dimensions of law's relation to the new ICTs, while we situate some of those dimensions in the context of a particular history, we do not propose or purport to be offering a comprehensive history of law's relation to the new ICTs. Our talk of 'opening' and 'closing' of systematic, state-based legality by the new ICTs is an intentional use of contrastive metaphors to provide an organizational scheme for what we intend to be independently valuable steps in an analysis and descriptive-explanatory account of legality as illuminated by its relation to the new ICTs.

THE NEW ICTS AND THE PROBLEM OF CONTINUITY IN THE CONTEXT OF LEGAL SYSTEM

In a 2004 article, 'How the New ICTs Matter to the Theory of Law', Culver reflected on early developments in e-government and their potential effect on law, and in particular, the relations between legal authorities and legal subjects. That article departed from the observation that while advocates of renewal of the practice of democracy were working to understand how the new ICTs might advance their cause, legal theorists were relatively unconcerned with the implications of the new ICTs for thinking about the nature of law, legal system, legal obligation and adjacent concepts.[5] Here we reproduce and

[5] As a snapshot of the era, see, e.g., B. N. Hague and B. D. Loader, *Digital Democracy* (London: Routledge, 1999); J. Hoff, I. Horrocks and P. Tops (eds), *Democratic Governance and New*

update the argument offered by Culver, while maintaining the core of the argument's assertion: that particular uses of the new ICTs may disrupt and perhaps even make impossible certain facts functioning as presumptions in analytical accounts of law presuming its basic form to be found in hierarchically organized state systems operated in their most minimal form by officials who accept the norms of the system, and citizen norm-subjects who may simply obey the norms of the system.[6] As deployment of new ICTs disrupts the factual presumptions undergirding this familiar account of law, the new social phenomena challenge the capacity of this view of law as both a 'momentary' account and as an account capable of explaining continuity of legality.

The system-centred view of law we have sketched is usefully characterized as a 'practice theory of law', to the extent that it satisfies the descriptive dimensions of its descriptive-explanatory aims by observation of what it argues are central, even if logically contingent[7] characteristics of law's actual use in social life. In proffering the combination of primary and secondary rules Hart memorably claimed to have found the 'key to the science of jurisprudence', provoking a great deal of discussion of this claim which tended to give much less attention to the question of just who is to turn the key, and how and why. Legal 'officials' are identified as key-turners, albeit in terms so general that new readers of analytical legal theory are often left wondering whether the term is meant to extend to court officials only, or further into various social institutions. It remains nonetheless a presumption and feature of the state-centred account

Technology (London: Routledge, 2000); P. Norris, *Digital Divide?* (Cambridge: Cambridge University Press, 2001); S. Coleman and J. Gøtze, *Bowling Together* (London: Hansard Society, 2001); Office of the e-Envoy, *In the Service of Democracy* (London: Office of the e-Envoy, the Cabinet Office, 2002).

6 We aim to depict here in general terms a version of many analytical legal theorists' account of the nature of legality. Our starting point is Hart's claim that 'there are therefore two minimum conditions necessary and sufficient for the existence of a legal system. On the one hand, those rules of behaviour which are valid according to the system's ultimate criteria of validity must be generally obeyed, and, on the other, its rules of recognition specifying the criteria of legal validity and its rules of change and adjudication must be effectively accepted as common public standards of official behaviour by its officials'. H. L. A. Hart, *The Concept of Law*, 3rd edn (Oxford: Oxford University Press, 2012), p. 116. Here we follow many analytical legal theorists in understanding the rule of recognition as rooted in the practice of officials, notwithstanding the existence of illuminating argument to the contrary. See, e.g., Zipursky's argument for the rule of recognition as a propositional entity. B. C. Zipursky, 'The model of social facts', in J. Coleman (ed.), *Hart's Postscript* (Oxford: Oxford University Press, 2001), pp. 224–227.

7 We are mindful of Hart's claim that the minimum natural law content of a legal system precludes the free use of violence for the naturally necessary but logically contingent reason that humans lack the carapaces of crabs and so are naturally vulnerable to free use of violence. H. L. A. Hart, 'Positivism and the separation of law and morals', *Harvard Law Review*, 71 (1957), p. 623.

that life under law is inhabited by law's officials and law's subjects. Even while legal officials are simultaneously subjects, these officials are presumed to play a special role with distinctive attitudes, knowledge and uses of law, all within the system shown by officials' practice of a master rule or rule of recognition.

The central insight of Culver's 'How the New ICTs Matter to the Theory of Law' addresses this relationship and the way it has been changed by the rise of two new ICT-driven practices: e-petitions and e-consultations. While these practices are instances of e-democracy, using the new ICTs to offer modernized versions of familiar practices, they nonetheless have significant effects on the presumption of the system-centred view of law. These new practices, arguably and demonstrably just initial instances of deeper and broader changes to social life driven by the new ICTs, tend to show that differences between officials and subjects are no longer what they were. Indeed, the changes driven by the new ICTs are so significant as to seriously decrease, or perhaps entirely defeat, the viability of an account of legality, and legal system, which tracks officials' conduct as the key indicator of the momentary and continued existence of legal system as the principal form of legality worthy of jurisprudential attention. This argument requires two steps, which can be undertaken in parallel. The first step is demonstration of the importance of three particular states and differences between officials and subjects – three asymmetries, as we will put it. The second step is demonstration that e-petitions and e-consultations – amongst other uses of the new ICTs – do in fact disrupt the factual basis of the asymmetries we see, in ways depriving the system-centred explanatory view of the presumptions it requires for its plausibility. As we set out this argument we will add further reflections on the sense in which e-petitions and e-consultations represent an 'opening' of legality in ways challenging the adequacy of system-centred approaches to the theory of law in the particular context of the problem of continuity.

The three asymmetries we see affected by the new ICTs are familiar to readers of analytical legal theory: differences between officials' and citizens' *legal knowledge*, *attitudes to law* and their conception of *law as an object of their allegiance*.

Knowledge of Law

Officials clearly differ from citizens in a formal or role-specific way insofar as officials have special powers and duties with respect to legal norms. Beneath this obvious difference there is a complex assumption that officials typically *relate* to legal knowledge in ways that citizens typically do not. Stated more intuitively, an official's knowledge of law cannot be matched by just anyone mimicking the operations of the official's office.[8] But why not?

The system-centred view of law seems to presume a social situation something like the following. Officials typically gain a special education, often a shared education, involving shared standards of adequate minimum knowledge of law or some department of law. This is not a process of merely learning 'what' law is as a matter of doctrine. It is additionally a process of learning 'how' to use various modes of manipulation of legal knowledge with proper regard for fellow officials' likely attitudes towards particular modes of argument regarding use of particular legal norms. Fully qualified officials maintain and deepen their knowledge through shared cooperative activities[9] in use of legal norms for official purposes.[10] Officials also typically have easy access to the 'dependent reasons'[11] underlying particular legal norms, and the particular histories

[8] It is not easy to identify the presuppositions embodied in this part of the system-centred view, in part because the analytical commitment to a descriptive-explanatory method does not entail the further claim that the system-centred view is properly evaluated according to its descriptive accuracy with respect to any particular social situation. The method's distinctive feature is instead the way in which its explanation of legal phenomena ascribes salience to the various social facts described. In identifying what we take to be presuppositions undergirding the explanation of legal normativity which ascribes a certain primacy to officials' intermediary role, we are necessarily engaging in an equally general exercise departing from 'central case' features of officials' and subjects' life under law.

[9] This phrase is borrowed from J. Coleman, *The Practice of Principle* (Oxford: Oxford University Press, 2001), pp. 96–100. Coleman derives his application of 'shared cooperative activity' from M. E. Bratman, 'Shared cooperative activity', *Philosophical Review*, 101 (1992), p. 327, and Bratman, 'Shared intention', *Ethics*, 97 (1993), p. 104.

[10] This might be expressed in Hartian terms as knowledge of secondary rules of introduction, change and elimination of primary rules.

[11] This use of 'dependent reasons' follows Raz. Raz characterizes authoritative reasons for action (such as legal norms) as preempting and taking the place of other reasons for action on which norm subjects might otherwise depend, in a situation where an authority's directives apply and norm subjects must act. As he puts it in discussion of the authority of an arbitrator, 'the arbitrator's decision is for the disputants a reason for action. They ought to do as he says because he says so. But this reason is related to the other reasons which apply to the case. It is not . . . just another reason to be added to the others, a reason to stand alongside the others when one reckons which way is better supported by reason. The arbitrator's decision is meant to be based on the other reasons, to sum them up and to reflect their outcome. For ease of reference I shall call both reasons of this character and the reasons they are meant to reflect dependent reasons'. J. Raz, *The Morality of Freedom* (Oxford: Clarendon Press, 1985), p. 41. Our discussion here uses the notion of dependent reasons to capture those reasons for action which continue to bear on abstract reasoning regarding action in some situation even while their employment in practical reasoning in that situation may be precluded. These dependent reasons arrive at their subsidiary and merely abstract relevance when some one or more of these reasons for action gains practical priority via its special endorsement by an authority whose reach extends to the matter under abstract debate. We take it that debate regarding legal reforms, for example, often involves attention to the dependent reasons which are subsumed into a particular legal

of dependent reasons which gained particular force in legal practices. Officials may as a matter of habit or duty maintain their awareness of economic or philosophical or some other kind of analysis or history which contributes to understanding the operation of legal norms. Alternatively, officials' ordinary activities may expose them to the reasoning of those persons who use dependent reasons in advocating introduction, change, maintenance, elimination or application of their system's legal norms. Exposure to these dependent reasons might occur in various available fora, ranging from, perhaps, personal pleading on the part of subjects, to pamphlet, to legislative chamber to adjudicative process. The officials envisioned in the system-centred view are typically conceived to be judges, but there are of course other kinds of officials in a legal system and they too are included in the presumption at least loosely in the use of the inclusive term 'officials' and not the more restrictive term 'judges'.

By contrast, subjects' relation to legal knowledge is one of relative privation, especially in the case of borderline legal systems whose recognition as legal systems is a matter of reasonable dispute. In the modern municipal legal systems from which the system-centred view derives its descriptive-explanatory claims, subjects usually lack specialized education in law, gaining instead in various ways a partial picture of the specific requirements of some particular department of law. In learning something of legal norms, subjects typically do not do so in ways which are simultaneously acts of learning and acts of affirmation of membership in a cohort or class. Similarly, subjects typically use legal norms for private purposes in an occasional and limited way, and do not by their use of legal norms contribute as officials do to a shared cooperative activity of affirming particular modes of argument regarding use of legal norms.[12] Subjects' typically limited and partial legal knowledge is paralleled by their equally limited knowledge of the dependent reasons associated with particular legal norms and their relation in turn to other legal norms and modes of argument regarding use of legal norms.

Attitudes towards Law

In the system-centred view, officials' and subjects' asymmetric knowledge of law is closely tracked by asymmetry in attitudes to law. It seems to be taken

norm whose special, authoritative force is partly grounded on the practical meaningfulness of the dependent reasons it summarizes, reflects and replaces.

[12] Subjects may of course individually or collectively in their capacity as private citizens use legal norms to advance what they believe to be in the public interest – but this typically occasional convergence of purposes remains quite unlike officials' collective practice of using, modifying and reaffirming modes of use of legal norms.

as a social fact that certain norm-subjects – officials – operate and regard one another as subject to both primary and secondary legal rules. Operators of secondary rules do not do so willy-nilly as if the capacity to do so arrived by accident, but rather in an intentional, collective fashion as a matter of shared cooperative activity predicated on shared doctrinal and operational knowledge. Intentional, shared cooperative activity in manipulating a shared body of normative knowledge is presumed to be characteristic of the class of officials, whereas not doing just that is presumed to be characteristic of subjects, no matter what their intentions with respect to law.[13]

Conditions for membership in the class of officials may vary, as might numbers of officials relative to subjects, all without affecting the viability of this assumption. What seems to be at the core of the asymmetry is a fact about possession of legal knowledge. In the minimal legal system subjects lack the kind of robust relation to legal knowledge necessary for a meaningful relation of fidelity to law, a sense of allegiance which includes knowing with some consistency the conditions for successful demonstration of fidelity. Even in more typical systems which do enjoy the allegiance of subjects, that knowledge-based allegiance is somewhat muted and uncertain in contrast to the allegiance of officials – the difference, perhaps, between citizenship and patriotism, where citizenship is rooted in knowledge and patriotism is rooted in sentiment.

The Roots of the Asymmetry in Knowledge and Attitude

These asymmetries in knowledge and attitude have causal roots in both time and geography. In the social situation presumed by the intermediary view, aspiring and full-fledged officials can arrange their affairs such that they have time to acquire legal knowledge as a matter of doctrine, and time to engage in the shared cooperative activity of learning how to use legal norms in legal modes of argument. Time matters also in ordinary use of norms, after the typical period of intensive acquisition of legal knowledge and shared activities cementing a sense of membership in the corps of officials. Officials can arrange to be free to use legal norms at the proper times, and to devote time to learning of dependent reasons bearing on legal norms.

[13] On some system-centred views, it may even be the case that subjects lack any intentions with respect to legal norms, perhaps merely complying with threats in a sheerly prudential way not properly characterized as reasons-responsive in the manner characteristic of the intention to comply with what is presented as an authoritative, non-optional legal norm. As Raz argues, 'what counts, from the point of view of the person in authority, is not what the subject thinks but how he acts. I do all that the law requires of me if my actions comply with it'. Raz, *Morality*, p. 39.

Time and geography are of course linked here. Officials' acquisition of legal knowledge does not, or at any rate historically has not, occurred just anywhere. Legal knowledge has been neatly warehoused in geographically fixed seats of government, courts and universities and their libraries. The geographic stability of centres of legal knowledge has contributed significantly to maintenance of a sense of cohort membership with a set of shared cohort standards. Once near the sources of legal knowledge, officials have often found themselves near fellow officials for shared cooperative activity in developing understanding of law, and near those with expert knowledge of particular sets of dependent reasons for action which law authorizes as binding legal norms.

Time and geography are typically barriers to those subjects who might intend to engage with law in something like the manner of officials. With the exception of a few subjects with wealth and extraordinary social influence, subjects lack time to acquire doctrinal legal knowledge, to learn modes of legal argument, and to engage in shared cooperative activities setting the boundaries for acceptable use of legal norms. As we have suggested in discussion of officials, legal knowledge and legal processes are typically concentrated in particular geographical locations. Subjects do not always have ready access to geographical centres of legal knowledge and dependent reasons bearing on legal norms. We shall turn in a moment to the contingency of these underpinnings of the asymmetry between officials and subjects; but first we must capture one further asymmetry rooted in an assumption about attitudes towards law as an object of allegiance.

Law as an Object of Allegiance

The system-centred general theory of law is something of a chimera: its account of law is expressed in the context of an associated account of the boundaries of specific instances of law characteristic of particular forms of life under law. The boundaries identified provide both an account of the identity of a particular legal system, and an identification of the object to which allegiance or fidelity is shown. This discrete entity is typically identified as the state or modern municipal legal system, an entity whose specific claims to authority within some set of boundaries are visible in its officials' practice of a rule of recognition.[14] While the system-centred general theory of law begins from the

[14] While Hart certainly thought about law in a broad fashion not entirely aligned with the notion of the state, subsequent positivist writing is often quite explicit in its focus, as, for example, J. Raz's *The Concept of a Legal System*, 2nd edn (Oxford: Clarendon Press, 1980), and L. Green, *The Authority of the State* (Oxford: Clarendon Press, 1988).

experience of the modern sovereign state, it is compatible with the emergence of international legal norms whose force extends into the internal affairs of sovereign states. Official practices can include treating as binding and so non-optional a range of legal norms which originate outside the state. As Hart put his project in the Postscript to *The Concept of Law*, 'The starting point for this clarificatory task is the widespread common knowledge of a modern municipal legal system which on page 3 of this book I attribute to any educated man'.[15] Yet Hart also writes that his theory accounts for law as a social institution which 'in spite of many variations in different cultures and in different times, has taken the same general form and structure'.[16]

An interestingly unstable presumption about the nature of attitudes of allegiance is embedded in this view. It presumes that the norms which constitute legal systems are primarily internal in origin, or at any rate develop into a distinctive form in a particular legal system even if adopted from an external original source, such that officials' norm-use is substantively and primarily a manifestation of allegiance to a particular norm-source state's claim to authority. There is no parallel presumption with respect to subjects: since all that is required is their obedience, nothing is presumed regarding the content of their attitudes of fidelity to law. The system-centred view is at least *prima facie* compatible with a familiar possibility, that subjects of a state obey its legal norms, yet hold what they regard as conduct-binding allegiance to the norms of some other authority, ranging from religious through political or state or other authorities.

THE DIFFERENCE THE NEW ICTS MAKE

Let us turn now to examine just why the asymmetries we have identified involve presuppositions of social fact liable to disruption by the new ICTs. As we have observed above, the term 'new information communication technologies' is typically used to describe the blend of software, hardware and specific technologies whose particular combinations have enabled ordinary persons and governments alike to manipulate, store and transfer information very rapidly across large distances, in diverse forms and in varying quantities, all within the control of the user. A number of caveats could of course be entered regarding the non-novel nature of the so-called new ICTs whose sudden social significance is really part of a continuum of technological development. Yet what is important here is not the sheer novelty of the technology found in new ICTs such as fax, email, mobile phones and internet tools. The new ICTs

[15] Hart, *Concept*, p. 240. [16] Ibid.

are important because of their social consequences as technologies which have removed many of the historical limits on communication posed by the technical *means* of communication.

In the emerging practices of e-government over the last roughly twenty years, the new ICTs are used to achieve various purposes. Interest in computing in government began in automation of back office functions to achieve performance and financial efficiencies, extending subsequently to use of ICTs such as databases at the point of contact with citizens, and eventually becoming citizen-facing with information-provision webpages, and finally, online services. Leading e-government jurisdictions have now begun to embrace a 'digital by default'[17] ideal asserting that online service delivery technologies should not be converted from paper-based processes, but should begin conception in an online form. When making services 'digital by default' in the internet era where all information can be made available to anyone with internet access, this service ideal, the latest incarnation of an ideal once spoken of as a 'spin the terminal' approach, lends itself easily to support for aspirations to open and transparent government. Digital services can enable subjects to see what officials see, and governments can thereby increase their performance with respect to a number of desired features of 'good governance', including transparency, effectiveness, public accountability and, on many views, eventually legitimacy. The rise of a second generation of e-government services and public engagement tools which are not translations but 'digital by default' is becoming known as 'Government 2.0', helpfully characterized by the Australian government as follows: 'Government 2.0 is about the use of technology to encourage a more open, transparent and engaging form of government, where the public has a greater role in forming policy and has improved access to government information'.[18]

[17] For example, the UK government uses this term and approach: www.gov.uk/service-manual/start. See also the New Zealand *Government ICT Strategy and Action Plan to 2017* at www.ict.govt.nz/assets/Uploads/Government-ICT-Strategy-and-Action-Plan-to-2017.pdf, p. 7.

[18] Australian Government Department of Finance: www.finance.gov.au/policy-guides-procurement/gov20/. This explanation asserts the practice of the Australian Government's 'Declaration of Open Government': 'The Australian Government now declares that, in order to promote greater participation in Australia's democracy, it is committed to open government based on a culture of engagement, built on better access to and use of government held information, and sustained by the innovative use of technology'. www.finance.gov.au/policy-guides-procurement/declaration-of-open-government/. See similarly how the New Zealand *Government ICT Strategy* frames one of its 'guiding principles': 'Openness and transparency. Non-personal information is a public asset that must be open by default for economic and social benefit' (p. 8).

The first wave of attempts to use the new ICTs to provide improved government services to citizens coincided with a burst of interest in what might be done to address declining trust in government and participation in democratic processes. The two-way communications enabled by the new ICTs in government service delivery were seen as equally adaptable to new styles of communication re-engaging citizens with government and law.[19] In the first version of the argument we have presented over the preceding pages, published in 2004, Culver focussed on e-petitions and e-consultations as two e-democracy devices which seemed at that time to be likely to gain widespread acceptance very rapidly, due to their technical feasibility and political usability in various contexts found in modern legal systems exhibiting varying levels of openness to citizens' engagement with government. Rehearsal of the argument regarding these applications of the new ICTs remains relevant, even while the post-2004 story of the career of these and similar applications of ICTs is rather different from Culver's anticipation, leading to the next section's discussion of how the new ICTs may be implicated in destabilization of state legality insofar as they are used to undermine the identity and continuity of state systems of law.

E-consultations are used to engage citizens in public policy issues, in ways ranging from officials' offering of information to citizens in 'tell and sell' fashion, through consultation on policy questions set by officials, and finally in active participation from citizens in issue-identification and further introduction and evaluation of options for resolution of issues via formal or informal norms.[20] Minimally, e-consultations enable officials to assess the practical feasibility of proposed norms by allowing citizens to comment on the 'fit' between proposed norms and the issue addressed. More constructively, e-consultations enable officials to solicit citizens' views to assist in honing officials' choice of norms without complete surrender of officials' decision-making power. In situations where officials have not yet chosen preferred normative solutions to the problems they address, citizens may take up authorship though typically not final authority for solutions citizens devise with or without the participation of officials. This last phase of active partnership is advocated by the Organization for Economic Cooperation and Development in its development of policy options aimed at redressing democratic disengagement in OECD member

[19] See, e.g., Office of the e-Envoy, *Service of Democracy*; *Engaging Citizens Online for Better Policy-Making*, OECD Policy Brief No. 00 2003 50 1 (March 2003); D. Lenihan, *Realigning Governance: From e-Government to e-Democracy* (Ottawa, Canada: Centre for Collaborative Government, 2002); J. E. Fountain, *Building the Virtual State* (Washington, DC: Brookings Institution Press, 2001).

[20] We draw this standard three-part division of engagement from *Citizens as Partners* (Paris: OECD, 2001); OECD Policy Brief, *Engaging Citizens*.

states. E-consultations of the first type are often provided through static webpages sometimes referred to as 'brochure-ware'. E-consultations emphasizing citizen-participation tend to use interactive technologies, promoting dialogue between citizens, and sometimes between citizens and officials. For various reasons including the need for reliability, e-consultations typically do not involve leading-edge technology, relying instead on mature technologies such as online questionnaires and moderated online discussion fora.[21] Yet even rudimentary technology allows access at the time and from the place of one's choosing and the opportunity for deliberation prior to response is opened. Both e-consultations and e-petitions can be accessed at any time and from any place. Participation in online discussion of issues is rapid yet asynchronous: while transmission of communications is nearly instantaneous, the data storage and retrieval capacities of the new ICTs mean that recipients can choose when to retrieve, interpret and respond to communications. Similarly, an online questionnaire, for example, can be completed and stored, then later modified as its author decides, within the period of the e-consultation.

This general account of e-consultation does not vary from Culver's 2004 explanation, significantly because the general account is still current as some of what was foreseen has not yet been achieved. There are many reasons for this state of affairs, including some associated with global political events giving rise to governments seeing openness as a danger, or perhaps as virtue only if appropriately accompanied by counterbalancing security measures. Incremental development has nonetheless occurred along the lines imagined in the OECD's 2001 consideration of the potential of e-democracy and e-government technologies to transform governance and government, in ways usefully summarized by the 'Government 2.0' aspiration reported above, in step with e-democracy tools captured under talk of the 'participative web' or 'web 2.0' or 'participation 2.0'.[22] The features of the participative web most

[21] Examples of e-consultation may be readily found: in Canada at http://www1.canada.ca/consultingcanadians/; in the United Kingdom at www.gov.uk/government/get-involved#engage-with-government; in Australia at www.australia.gov.au/news-and-media/public-consultations; and in France at www.vie-publique.fr/spip.php?page=debatsfiltres&motdebat=5205.

[22] As summarized by the OECD, 'the "participative web" is the most common term and underlying concept used to describe the more extensive use of the Internet's capabilities to expand creativity and communication. It is based on intelligent web services and new Internet-based software applications that enable users to collaborate and contribute to developing, extending, rating, commenting on and distributing digital content and developing and customizing Internet applications (O'Reilly, 2002, 2005; MIC, 2006; OECD, 2006a, 2006b). New web software tools enable commercial and non-commercial service providers to draw on an ever-widening array of content sources and what is often called the "collective intelligence" of Internet users, to use information on the web in the form of data, metadata and user resources, and to

relevant to legal theory are associated with so-called user-created content and the way user-created content interacts with other internet applications and users.[23] The applications on which the participative web relies are so fast-evolving that there is little point in enumerating them. What matters more is that there are many, and that they are emerging and changing with improved communications technologies. Their effect is to diversify, on the back of the internet, the ways in which communications are received, manipulated, shared and given response. Where once a government could be reasonably confident of controlling the form and audience of its consultation message together with the form of response from recipient subjects, today the participative web acts as a sort of metaphorical prism, where message and audience are varied by internet applications, as may be the form of response to governments. As an OECD report observed in 2009,

> The tools and practices of the participative web can help make both online and face-to-face public participation more open and inclusive. They are transforming three factors which contribute to successful policy making and service delivery:
>
> - **Knowledge** which flows freely with the move from an 'economy of scarcity' to an 'economy of surplus'.
> - **Connections** which are no longer binary, private and hierarchical but multiple, public and networked.
> - **Actors** who are not just isolated 'atoms' but are embedded in a dense network of loose links with many others.[24]

Much remains to be learned with respect to the way multiple, public and networked connections reduce 'atomic individualism' in bordered hierarchies; but it is clear even in these early days of government engagement with the participative web that there is little likelihood of a return to former hierarchical relations between authoritative voices and supplicant listeners. We might therefore be somewhat sceptical regarding the OECD's optimistic assertion

create links between them. A further characteristic of the participative web is the communication between users and between separate software applications via open web standards and interfaces'. *Participative Web and User-Created Content* (Paris: OECD, 2007), p. 17.

[23] By 'user-created content', many authors intend to capture the ideas and data with which users of the internet populate various applications of the internet as a means of communication for personal purposes. Familiar examples include from blogging applications enabling individual users to express their views in a diary-like format, and the applications enabling even users of relatively simple and inexpensive handheld devices to communicate brief messages to a global audience nearly instantly, and as frequently as desired.

[24] *Focus on Citizens* (Paris: OECD, 2009), p. 68.

that 'Government use of the participative web will enhance its external relations with stakeholders'.[25] We find more credible, in light of the nature of the phenomena reported, the immediately subsequent observation that 'Government is just one of the nodes in the network – albeit a large one which is well endowed and highly connected. It is obliged to struggle for the attention of those online, prove its relevance and add value in the same way as any other node'.[26]

E-consultations of various kinds have become a standard part of 'government 2.0', in variations ranging from 'digital by default' to electronic versions of existing practices. Since evaluation of e-consultations is conducted sporadically and by reference to a rapidly developing set of standards, it is difficult to say with any precision what substantial difference e-consultation has made to the practice of governance and the nature of government. It is rather easier to see the potential and emerging reality of e-democracy tools in the context of *e-petitions*. This form of citizen-driven engagement with government is rooted in past petition practices whose prevalence and effectiveness provide a history against which e-petitions can begin to be measured. Most visibly pioneered in Scotland's new Parliament,[27] an e-petition is a form of engagement in which citizens can propose norms to officials, typically via a website containing information, discussion and online signature components. E-petitions differ from traditional petitions in several crucial ways involving enhancement of the valuable features of traditional petitions. Traditional petitions typically involve brief expression of a proposal together with signatures of proponents of the proposal, sometimes bolstered by information meetings. The proposal proffered by an e-petition may have a simple summary form, yet the information storage capacity of the new ICTs opens the way for complex proposals, including, for example, provision of model legislation drawn up by the e-petition's proponents. Similar sophistication is brought to provision of information on the e-petition's topic. The new ICTs permit a variety of forms of presentation of information, in nearly infinite quantity. An e-petition offers the possibility of connection to a web of knowledge relevant to the proposal, through links to relevant information and immediate provision of, e.g., photos, maps, letters of support, video recordings of images or audio recordings of sound. Provision of information can become more than a set-piece established by initial proponents of the petition as other participants add information for consideration by fellow-citizens. The participative web offers further possibilities within and beyond the control of governments establishing e-petition facilities: from subjects creating parallel yet separate deliberative opportunities using online fora,

[25] Ibid. [26] Ibid. [27] See www.scottish.parliament.uk/gettinginvolved/petitions/.

shared access to comparative modelling, or a different form of response to an issue raised by an e-petition, e.g., collaborative construction of an alternative to current legislation.

These features of e-petitions are not, as we have said, wholly novel. They are better viewed as enhancements of processes previously available yet difficult to integrate into the traditional petition process. Where e-petitions differ crucially is in their standing for a prolonged period of time in which discussion and reflection are possible, as is addition of relevant information in light of queries or criticism. E-petitions are not just the result of a quick signature given to a canvasser in an effort to be polite, or civic-minded on little or no clearly evident basis. An e-petition viewed arrives as a set of signatures relative to a particular body of knowledge presented within the petition, and open to debate over time in the e-petition's discussion forum. At the very least, e-petitions provide the means for demonstration of e-petitioners' demonstration of their sincere and enduring commitment to their proposal. At best it may represent something like an attempt at self-legislation, a communal demonstration of the capacity to face up to a pressing issue with a viable normative solution resulting from deliberation and choice amongst viable options.

This discussion is not meant to gloss over the admittedly difficult issues of a digital divide, or the question of whether subjects really can develop adequate legal knowledge from exposure to online sources of knowledge. What is more important to our argument is that the time- and geography-surmounting capacity of these information-transferring technologies is the precondition for breach of the presumed asymmetries between officials and subjects. The time-independent character of data storage and retrieval can make legal doctrine equally available to officials and subjects, and while a shared education in legal knowledge and its characteristic modes of argument may be quite limited in single-issue policy consultations, the new ICTs ease self-organization and mutual education on the part of the subjects.[28] These devices taken as a pair exhibit a further characteristic relevant to the knowledge asymmetry – the potential for a shift of control of legal knowledge from officials to citizens, even if only on particular issues and in particular departments of law. On a continuum capturing the identity of those who control the flow and form of presentation of knowledge, e-consultations represent the end of the continuum most closely associated with officials' control of legal knowledge,

[28] Low- to no-cost internet applications are flourishing in variety and complexity, with corresponding user-determined use, from the rise of massively open online courses (MOOCs) delivering educational opportunities, to internet applications assisting 'blended' learning online and offline, to nearly ubiquitous applications such as Facebook enabling rapid rallying of attention to issues, alongside fund-raising devices such as GoFundMe.com.

modes of legal argument and knowledge of dependent reasons. The middle part of the continuum is occupied by the conception of consultation which includes citizens in agenda-setting on policy issues, and the continuum then sees a decisive shift as e-petitions represent a citizen-generated identification of issues needing normative solutions. E-petitions involve a crucial shift in control of communication and manipulation of legal knowledge. The issues are set by citizens, the set of dependent reasons thought relevant in various ways is set by citizens, and citizens control at least proposition of a specific normative solution to issues raised.

ICTS AND ANALYTICAL APPROACHES TO LEGAL SYSTEM AND LEGALITY

What does this matter to the theory of law? To the extent that e-consultation involves citizens in formation of norms, the identity of officials is blurred, especially in the post-legislative domain where regulations and policies devised to interpret the open-textured norms set by legislators gain their content from the intentional action and practices of recognition driven by citizens. Where citizens participate actively in norm formation, officials' role may be reduced to that of authoritative certification of the adequacy of the process. Some of these features are especially forcefully expressed in e-petitions: such petitions breach temporal and geographical limitations on gaining knowledge of normative options and associated dependent reasons in modern municipal legal systems. More importantly, e-petitions represent the potential for a reversal in the source of norms, particularly post-legislative norms, in a way which may leave officials' offices and formal capacities untouched. E-petitioning offers the possibility of a revival of customary law, by which citizens participate in norm-setting, variation, and elimination on an 'as needed' basis in which need and relevant dependent reasons are identified by citizens themselves. It may even be the case in some situations that citizens' demonstrable legal knowledge and knowledge of particular, relevant dependent reasons augur in favour of community-based normative solutions. Community-based alternative dispute resolution may, for example, produce what are generally regarded and spoken of as binding, non-optional norms of conduct.

Talk of customary law may raise the spectre of direct democracy in various forms. Yet e-petitioning should be distinguished from a direct democracy where all issues are settled by plebiscite, or a kind of shared governance in which certain issues are required to be put before citizens. E-petitioning certainly might be used in novel governance models in our existing democracies, yet e-petitioning is equally compatible with existing models of representative democracy, and indeed, any social situation in which it is permissible for citizens to express their views on law. What is different in e-petitioning is not the fact of popular political expression, but the new potential for that expression to be legally well-informed and to be representative of precisely the class of norm-subjects whose active understanding and subsequent acceptance of legal norms was not previously sought because it could not be had. E-petitions may have the force of knowledge, on the back of a shared activity of deliberation and identification of best practice needing authoritative certification in law. E-petitions may even bring new forces to bear on norm creation and execution: in the case of Scotland e-petitions are not just unsolicited expressions of the views of Scottish citizens, but can be raised by anyone whose concern is within the jurisdiction of Scottish Parliament.[29] All of this threatens the explanation of life under law which presupposes a limited audience for competent understanding of promulgation of legal norms, limited expertise in use of norms, and so presupposes various contingent limits on the capacity of norm-subjects to participate in the practices said to constitute the rule of recognition.

The way e-consultations and e-petitions breach the knowledge and so the attitudinal asymmetry may simply bring an end to the probative value of the idea of a rule of recognition, forcing adoption of some other way to account for the legal character and identity of valid legal norms in some social situation. If it is true, as the system-centred view holds, that subjects in modern municipal systems of law may obey law for any reason at all and may in fact have a plurality of allegiances, there is a fundamental problem in understanding the identity of legal systems as being constituted by officials' practice of the rule of recognition. As the knowledge and attitudinal asymmetry between officials and subjects is reduced, subjects may become equally capable of acquiring legal knowledge prerequisite to substantial allegiance to law, and in turn increasingly capable of contributing to or simply undertaking the legal operations previously only undertaken by officials.

[29] As explained in Scottish Parliament's 'How to submit a public petition' leaflet, 'Members of the Scottish Parliament (MSPs).... may not themselves submit petitions but otherwise there are no restrictions on who can submit a petition and there is no requirement to collect numerous signatures in support of a petition, only one signature is required. Petitions can be lodged in any language'. See www.scottish.parliament.uk/PublicInformationdocuments/HTSAPP-190712.pdf. It is worth noting in this context the Scottish Parliament's embrace of the participative web, going so far as to suggest to e-petition users just how each may 'Promote your petition'. Petitioners are advised that they may create links to other internet applications supporting user-created content, or to other forms of communication: 'You can link your petition to your own website, social networking site, video etc. You can even create your own petition web address'. www.scottish.parliament.uk/gettinginvolved/petitions/HowToPetition.aspx.

In legal systems (or for that matter, sub-systems or non-systemic orders) where subjects regularly use with substantive effect devices such as e-consultations or e-petitions with generally recognized law-making, varying or eliminating effect, subjects effectively merge with the class of officials no matter what process-certification power officials retain by virtue of the formal character of their office. In this situation, the plurality of subjects' allegiances becomes a plurality of allegiances amongst officials. If officials or the blend of officials and norm-setting subjects have a plurality of allegiances, there arises at least a factual difficulty in assessing which of their practices in official use of law is associated with which allegiance. There is a further possibility that the plurality of allegiances will be represented in each instance of official use of law in nominally discrete legal systems, leading to an elision of their boundaries if this occurs on a sufficiently large scale. Stated more bluntly, once the knowledge and attitude asymmetries are breached, the legal theorist loses the option of looking to officials as the source of a shared cooperative agreement in use of legal knowledge in a system-constituting way.

What does this mean for analytical legal theory's account of law, and more particularly, for its response to the problem of continuity we have taken up as a test for that theory? Our view here is consistent with our remedial rather than revolutionary views expressed elsewhere, particularly in *Legality's Borders*. Where there are new social phenomena affecting life under law, those phenomena need explanation, using appropriate explanatory devices. We have demonstrated the existence of e-democracy exercises sponsored by governments and enabled by the participative web, affecting life under law by challenging the theoretical meaningfulness and descriptive-explanatory availability of an official-subject divide, giving rise to a need for a novel approach to identifying and explaining legality in forms including but not limited to state-based legal systems. Our identification of this need is not simultaneously a rejection of all dimensions of what we have characterized as state-centred analytical approaches. While we believe we have shown that it is no longer warranted to presume hierarchically organized systems as the sole instance of legality worthy of explanatory efforts, we do not suppose a departure from a system-centred approach to characterization of legality must include jettisoning other tools of analytical legal theory. The norm-level account of legal norms as peremptory content-independent reasons for action remains viable, in our view, as does the merit of commitment to morally neutral descriptive-explanation. What changes most is the set of problems we choose to take up, motivated by theoretical and practical considerations raised by the new phenomena – whether familiar problems or novel problems. The problem of the continuity of legal systems is unquestionably familiar, even if subject to varying attention. Our preceding argument regarding the disruptive effects of the new ICTs for a presumed official-citizen divide, for example, might motivate renewed attention to problems in the context of characterization of legal systems, and not just problems of continuity but more basic problems presumed solved in accounts of what Raz called 'momentary' legal systems. We have argued in Chapter 2 that Raz's assertion of an intimate relation between the norms of a legal system and supporting social norms is just that – assertion without argument to specify just what is accepted, and why, in treating as reliable the claim that a legal system sits in a relationship of non-symmetric supervenience with a supporting 'comprehensive' social system of which the state is one (political) sub-system. Raz, on our view expressed in Chapter 2, lacks not just an account of continuity of legal system, but an account of the momentary existence of a legal system. Our argument above regarding the frailty of the official-citizen distinction simply adds weight to the set of concerns we have raised regarding the adequacy of analytical accounts of legal system to succeed on their own terms, never mind the further question of whether they are capable of and do in fact address other legal phenomena needing descriptive-explanation. Here, however, we part from that set of questions and familiar problems, facing instead what seem to us to be far more pressing problems in the context of our twenty-first-century citizen who travels. Here we turn to what we described at the beginning of this chapter as 'closings', or better 'failed closings' of state legal systems during the rise of the new ICTs, raising new problems for general accounts of law.

THE NEW ICTS AND THE CLOSED LEGAL SYSTEM

On what we might call the received analytical view of legality we have explored in preceding chapters, where the problem of continuity is considered, it is taken to be the problem of continuity of legal system. And where a legal system is under investigation as a continuous set of social phenomena, that set is taken to comprise relations between phenomena usefully individuated as state, law and society. The preconditions of continuous legality are accordingly taken to be the preconditions of legal system qua state law–society complex. In the terms we have asserted in preceding argument, we take the ordering state law–society as the interacting situations of possibly increasingly asymmetric superveniences asserted by system-centred analytical legal theory, in that order or set of layers. Why? Hart and Raz and followers all suppose in various ways that legality is practically and logically dependent on an underlying social order or orders, and that the state qua Hart's 'modern municipal legal system' is a modern manifestation of a particularly sophisticated political organization atop a legal system. System-centred approaches are in a sense self-contained, to the extent that they presume the ready availability of at least analytical borders for their investigation even while system borders may run unmarked and undefended on physical geography. This self-containment is not, however, simply a retreat to a set of modelling conventions intended to render a difficult object of study more tractable. Analytical legal theory's self-consciousness with respect to the fact that legal systems relate to one another in various ways is so familiar as to demand only a quick reminder of familiar arguments. Hart, for example, criticized Austin's doctrine of sovereignty as failing to account for various kinds of interdependence between states, including treaties voluntarily entered into. More recently, theorists of the European Union have found explanatory value in Raz's argument that legal systems may adopt non-system so in that sense 'foreign' norms without their becoming part of the system.[30] Analytical legal theorists are unquestionably alive to the question of demarcation of one state system from another – at least in the context of momentary systems – and equally unquestionably productive insights have been gained from investigations of this question.

There are nonetheless reasons to worry that the productivity of the system-centred approach might be diminished by the rise of phenomena not well-captured by the approach, as we have demonstrated above. As we proceed to demonstration of ways in which the system-centred approach needs supplementation or partial replacement to account for the rise of the new ICTs as phenomena which make demarcation amongst state systems and other legal orders increasingly difficult, it may be worth being mindful of observations from analogous investigations similarly challenged by the question of how to characterize and revise characterization of an object under investigation, particularly when changes to the object of investigation appear to demand new methods. One source of cautionary insight may be found in Weber, whose methodological reflections on the possibility of an 'ideal-type' of the state remind us of an insight articulated by Raz in a different way and for different reasons: that concepts built and used for explanatory purposes in social inquiry bear the marks of their inquirer's particular purpose, such that we are mistaken if we suppose we are cutting nature at its joints, when instead we are developing a heuristic for purposes which might be appropriate at one time and context, and inappropriate in another. Weber writes of the state that:

[30] J. Dickson, 'How many legal systems? Some puzzles regarding the identity conditions of, and relations between, legal systems in the European Union', *Problema*, 2 (2008), pp. 9–50.

> It is necessary for us to forego here a detailed discussion of the case which is by far the most complicated and most interesting, namely, the problem of the logical structure of the concept of the state. The following however should be noted: when we inquire as to what corresponds to the idea of the 'state' in empirical reality, we find an infinity of diffuse and discrete human actions, both active and passive, factually and legally regulated relationships, partly unique and partly recurrent in character, all bound together by an idea, namely, the belief in the actual or normative validity of rules and of the authority-relationships of some human beings towards others. This belief is in part consciously, in part dimly felt, and in part passively accepted by persons who, should they think about the 'idea' in a really clearly defined manner, would not first need a general theory of the state which aims to articulate the idea. The scientific conception of the state, however it is formulated, is naturally always a synthesis which we construct for certain heuristic purposes.[31]

Without claiming analytical legal theorists are Weberians, and while noting Weber's preliminary remark that he is not providing 'detailed discussion' of the nature of the state, useful insights may nonetheless be extracted from Weber's approach to objectivity in social science and the proper limits of the epistemic ambitions of those creating or better reconstructing an 'ideal-type'. The usefulness of an 'ideal-type' of the state or other legal concepts for heuristic purposes is sufficient justification for its construction even while its content does not pretend to provide some sort of one-to-one correspondence of explanation to empirically verifiable fact in the world. What matters and may be forgotten, however, is that the concept is a synthesis constructed for heuristic purposes that must be front of mind, and subject to evaluation and re-evaluation to ascertain their fitness in a particular context. As Weber summarizes his sociologically purposed use of ideal-typical concepts, 'The goal

[31] M. Weber, 'Objectivity in social science and policy', in E. A. Shils and H. A. Finch (eds), *Max Weber on the Methodology of the Social Sciences* (Glencoe, IL: Free Press, 1949), p. 99. In order to ensure that we demonstrate recognition of the full context of Weber's observations, we should note that Weber goes on to suggest a particular kind of relation between ideal types and concepts in use for practice purposes, articulating a particular kind of mutual relation: 'But on the other hand, it is also abstracted from the unclear syntheses which are found in the minds of human beings. The concrete content, however, which the historical "state" assumes in those syntheses in the minds of those who make up the state, can in its turn only be made explicit through the use of ideal-typical concepts. Nor, furthermore, can there be the least doubt that the manner in which those syntheses are made (always in a logically imperfect form) by the members of a state, or in other words, the "ideas" which they construct for themselves about the state – as for example, the German "organic" metaphysics of the state in contrast with the American "business" conception, is of great practical significance. In other words, here too the practical idea which should be valid or is believed to be valid and the heuristically intended, theoretically ideal type approach each other very closely and constantly tend to merge with each other'.

of ideal-typical concept construction is always to make clearly explicit not the class or group average character but rather the unique individual character of cultural phenomena'.[32] Leaving aside the question of the influence of Weber on legal theory and legal theory on Weber, a methodological cousin's concerns and the reasons for those concerns can have a salutary effect as we consider how and why we differ from the cousin's approach. In this instance, Weber's emphasis on the 'unique individual character of cultural phenomena' captured even by a generalized ideal-type seems quite strikingly different in commitment and detail from the analytical legal theory of Hart, Raz and heirs. Whether Weber's commitment is justified in its own right matters less than the fact that he specifies a particular, testable goal for evaluation of a heuristic ideal-type: successful explanation of 'unique individual character'. That test, however embryonic, at least points to further tasks associated with deciding what data in an individual situation need inclusion in explanation, and by what means data will be sourced, revisited over time for assessment of continued relevance, and so on. This example is a useful reminder to analytical legal theorists of the need to state explicitly and to revisit the object of their approach, the purpose of the concepts emerging from application of morally neutral descriptive-explanatory methods, and the basis on which those methods include or exclude data potentially included within the explanatory scope of the investigation. Is the object of analytical legal theory's investigation really still Hart's 'modern municipal system' – and under what conditions might that object be expected to change? Is the purpose of our construction of an understanding of law still something like the substance of Hart's explanation of his contributions to legal philosophy? In response to an interviewer's raising this question, Hart replied, 'I hope it has both enabled people to take a wider view of the nature of law and the problems that arise in the running of the legal system and [also that] it has given them a sensitivity to accuracy, clarity of expression, and its details'.[33] In seeking to enable not just academics but 'people' more broadly to take a 'wider view' of what must be not just theoretical but practical problems in 'the running of the legal system', are we adequately responsive to changes in the phenomena of the legal system and its operational context – its 'unique individual character', as we might say, borrowing from Weber? Whatever we may say of the adequacy of analytical legal theory's characterization of the state law–society relation – according to Raz simply absent in some respects in Hart's work, and according to us, asserted but seriously

[32] Ibid., p. 101.

[33] D. Sugarman, 'Hart interviewed: H. L. A. Hart in conversation with David Sugarman', *Journal of Law and Society*, 32 (2005), p. 293.

under-explored by Raz – there is in the adjacent methodological reasoning of Weber a reminder that these questions need answers. These questions are particularly acute when novel phenomena arise, particularly novel phenomena with potential to change substantially the object of investigation, raising in the case of analytical legal theory the danger not just that theorists lack an account of how they include new necessary features of legality into their accounts, but worse, a mistake because historic and not contemporary account of necessary features of legality. Without answers to these questions, analytical legal theory risks being not a general-level descriptive-explanatory approach to legality as it is, even if in a form analogous to a Weberian ideal-type, but rather a history. Analytical legal theory might fall further into being an idealized history relying on abstractions that are quite unnecessary because data for a comprehensive history exist to be gathered by those minded to do so. Still worse, without an account of the state-society-law asymmetric supervenience relations, their preconditions, and the evidence to be consulted to validate the theoretical account of the social situation, analytical legal theory risks becoming not a morally neutral explanation but a co-opted defender of a past order. We might borrow from Marx an insight into what analytical legal theory might yet find itself observing and needing to characterize in transition. Marx famously claimed that 'No social order ever disappears before all the productive forces for which there is room in it have been developed, and new, higher relations of production never appear before the material conditions of their existence have matured in the womb of the old society'.[34] Analytical legal theory must not only track the career of legality in the historically contingent post-Westphalian law-state, but it must do so while recognizing that characterization of legality in that context cannot proceed without an eye to the likelihood that this form of legality is unlikely to be the final or only form of legality, and approaches to currently dominant forms of legality are equally unlikely to be permanently applicable and sufficient without substantial variation.

[34] K. Marx, *A Contribution to the Critique of Political Economy* (1859), reprinted in *The Poverty of Philosophy* (New York: International, 1936), p. 44. On the origin of this insight, Gerald Cohen observes, 'Central formulations in Hegel's philosophy of history re-appear transmuted in Marx. For example: 'the world spirit has had the patience to pass through these [cultural] forms in the long expanse of time, taking upon itself the tremendous labour of world history *in which it imparted as much of its content to every form as that form was capable of holding*'. Cohen's accompanying note is to "Preface" to *Phenomenology*, p. 404, our italics. The above belongs to the provenance of "No social order ever disappears before all the productive forces for which there is room in it have been developed'. G. A. Cohen, *Karl Marx's Theory of History*, expanded edn (Princeton, NJ: Princeton University Press, 2009), pp. 26–27.

APPLICATIONS OF THE NEW ICTS CHALLENGING THE CAPACITY OF STATE SYSTEMS AND SYSTEM-CENTRED THEORY TO DEMARCATE A MEANINGFULLY CLOSED SYSTEM OF LAW

Analytical legal theorists, while generally state-focussed, are unquestionably engaged with the possibility that novel social phenomena may require changes to descriptive-explanatory accounts of state systems of law. Even state-centred jurisprudence recognizes that modern states are increasingly interconnected and affected by legal structures atop changing flows of inter-state trade, immigration, pollutants and other changes to social life, giving rise to questions regarding the sense and extent to which legal systems are meaningfully closed and susceptible to demarcation from one another and other forms of legal order. The rise of the legal structure of the European Union, for example, has raised questions as to whether it is the set of sovereign state's individual commitments, a novel supra-state legal order, or something else, with various further accounts of what this means for participating states (or post-states). What is less frequently considered is the possibility that technological choices may carry significant implications for the nature of the state legal system as the central object of legal theory. Here we turn to two areas of technology and representative choices which, we shall argue, are in the midst of disrupting the insufficiently examined set of asymmetric supervenience relations preconditional to possibility of a state law–society relation, whether momentary or continuous. The consequences of these disruptions have yet to be fully explored; but they may yet include, we shall argue, revision of both what is taken to be the central object of analytical legal theory and the most salient problems associated with understanding that object.

We draw our first example from what has become called the 'internet of things', referring to the networked communication of information amongst physical objects.[35] Whether those physical objects are specifically designed to be communications devices or whether communications technologies are embedded within them, they bridge the divide between the physical world and the computational capacity of information systems. Familiar examples abound: from uni-directional communications from webcams useful for remote viewing of traffic and weather conditions, to the rapid rise of bi-directional communications devices enabling remote monitoring and adjustment of a thermostat controlling room temperature. Our second example is drawn from the 'social web', sometimes called 'Web 2.0', referring to the

[35] See generally R. H. Weber and R. Weber, *Internet of Things* (Dordrecht, Netherlands: Springer, 2010).

choice to use the internet for information sharing and co-creation,[36] anticipated yet not evident in early use of the internet to enable rapid access to widely distributed sources of information. Ready examples include Facebook, functioning as a kind of online public diary and meeting place, and Twitter, a means of communicating brief messages rapidly to a specified network of contacts, using simple, highly portable technology. While these two application areas of the new ICTs each serve quite different purposes, they share an important feature relative to the state law–society relation: they breach the divide between the virtual world and the real world, between cyberspace and 'meatspace'.[37] So much, perhaps for just the moment, for Gibson's video game-inspired vision of a virtual world largely separate, or increasingly separating from an original physical world. At least some applications of the new ICTs seem not to create a separate virtual world, but to intensify opportunities for social and physical interconnectedness in the already-present physical world. To the extent that the new ICTs are functions of the internet as a centre-less globally distributed set of physical nodes and connections enabled by shared protocols, opportunities for intensified social and physical connectedness are as widely available as the technology enabling those opportunities. The emergence and use of these socio-technical opportunities gives rise to our argument regarding the stability of the preconditions of the state law–society amalgam serving as the principal explanatory object of analytical legal theory.

Electricity Grids, Smart Grids and Super Grids: Decentralizing Production, Consumption and Control

Popular media coverage of the internet of things has varied from utopian to catastrophist sentiments and in between. Some recent celebrity pronouncements in light of novel technological developments have made an intuitively plausible case for a catastrophist view. On this view, the internet of things is at best a worrisome pathway towards ubiquitous surveillance, and at worst the harbinger of an era of autonomous weapons enabling automated warfare[38]

[36] Tim O'Reilly claims credit – and is widely acknowledged – for coining the term. See www.oreilly.com/pub/a/web2/archive/what-is-web-20.html.

[37] The origin of the term 'meatspace' is unclear, even while its appeal as an earthy contrast to cyberspace is plain. See, for example, use by a character in celebrated novelist T. Pynchon's *Bleeding Edge* (New York: Penguin, 2013), p. 168: 'It was like they actively went seeking it, this life they have now, this faraway, virtual life, leaving the rest of us stuck back here in meatspace, blinking at images on a screen'.

[38] See generally A. Krishnan, *Killer Robots* (Aldershot: Ashgate, 2009).

and human-replacing artificial intelligence.[39] Some or all of these forecast situations may yet occur. For the moment, however, they seem avoidable and a significant distraction from applications of the internet of things which are closer to practical realization, and more interesting as possibly positive transformations of long-standing social formations such as the state. One such application may be seen in the course of development of energy generation, transmission, distribution and storage and more specifically, the consequences of the technological transition from an electrical 'grid' to the 'smartgrid' and on to the 'supergrid'. A brief rehearsal of the history of this transition will lay the groundwork for our reflections on its jurisprudential significance.

Throughout the process of electrification of industrialized economies and their states, systems developed in a pattern known as a grid. A typical grid consisted of a generation point using a source such as hydropower, coal, natural gas, or nuclear, transformation of the alternating current (AC) generated into direct current (DC) for transmission over a high voltage transmission, and transformation of DC into AC in a lower-voltage final distribution network bringing electricity to users. Operation of such grids typically involved forecasting demand over a relatively short future period (e.g., twenty-four hours), and increasing or diminishing production at one or more generation points to meet demand. As grids developed and stretched across regions and national borders, techniques were developed to connect grids and to manage multiple generation sources to meet predicted demand. In practice, notwithstanding carefully designed models and safeguards, these grids are subject to malfunctions experienced as 'blackout' failures of power delivery to users, and 'brownouts' as demand exceeds supply and voltage available to users is intentionally or unintentionally reduced. In complex systems comprising multiple power generation sources, some failures exhibit 'cascading', where a failure at one point in the grid has follow-on effects for other parts of the grid. Some of the governance challenges and jurisprudential questions arising from development of grid technologies can be usefully elucidated by consideration of

39 Popular media have given extensive attention to an open letter signed by luminaries including Stephen Hawking, Elon Musk and Steve Wozniak, warning of an artificial intelligence 'arms race' posing grave danger to humanity. For media coverage see, e.g., 'Hawking, Musk, Wozniak warn of military artificial intelligence arms race', CBC News (27 July 2015). Available from www.cbc.ca/news/trending/hawking-musk-wozniak-warn-of-military-artificial-intelligence-arms-race-1.3169193. See also S. Gibbs, 'Musk, Wozniak and Hawking urge ban on warfare AI and autonomous weapons', *The Guardian* (27 July 2015). Available at www.theguardian.com/technology/2015/jul/27/musk-wozniak-hawking-ban-ai-autonomous-weapons. The letter is hosted by the Future of Life Institute: www.futureoflife.org/open-letter-autonomous-weapons/.

the consequences of a grid failure whose scale and negative consequences warranted an investigation giving rise to significant changes in law.

In its 2006 report, a bi-national US-Canada task force inquiring into a 2003 cascading failure in a trans-boundary grid summarized the failure as follows: 'On August 14, 2003, the largest power blackout in North American history affected an area with an estimated 50 million people and 61,800 megawatts (MW) of electric load in the states of Ohio, Michigan, Pennsylvania, New York, Vermont, Massachusetts, Connecticut and New Jersey, and the Canadian province of Ontario'.[40] Amongst the forty-six recommendations of the task force, legal theorists might note particularly some of the fourteen recommendations summarized as 'Institutional Issues Related to Reliability'.[41]

The first recommendation of the task force, later accepted by the US government, urged co-operation to support *non-optional* reliability standards:

> R1. Appropriate branches of government in the United States and Canada should take action as required to make reliability standards mandatory and enforceable, and to provide appropriate penalties for non-compliance.
>
> To emphasize the importance of making reliability standards mandatory and enforceable, the Task Force focused its first recommendation on this fundamental goal. The recommendation has five components:
>
> > R1.A. The U.S. Congress should enact the reliability provisions proposed in the pending comprehensive energy bill.
> >
> > Actions Taken: The U.S. Congress passed H.R. 6, the Energy Policy Act of 2005 (EPAct 2005), on July 29, 2005, and the President signed the bill into law on August 8, 2005.[42]

The third of the five parts of Recommendation 1 calls for development of 'identical or compatible reliability standards',[43] and further expresses how this

[40] *U.S.-Canada power system outage task force* (2006): www.energy.gov/sites/prod/files/oeprod/DocumentsandMedia/BlackoutFinalImplementationReport%282%29.pdf, p. 3. To put the significance of this critical infrastructure failure in context, it is worth noting that the report indicates at the close of the paragraph quoted earlier that 'estimates of the total costs caused by the blackout in the United States ranged between $4 billion and $10 billion (U.S. dollars). In Canada, the gross domestic product was down 0.7 per cent in August, there was a net loss of 18.9 million work hours, and manufacturing shipments in Ontario were down $2.3 billion (Canadian dollars)'.

[41] Ibid., p. 5. [42] Ibid.

[43] 'R1.C. The Canadian federal and provincial governments should work together, and with U.S. authorities, to develop a framework to ensure that identical or compatible reliability standards apply in both countries'. Ibid., p. 7.

might be done in parallel in each country.[44] The fourth part of Recommendation 1 proposes establishment of a Bilateral Group to provide oversight of the existing North American Electric Reliability Council.[45] The Council was subsequently replaced 1 January 2007 by a not-for-profit international regulatory authority, the North American Electric Reliability Corporation (NERC), operating as the US national authority for electric reliability, and under memoranda of understanding with Ontario, Quebec, Nova Scotia and the National Energy Board of Canada.[46] The Corporation now serves as

> the electric reliability organization (ERO) for North America, subject to oversight by the Federal Energy Regulatory Commission (FERC) and governmental authorities in Canada. NERC's jurisdiction includes users, owners, and operators of the bulk power system, which serves more than 334 million people.[47]

The jurisprudential interest in this story lies less in its details and more in the technologies which will succeed the grid architecture described above, and presumed in the emerging governance arrangements designed to avoid the serious negative consequences of cascading failures. What we have seen so far is a technological failure with further socially experienced negative consequences, motivating a lengthy process of bi-national investigation and creation of a new international institution to enable application of non-optional norms. The content of those norms is necessarily nearly identical in both member states to the extent that the operation conditions of the chosen technology remain constant across borders. The structure of this history is familiar: each

44 For example, see:

> 'Action Required to Fully Implement Recommendation 1.C:
>
> > The actions of the individual jurisdictions and of the Canadian Federal-Provincial-Territorial Electricity Working Group (FPT Electricity Working Group) have developed a frame-work to ensure compatible reliability standards apply in Canada. However, as in the United States, implementation of an identical or compatible system of mandatory standards will require the ERO [Electricity Reliability Organization] to be established and for it to submit proposed reliability standards to appropriate authorities in Canada'. Ibid.

45 'R1.D. An international mechanism should be developed to provide for government oversight of NERC and the proposed ERO. Actions Taken: In order to provide coordinated oversight of NERC and the proposed ERO, the US Department of Energy (DOE), FERC and the FPT Electricity Working Group, with the assistance of the US State Department and the Canadian Department of Foreign Affairs and International Trade, established the Bilateral Group. Terms of Reference for the Bilateral Group were signed by the various agencies on June 30, 2005'. Ibid., pp. 7–8.

46 See NERC history document: www.nerc.com/AboutNERC/Documents/HistoryAUG13.pdf.

47 www.nerc.com/AboutNERC/Pages/default.aspx.

state has voluntarily assumed obligations to enable governance of critical infrastructure whose operation depends upon coordination amongst participating states. The only jurisprudentially noteworthy phenomena might be found in the interdependency relation created by shared critical infrastructure warranting creation of a joint institution operating relatively independently from a US base with joint US-Canadian oversight. Yet beyond the consequences of this development for state sovereignty the remainder of the legal content of this situation seems readily available from a system-centred analytical approach to legality – except, perhaps, the fact that state autonomy is surrendered in an uncertainty-generating way insofar as jointly made technological consequences may carry future consequences unforeseeable today, with significant consequences for the state's authority over its critical infrastructure.

This last possibility becomes much more salient when considering the technology and management practices associated with 'smart grids' and planned 'super grids'. Smart grids are a technological and normative response to several social and technological facts including a desire to use existing grid infrastructure as effectively as possible in the face of growing demand, particularly peak demand (in e.g., periods of unusually hot or cold weather), and limited user appetite for large investment in grid extension. More significantly, both technologically and normatively, smart grids are an answer to the challenge of integration of renewable energy sources into electricity systems. This challenge has arisen as one consequence of the interaction between the maturation of renewable energy production technologies, and the decarbonization of industrialized economies in response to climate change and predicted fossil fuel shortages (at least at prices supporting use of hydrocarbons for energy production as opposed to other applications, such as chemical production). The idea of a smart grid builds on the base of the post-war electricity grid, now taking advantage of the computational and two-way communications capacities of the internet of things. These capacities – extremely rapid algorithm-driven decision making, and remote monitoring and control – change decisively the capacity of grids to match electricity generation to electricity demand.

In a smart grid, multiple methods of electricity generation (and storage) can be effectively integrated, while demand can be both monitored and controlled. Where conventional grids rely on a few 'always on' generation points varying production according to forecast and actual demand, smart grids seek to integrate many, typically highly distributed generation points whose output is intermittent and variable. Whether large-scale installations such as wind farms comprising many turbines, or the single turbine of a small scale 'prosumer' producer-consumer, wind generation of electricity is constrained by the fact that suitably windy generation sites may be distant from final users. Moreover, even suitable sites are intermittently windy, and wind velocity is not constant so generation capacity varies. Similar considerations apply to solar electricity generation, hydro electricity generation from dammed rivers, and tidal electricity generation. Variability and intermittency challenges can be met in various ways. The first is to store energy, by familiar means including chemical batteries and pumping water to a height from which it is later released, and by less familiar means such as compression of air later released and flywheel energy storage systems. Such responses are widely considered to be just a partial contribution to resolution of variability and intermittency problems, to the extent that storage technologies are relatively immature, and require additional investment which might be avoided by two further responses. A second response, of greater interest to us, lies in recognition that if a smart grid's renewable energy sources are sufficiently broadly distributed, their combination will nearly always generate energy – somewhere, even if distant from electricity users, the sun is shining, the wind is blowing and marine currents are flowing. This response is gaining a great deal of attention, with issues of jurisprudential interest arising, alongside an equally logically obvious, if not technically simple third approach to grid management via selective reduction of demand. So-called load-shedding approaches seek to use the two-way communications capacity of the internet of things to reduce demand on electricity grids in various ways. Readers in many jurisdictions will be familiar with domestic 'smart meters' which not only measure electricity consumption, but transmit information regarding consumption to grid operators, who can develop histories of use alongside moment-to-moment measurement of use in specific contexts – particularly those associated with peak demand. It is only a small step from these meters to use of devices capable of receiving and responding to signals regarding use of electricity under particular specified conditions, i.e., a dishwasher which only operates in off-peak demand periods (with demand levelled across time-zones), or when the price of electricity falls beneath a particular threshold.

As renovation of aging grids meets demand for integration of renewable sources of energy, all three of these approaches are evident in development of smart grids. Some aspects of smart grid development are already receiving jurisprudential attention for what might be called quite conventional reasons. Smart meters and load-shedding are conceived by some to involve privacy issues to the extent that consumption patterns are measured and profiles of users are easily generated. More significantly, interconnection of vast numbers of devices provides an opportunity for hackers to remove control of devices and electricity consumption from the control of rightful owners and consumers.[48]

[48] C. Bosch, 'Securing the smart grid: protecting national security and privacy through mandatory, enforceable interoperability standards', *Fordham Urban Law Journal*, 41 (2013–2014), pp. 1371ff.

These issues are of significant interest to authorities in state systems of law seeking to protect expectations within those systems, excluding increasingly geographically distributed malfeasors. The significance of these issues pales, however, when considered in light of the jurisprudential implications of 'super grids', emerging from lessons learned in smart grid development and responding to variability and intermittency challenges at a far greater scale than thought plausible until very recently. The notion of the super grid (or mega grid) is simply that of the smart grid but at larger scale, integrating many very distant generation sources, typically sufficiently distant from end users of electricity that the grids cross several local, regional and state boundaries. Various supergrids have been envisaged, including, for example, the 'Desertec' initiative aiming to link solar electricity generation in desert areas of North Africa to consumers up to 3,000 kilometres away.[49] Other, less operationally ambitious supergrid efforts are much closer to realization. A North Sea supergrid, under development in a series of studies since November 2008, seeks to connect abundant offshore wind, wave and tidal energy in the North Sea to markets in the UK and continental Europe.[50] The North Seas Countries' Offshore Grid Initiative joins together Norway with European Union members Belgium, Denmark, France, Germany, Ireland, Luxembourg, the Netherlands, Sweden and the United Kingdom.[51] As planning for this grid has advanced, with recent confirmation of investment from the European Commission, questions have arisen regarding the technical standards to be employed, ownership of infrastructure and responsibility for management of the supergrid. The initiative's working group on market and regulatory issues reported in 2012 that:

> While certain barriers have been identified, they are not insurmountable. There is currently no regulatory regime in Europe which provides an explicit regulatory framework for the development of 'hybrid' assets. An agreed and compatible approach to the development of such assets is recommended in order to foster their development when this fits with government generation ambitions and when it is economic and cost-efficient to do so.[52]

49 www.desertec.org/en/concept/.

50 C. Macilwain, 'Supergrid: is a vast undersea grid bringing wind-generated electricity from the North Sea to Europe a feasible proposition or an overpriced fantasy?', *Nature*, 468 (2 December 2010), pp. 624–625. Available at www.nature.com/news/2010/101201/pdf/468624a.pdf.

51 The North Seas Countries' Offshore Grid Initiative Memorandum of Understanding (7 December 2009). Available at www.benelux.int/files/8113/9625/9202/MoU_NSCOGI.pdf.

52 The North Seas Countries' Offshore Grid Initiative: Recommendations for guiding principles for the development of integrated offshore cross border infrastructure (23 November 2012). Available at www.benelux.int/files/4714/0923/4575/recommendations.pdf, p. 2.

The 'hybrid assets' of concern are those 'transmission assets which includes both interconnection and grid connection',[53] such as a set of interconnected wind turbines over some area, connected to a grid and its conversion of generated AC into DC for long distance transmission, conversion back to AC and distribution to users. As options for governance are explored, the working group is very much aware of the claims of state-based legal systems, and further aware of complexities involving their life in the European Union. Alongside consideration of governance options involving coordination across nominally independent state and non-state parties such as Transmission System Operators (TSOs), the working party notes in passing that:

> Another option which was considered but rejected was the establishment of a North Seas TSO and North Seas Regulatory Body to oversee all developments in the North Seas region including identification of the need for coordinated projects. This option cuts across Member State sovereignty, and is thus not a credible option for consideration. Although we do remain open to the benefits of centralised coordinating efforts that will help to bring aspects of the North Seas development together.[54]

The terse language of multi-author working groups can of course be misleading insofar as it represents tentative steps taken by a group well prior to finalization of agreements and their application to practice. The working group's framing of the issues is nonetheless very helpful as an introduction to the jurisprudential issues arising from this instance of the internet of things.

States choosing to participate in supergrids may do so for a range of reasons. Some may be convinced of the importance of decarbonization as a response to global climate change. Others may be subject to geopolitical concerns regarding the political stability or price availability of existing sources of energy, warranting investment in supergrids to support diversification of sources of energy and increased reliability of access. Whatever the motivations of states embracing supergrids, the consequences are likely to be the same. The choice to participate in the creation and use of a network of critical infrastructure is a *de facto* acceptance of an increased degree of interdependence and correlative diminution of both political and legal autonomy. The physical penetration of borders by transmission networks connected to generation, storage and users is symbolically important; but what is more important than these visible ties amongst states is the nature of the commitment they demonstrate, and the normative content of their operation. Choice to participate in a supergrid generating energy in one location and transmitting it over long distances, often

[53] Ibid. [54] Ibid., p. 5.

across state borders, is a choice to accept a multi-part jointness. That jointness is significant in part because very large financial investments are required – *Nature* reported in 2010 that the North Sea supergrid would cost an estimated €20 billion.[55] The jointness of choice of a supergrid is still more significant because the required investments are in critical infrastructure – the infrastructure required for the state to operate in the manner expected by its members. Planning, construction and operation of critical infrastructure proceeds best on the basis of a shared set of both technical standards and operating policies. As choice of coordinative conventions proceeds, and operating agents are chosen, a particular set of technological choices and investments are made. These choices are in principle reversible, but such reversals are so costly that there is no practical means of turning back: a particular 'path dependence' is chosen and accepted.[56] It is important in this context to understand that the path dependence involved is not merely a matter of one-off construction of like physical objects. Further factors are involved: as Woolley argues persuasively, technological choices require mobilization of supply chains in which private investors are typically involved, typically seeking protected expectations regarding return on investment.[57] Once constructed, operation of the supergrid requires coordination in continued development of the algorithms enabling its operation in a dynamic context, alongside surveillance of possible human and natural threats, ongoing maintenance, response to inevitable unplanned failures, and so on through the many factors affecting operation of a complex system. The jointness of purpose evident in commitment to supergrids is therefore a commitment to a shared socio-technical pathway even as that pathway embodies significant uncertainties regarding future social and natural states of affairs – political stability, climate change and resource exhaustion, to name just a few.

From this analysis we can infer that the normative structure of the supergrid follows networked critical infrastructure as much or more than it does the boundaries of states: the norms of its establishment and operation are jointly chosen, are jointly implemented and require joint variation on an ongoing basis. This sort of dispersion of authority and control in the context of technological path dependence has many analogues served by various explanatory approaches. Military alliances and states' purchasing inter-operable equipment serves as a useful illustration of the kinds of considerations which have guided

55 Macilwain, 'Supergrid', p. 624.

56 See O. Woolley, 'Governing a North Sea grid development: the need for a regional framework treaty', *Competition and Regulation in Network Industries*, 14, no. 1 (2013), pp. 73–97, Section 2, 'The North Sea grid and path dependency', pp. 76ff.

57 Ibid., p. 85.

states' choices regarding inter-dependence, and in some cases, *de facto* control of dimensions of other states' autonomy via control of supply of military equipment. A more useful analogy may be found in thinking by environmental law scholars and others in the context of what are sometimes called trans-boundary issues, but are perhaps better framed as global issues for which regional resolutions are sought. In attempting to reconcile *de facto* responses to phenomena such as global climate change, some scholars have taken up a notion of 'network governance', which seeks to supplement rather than supplant explanations rooted in the presumed primacy of states as actors. These analyses observe that considerable governance of environmental matters occurs in a range of non-hierarchical interactions at multiple scales, amongst multiple actors and kinds of actors, including local, regional, and supra-regional civil society organizations, treaties, state systems of law, etc. Craik and Van Nijnatten, for example, suggest viewing North American climate policy not as 'a loose collection of disparate governance activities, but as a dynamic and adaptive system'.[58] In advocating this approach, scholars such as Craik and Van Nijnatten appear to embody a kind of naturalized jurisprudence insofar as they are both responsive to particular kinds of empirical phenomena and further accept the possibility that those phenomena determine the nature of law in various ways. As they frame their interdisciplinary method:

> Our relational approach draws on several emerging strands of literature that focus on such linkages, most notably work on socio-ecological systems, or SES. In light with SES thinking, we portray North American climate governance as a 'complex system' composed of interactions among a diverse array of climate policy institutions and mechanisms, which are themselves rooted in bio-physical reality.[59]

The central focus of these and similarly minded scholars of climate change is to detect and characterize change in normative approaches to climate change, so hierarchical state systems of law are not a primary object of inquiry, and the possibly changing role of states in life under law receives relatively little direct examination. These investigations are nonetheless of interest to our similarly relational approach, concerned with the capacity of novel phenomena – whether environmental or technological or other – to vary law's form

58 N. Craik and D. Van Nijnatten, 'Designing integration: the system of climate change governance in North America', in N. Craik, I. Studer and D. Van Nijnatten (eds), *Climate Change Policy in North America* (Toronto, Canada: University of Toronto Press, 2013), p. 7.

59 Ibid. Craik and Van Nijnatten refer to the seminal socio-ecological system article by Ostrom: E. Ostrom, 'A general framework for analyzing sustainability of social-ecological systems', *Science*, 325 (2009), p. 419.

and content. Where environmental changes and response to them occur in what from a state-centred perspective are shared borders or overlapping areas of concern (e.g., fish swimming across state borders), descriptive-explanatory accounts of governance responses are noting a diminution of the role of the state as novel devices emerge, demanding characterization in networks at least alongside and including hierarchically organized states, and potentially supplanting them. Notwithstanding state-supporting language from analysts such as those in the North Sea Grid working groups, legal theorists sensitive to changing phenomena must ask just when normative responses to novel phenomena compel rejection of explanations taking states to be implicitly or explicitly authorizing or using norms without thereby including them in their legal systems. While climate change governance across state boundaries has yet to coalesce, for various reasons in various regions, into readily identified regional legal institutions then compelling reconsideration of the role of states in climate governance, such developments are not impossible to imagine as 'biophysical reality' compels novel normative responses to climate change. The case of supergrids is less prominent yet likely more compelling as an instance of phenomena driving changing normative responses changing the centrality of the state as a source of legality.

A series of contrasts will help to elucidate the challenge to state-focussed accounts of legality posed by supergrids as an instance of the internet of things. Unlike compatible defence equipment distributed amongst allies in an 'on demand' state of organization until the unusual and typically relatively brief situation of warfare involving modern states, smartgrids and the new supergrids are 'always on' critical infrastructure whose continued operation, however adaptive and varying in a controlled network, is a functional precondition to the existence of the states bringing it into being. Like climate change governance, smart and supergrids and the norms enabling their well-functioning are intrinsically connected to 'biophysical reality' which cannot be re-shaped by fiat by states contributing to the existence of the smartgrid or supergrid. Yet unlike climate change governance where the need for political will to 'harden' currently 'soft' normative approaches is accompanied by ongoing scientific debate regarding the best means to respond to climate change – e.g., from reductive approaches seeking limitations of greenhouse gas emissions to carbon capture systems independent of emitters and their conduct choices – smart and supergrids are relatively well-defined objects of governance. For example, 'hybrid assets' as discussed above are well understood as a genus even while species-level selections of particular technology packages await further deliberation. Most importantly, the regional interdependence created by smart and supergrids is part of ongoing bi- and multi-directional communications monitoring and controlling generation, transmission and use of electricity. Moreover, smart and supergrids are systems explicitly designed to be 'self healing' in response to failures such as the cascading failure of 2003 described above, and resistant to attack. So where sharing of military equipment types and standards is an option held in reserve and climate change governance awaits political will to give particular institutional force to particular regional legal institutions likely to effectively take the place of state action notwithstanding claims to continued state oversight, smart and supergrids in their constant interaction in a chosen relation of interdependence seem to create a novel normative union. That union may take various shapes, as we have seen. Some unions appear entirely novel, e.g., the North American choice to create the North American Electric Reliability Corporation (NERC) as 'a not-for-profit international regulatory authority', nonetheless 'subject to oversight by the Federal Energy Regulatory Commission (FERC) and governmental authorities in Canada'.[60] Others are more familiar, as the North Sea supergrid appears to be a 'union within a union' of largely European Union member countries. Whatever the particular shape of supergrid-contributor relations, norm formation appears to follow technology and geography such that choices to create resilient, attack-resistant critical infrastructure does not so much reform state interactions as transcend them in ways recreating boundaries as much virtual as physical, creating communications networks less vulnerable to external attack or internal failure. To the extent that those virtual boundaries corresponding to socio-technical systems in the 'biophysical' world of 'meatspace', the internet of things controlling those socio-technical systems disrupts the law-state relation and offers the opportunity to regard state systems less as authorities than authors of socio-technical systems and legal orders which transcend them. Supergrids as an application of the internet of things might be greeted in the spirit of Neil MacCormick's suggestion that the European Union offers states a more mature mode of existence. Where there are supergrids their state authors transform an independence marked by vulnerability and threats to continuity of legal order, moving instead towards interdependence marked by resilience and continuity of critical infrastructure pre-conditional to continued legal order of the kind desired by and associated with the ordinary citizen of the twenty-first century. This state of affairs is already emerging in the North American smartgrid, and is gaining speed in Europe as the European Commission advances a European

[60] www.nerc.com/AboutNERC/Pages/default.aspx.

Energy Union[61] and is reported to be on the brink of committing seed funding for the North Sea supergrid from the Investment Fund for Europe.[62]

The internet of things as applied in supergrids demonstrates how states may be choosing out of the kind of contingent state-law asymmetric supervenience enabling legal systems to be demarcated from one another and taken as the basic object of jurisprudential investigation. At this particular point of intersection of virtual and real worlds, seeking to find ways in which supergrid governance is really state-authorized and state-based so still ultimately hierarchical may be theoretically unprofitable. The internet of things breaches state-law claims to authority by subverting and re-distributing control of knowledge and extension of that knowledge into the real, biophysical world. Once societies under law choose interdependent critical infrastructure networks over state-based grids, reduced jurisprudential and practical prominence of the state is no longer a temporary aberration before the state reasserts its claims and re-establishes hierarchy. Rather, the rise of a new socio-ecological system gives rise to new forms of legal order requiring fresh explanation, using methods old and possibly new, in any case departing without the presumption of the priority of the state system of law as the object of investigation and without the further presumption that where there is law, it exists in a relation of asymmetric supervenience – so a closed system – with an authorizing state.

Bitcoin: Borderless Distribution of the Power to Make Determinations of Law

Let us turn now to the social web and the software-driven social phenomena of Bitcoin and bitcoins for an example of the way the new ICTs may change life under law, and the objects of legal theory and the associated problems of legal theory. Like the example of supergrids discussed above, our example drawn from the social web is still emerging. Yet it has sufficient practical effect to date to warrant investigation as a real and not merely potential instance of the way the new ICTs may disrupt the state legal system's constitutive asymmetric supervenience relations creating a bordered system with limited and specifiable points of intersection with other systems. Our example drawn from the social web is different, however, insofar as its nature and effects are features and options for social organization and the law–society relation, with relatively limited direct engagement with physical objects in the way typical of

61 European Commission priority: energy union. See http://ec.europa.eu/priorities/energy-union/index_en.htm.

62 M. Latham, 'EU set to pledge billions in support of "top priority" North Sea supergrid', *Herald Scotland* (18 July 2015). Available at www.heraldscotland.com/business/13463812.EU_set_to_pledge_billions_in_support_of__top_priority__North_Sea_supergrid/.

applications of the internet of things. In summary terms we shall expand below, Bitcoin and similar technologies are capable of decentralizing and distributing in a non-hierarchical way a process for making determinations of validity with respect to exercise of claim-rights. So far the bulk of focus on Bitcoin has arrived with its application as a virtual currency, whose additional use of cryptographic techniques places its application in the set of cryptocurrencies. As we shall observe below, however, it is already easy to recognize that initial use of Bitcoin technology as a cryptocurrency is just one of its uses. Focus on this species-level application at the expense of understanding the implications of the Bitcoin genus distracts attention away from the genuinely novel effects of Bitcoin on decentralized supply of reliable agent-to-agent transactions whose validity is determined in a quasi-automated way, all without regard for physical borders.

The history of the Bitcoin software and exchange system is brief, recent and tumultuous. Through Bitcoin's rapid development replete with rises and falls, the relatively slower pace of academic investigation and publication has left inquiry into Bitcoin poised between academic publication and journalists' no less thoughtful though typically quite brief tracing of actions and effects. The origin of Bitcoin is uncontroversially found in the 2008 web posting of an article written by 'Satoshi Nakamoto' in a techno-academic vernacular to a cryptography mailing list at metzdowd.com. The author, now commonly viewed as likely a pseudonymous group of authors, posted an abstract and link to a paper, prefaced by the simple assertion that 'I've been working on a new electronic cash system that's fully peer-to-peer, with no trusted third party'.[63] What we view as the most jurisprudentially significant element of this claim and its technical instantiation is the absence of a 'trusted third party' or centralized validator of certain kinds of agent-to-agent transactions. The significance of this claim emerges from a history of trial and error which must be traced in order to disentangle a history and apparent failure from a more significant underlying potential and actual change to determinations of law.

Perhaps the best starting point for a general understanding of Bitcoin is the abstract to Nakamoto's original paper:

> Abstract. A purely peer-to-peer version of electronic cash would allow online payments to be sent directly from one party to another without the burdens of going through a financial institution. Digital signatures provide part of the solution, but the main benefits are lost if a trusted party is still required to prevent double-spending. We propose a solution to the double-spending problem using a peer-to-peer network. The network timestamps transactions

[63] www.metzdowd.com/pipermail/cryptography/2008-October/014810.html.

> by hashing them into an ongoing chain of hash-based proof-of-work, forming a record that cannot be changed without redoing the proof-of-work. The longest chain not only serves as proof of the sequence of events witnessed, but proof that it came from the largest pool of CPU power. As long as honest nodes control the most CPU power on the network, they can generate the longest chain and outpace any attackers. The network itself requires minimal structure. Messages are broadcasted on a best effort basis, and nodes can leave and rejoin the network at will, accepting the longest proof-of-work chain as proof of what happened while they were gone.[64]

The initial, technical advance in the Bitcoin software is found in its solution to what Nakamoto calls the 'double-spending' problem, set in the context of cash but appearing in other contexts as well. As Peck explains this function of Bitcoin,

> The simplest way to understand Bitcoin is to think of it as a digital ledger book. Imagine a bunch of people at a table who all have real-time access to the same financial ledger on laptops in front of them. The ledger records how many bitcoins each person at the table has at a given time. By necessity, the balance of each account is public information, and if one person wants to transfer funds to the person sitting across from him, he has to announce that transaction to everyone at the table. The entire group then appends the transaction to the ledger, which they all need to agree on. In a system like this, money never has to exist in a physical form, and yet it can't be spent twice.[65]

The key to this advance lies in the Bitcoin software's generation of a unique history for every bitcoin, the accounting unit for bitcoins – whether conceived as currency or simply units of private property. Following the above analogy, the process of group recognition of a transaction as valid is carried out by multiple, distributed computational acts constructing a 'block chain' enabling verification of unique occurrence of a transaction regarding a specified object. The Bitcoin system provides incentives for these distributed processing acts conducted by 'miners'. As Böhme, Christin, Edelman, and Moore characterize this 'foundation of the entire Bitcoin system',

> Every new transaction that is published to the Bitcoin network is periodically grouped together in a 'block' of recent transactions. To make sure no unauthorized transactions have been inserted, the block itself is compared to

64 Ibid.

65 M. E. Peck, 'Bitcoin: the cryptoanarchists' answer to cash', *IEEE Spectrum* (30 May 2012). Available at http://spectrum.ieee.org/computing/software/bitcoin-the-cryptoanarchists-answer-to-cash.

> the most recently published block – yielding a linked sequence of blocks, or 'block chain'. A new block is added to the chain roughly every ten minutes. With this data structure in place, any Bitcoin user can verify that a prior transaction did in fact occur. Keeping the transaction record operational and updated is a public good, as it is the foundation of the entire Bitcoin system. To encourage users to assist, the Bitcoin system periodically awards newly minted bitcoins to the user who solves a mathematical puzzle that is based on the pre-existing contents of the block (which prevents tampering with the block and hence modifying prior transactions) and which can only be solved by computationally intensive methods that include a random component.[66]

The resulting system offers a decentralized yet public record of transactions regarding a finite number of bitcoins introduced slowly over time by Bitcoin .org, anticipated to reach a total of just 21 million.[67] The system's authors appear to be software engineers, and supporters range from libertarians to traders in morally questionable goods, to banks and small businesses seeking new means of exchange. State sponsors and regulators have appeared sporadically and in various roles. Böhme, Christin, Edelman, and Moore summarize Bitcoin and its context as follows:

> Bitcoin's rules were designed by engineers with no apparent influence from lawyers or regulators. Rather than store transactions on any single server or set of servers, Bitcoin is built on a transaction log that is distributed across a network of participating computers. It includes mechanisms to reward honest participation, to bootstrap acceptance by early adopters, and to guard against concentrations of power. Bitcoin's design allows for irreversible transactions, a prescribed path of money creation over time, and a public transaction history. Anyone can create a Bitcoin account, without charge and without any centralized vetting procedure – or even a requirement to provide a real name. Collectively, these rules yield a system that is understood to be more flexible, more private, and less amenable to regulatory oversight than other forms of payment – though as we discuss in subsequent sections, all these benefits face important limits.[68]

In this system, these authors note, 'Compared with conventional payment systems, Bitcoin lacks a governance structure other than its underlying software'.[69]

[66] R. Böhme, N. Christin, B. Edelman and T. Moore, 'Bitcoin: economics, technology, and governance', *Journal of Economic Perspectives*, 29, no. 2 (Spring 2015), p. 217.
[67] Peck, 'Bitcoin'. [68] Ibid., pp. 213–214. [69] Ibid., p. 219.

In practice, notwithstanding the software's supporting 'complete decentralization (including the possibility of all participants acting as miners), significant economic forces push towards de facto centralization and concentration among a small number of intermediaries at various levels of the Bitcoin ecosystem'.[70] Böhme, Christin, Edelman and Moore survey currency exchanges, digital wallet services, mixers, mining pools and payment processors.

There is a great deal of interest in currency-related dimensions of Bitcoin, including, for example, how the supply of bitcoins is managed, from the initial 'genesis coin' to growth involving miners completing increasingly complex computations validating increasingly complex block chains, and further debate regarding whether bitcoins are a currency or simply a privately held commodity and whether and how states ought to recognize and regulate bitcoins.[71] Much of this debate has waxed and waned with Bitcoin's rapid rise as an exchange medium thought to have the potential to rival traditional currencies, followed by negative exposure as Bitcoin's anonymity was found attractive by 'dark web' users of illicit goods and services. Further concerns regarding the security and reliability of Bitcoin have been driven by technical and business failures, together with major regulatory changes. The collapse of the Tokyo-based Mt. Gox bitcoin exchange on February 25, 2014 received extensive media attention as an exemplar of a set of concerns arising regarding virtual and cryptocurrencies. At its peak influence in 2013, Mt. Gox was reported to have claimed that it 'handles 80% of all bitcoin trading',[72] a position of dominance naturally attracting special attention to its demise, since the fate of the Bitcoin technology could have been inextricable from the fate of a dominant user. When Mt. Gox admitted publicly to the magnitude of the crisis it faced, the result of a series of technical and management failures, it estimated that it had 'lost' US$480 million constituting a significant portion of all bitcoins then circulating. Reuters UK reported that 'Mt. Gox said on Friday that it had lost 750,000 of its users' bitcoins and 100,000 of its own. At the current bitcoin price of about $565, that would total some $480 million – representing about

[70] Ibid., pp. 219–220.

[71] For a US-focussed, comprehensive overview, see generally L. Trautman, 'Virtual currencies, Bitcoin and what now after Liberty Reserve, Silk Road, and Mt. Gox?', *Richmond Journal of Law and Technology*, 20 (2014), p. 13. Available at http://jolt.richmond.edu/v20i4/article13.pdf. See also K. V. Tu and M. W. Meredith, 'Rethinking virtual currency regulation in the Bitcoin age', *Washington Law Review*, 90 (2015), p. 271; N. Wenker, 'Online currencies, real world chaos: the struggle to regulate the rise of Bitcoin', *Texas Review of Law and Politics*, 19 (2014–2015), p. 145.

[72] J. Sparshott, 'Bitcoin exchange bolsters user verification', *Wall Street Journal* (30 May 2013). Available at www.wsj.com/news/articles/SB10001424127887324866904578515552017379238.

7 percent of the estimated global total of bitcoins'.[73] Mt. Gox later claimed to have found 200,000 bitcoins stored in a mislabelled 'wallet', reducing the total loss very slightly.[74] The causes of this loss have both technical and management roots. Mt. Gox was found to have been affected by 'transaction malleability'[75] caused by a known software defect it failed to remedy, permitting agents to induce the Mt. Gox site to send those agents bitcoins under the apprehension that Mt. Gox was receiving consideration in exchange when in fact it was not. Since the software defect was known in 2011 and various Bitcoin actors acted at that time to respond to it, the processes by which Mt. Gox 'lost' bitcoins is thought by some to have been relatively lengthy, from 2011 to 2013.[76] Mt. Gox's failure to respond to notice of easily resolved technical issues with Bitcoin raised further questions regarding the causal roles of the Bitcoin software and Mt. Gox's management and accounting practices.[77] In the aftermath of Mt. Gox's failure, former Chief Executive Officer Mark Karpelès is being investigated under suspicion of having illegitimately manipulated the firm's books to generate a personal financial benefit, adding a dimension of internal corruption to Mt. Gox's legacy of failed technology implementation and weak internal security and accounting.[78] And yet, after Mt. Gox, new exchanges have entered the market while others continued. Today a simple Google

[73] B. Wolf and E. Flitter, 'Mt. Gox: the brief reign of bitcoin's top exchange', Reuters UK (28 February 2014). Available at http://uk.reuters.com/article/2014/02/28/us-bitcoin-mtgox-insight-idUKBREA1R06C20140228.

[74] S. Knight, 'Mt. Gox says it found 200,000 bitcoins in "forgotten" wallet', Reuters US (21 March 2014). Available at www.reuters.com/article/2014/03/21/us-bitcoin-mtgox-wallet-idUSBREA2K05N20140321.

[75] As an extensive article by Alex Hern in the *Guardian* puts it, 'in Mt. Gox's case, it appears that what happened is that the site was expecting transactions to show up in the public ledger under the specific transaction ID it had recorded. When those transactions didn't show up – because the thief had edited the ID – the thief could then complain that the transaction had failed, and the system would *automatically* retry, initiating a second transaction and sending out more bitcoins'. A. Hern, 'How a bug in bitcoin led to Mt. Gox's collapse', *The Guardian* (27 February 2014). Available at www.theguardian.com/technology/2014/feb/27/how-does-a-bug-in-bitcoin-lead-to-mtgoxs-collapse.

[76] Ibid.

[77] Mt. Gox Chief Executive Officer Mark Karpelès has since admitted to management errors: '"The weakest point of my company was management", said Mr. Karpelès, who was the sole executive of the company. "I failed to lay out appropriate corporate structures"'. T. Mochizuki and E. Warnock, 'Mt. Gox head believes no more bitcoins will be found', *Wall Street Journal* (29 June 2014). Available at www.wsj.com/articles/mt-gox-head-believes-no-more-bitcoin-will-be-found-1403850830.

[78] Karpelès was charged with embezzlement by Japanese authorities in September of 2015, as reported by the *Guardian* (www.theguardian.com/technology/2015/sep/14/bitcoin-mt-gox-ceo-mark-karpeles-charged-embezzling) and the BBC (www.bbc.com/news/business-34217495).

query indicates that bitcoins are trading at US$419, and Bitcoin continues in plain view of the internet.

During the rise of Mt. Gox and other exchanges, regulators scrutinized Bitcoin and in some cases, adopted incremental response approaches emphasizing investigation and evaluation. In the US, the Chairman (Senator Carper) of the Homeland Security and Governmental Affairs Committee requested that the Law Library of Congress report on other states' and the European Union's views regarding the legal status of virtual currencies including Bitcoin.[79] Other states have taken a more robust regulatory approach, effectively removing the capacity of Bitcoin technology to enable a virtual cryptocurrency operating alongside state-sponsored currencies. The most striking regulatory intervention was seen in China, where on 3 December 2013 the central bank of China and associated ministries issued a notice banning banks from using bitcoins:

> It is required that, at this stage, financial and payment institutions may not use Bitcoin pricing for products or services, may not buy or sell Bitcoins, may not act as a central counterparty in Bitcoin trading, may not offer insurance products associated with Bitcoin, may not provide direct or indirect Bitcoin-related services to customers.[80]

This limitation of Chinese market exposure to bitcoins is not, however, so drastic as it might seem, since private citizens are not banned from use of bitcoins. CNBC report analysis conducted by Goldman Sachs in 2015 indicating that nearly 80 per cent of bitcoin purchases are conducted using Chinese yuan.[81]

These technical and management failures combined with regulatory responses offer vivid evidence of the susceptibility of Bitcoin software and processes to problems as old as banking itself. It is tempting to read the career of Bitcoin through a Hollywood lens, seeing a cyber-age version of a well-known tale: brash young innovators invent a promising form of commerce yet are ruined by a combination of excessively rapid growth, too-late

[79] The announcement of the report's completion (Report for Congress LL File No. 2014-010233 Regulation of Bitcoin in Selected Jurisdictions) and a link are available at www.hsgac.senate.gov/media/majority-media/new-report-outlines-treatment-and-regulation-of-bitcoin-around-the-world.

[80] 'People's Bank of China, Ministry of Industry and Information Technology of China, China Securities Regulatory Commission, China Banking Regulatory Commission and the China Insurance Regulatory Commission Notice on the Prevention of Risks Associated with Bitcoin' (Bank Notice [2013] No. 289), available at https://vip.btcchina.com/page/bocnotice2013. For media discussion, see also W. Yiyao and G. Changxin, 'Banks not allowed to use Bitcoin', *China Daily* (December 5, 2013). Available at www.chinadaily.com.cn/china/2013-12/05/content_17155306.htm.

[81] N. Chandran, 'This is why bitcoin won't go away anytime soon', CNBC.com (12 March 2015). Available at www.cnbc.com/2015/03/12/-bitcoin-wont-go-away-anytime-soon.html.

fixes to flaws in their business model, and a string of thefts and management errors driven by hubris and exacerbated by suspicious and protectionist regulators. There may even be a happy Hollywood ending available, as neither the Mt. Gox failure nor far-reaching Chinese regulatory intervention have stopped the next generation of innovators from continuing to use Bitcoin and bitcoins as a system and medium of exchange. Bitcoin itself continues to develop, as solutions to technical limitations are attempted and the community of Bitcoin users chooses to adapt or reject those solutions.

The vast majority of engagement with Bitcoin by users and commentators focusses on its use to enable currency exchange. Estimates of the significance and future of Bitcoin tend to focus on associated issues regarding the economic model supporting the mining process key to verification, the large swings in value of bitcoins, and so on. Yet as some commentators have been quick to point out, the lessons of Bitcoin are not restricted to its originators' intention to use the 'blockchain' technology and its maintenance community for currency exchange purposes. *Forbes* contributor Robert Rosenkranz suggests in an appropriately named short article that 'Bitcoin's Value Isn't Currency, It's Technology'.[82] Rosenkranz illustrates his title's claim via examples of applications of blockchain technology to transactions long subject to the apparatus of hierarchically organized state systems of law:

> Credit card companies charge fees around 2.5 percent for moving value from a customer to a merchant. Banks charge at least that much for international transfers. Block chain transaction charges are a small fraction – approximately one half of one percent and eventually should be much lower than that. Potentially, blockchain can also record and transfer ownership of physical assets like automobiles, real estate, and art and intangible assets such as patents and royalties. It can thus enable secured lending transactions between strangers.[83]

Novel socio-technical mechanisms for currency exchange are certainly worthy of jurisprudential attention. When those mechanisms are demonstrably applicable to the kind of exchanges historically governed under the law of contract as applied to various kinds of property under institutions of law and legal institutions providing state-guaranteed determinations of legal validity, much more

[82] R. Rosenkranz, 'Bitcoin's value isn't currency: it's technology', *Forbes* (7 July 2015). Available at www.forbes.com/sites/robertrosenkranz/2015/07/07/bitcoins-value-isnt-currency-its-technology/.

[83] www.forbes.com/sites/robertrosenkranz/2015/07/07/bitcoins-value-isnt-currency-its-technology/2/.

jurisprudential attention is warranted since there is the prospect of transformative innovation in the practice of contract. What might this transformation be, and how ought it to be characterized?

The Bitcoin model's use of blockchain may appear at least momentarily to be a novel socio-technical practice occupying a relatively subordinate point in a familiar hierarchical chain of validity where officials of some legal system or systems act as validators – so while there is something new about Bitcoin, its novelty fits within and is explained by familiar means. Yet closer attention shows this explanation misreads the significance of decentralized transaction validation within the Bitcoin model. Decentralization of determinations of validity is of course possible within state legal systems, but the way validity is determined in the Bitcoin model is much different from the practice of a cadre of officials jointly constituting a rule or rules of recognition. To begin with, while acts of determination of Bitcoin validity are not ethnographically observable as the actions of officials in state systems of law are presumed to be, the way determinations of validity are made in the Bitcoin approach clearly does not use or continuously construct a culture of shared meanings and object of allegiance as may be found in, e.g., reported decisions of appellate courts constituting a line of precedent and contributing to a system of legal norms. Rather, determinations of validity are solutions of software-generated corroboration problems where validity is constructed by the accumulation of six confirmations (an arbitrarily set confidence threshold) conducted by any miners who choose to tackle the problem.[84] Once users, not some set of miners, have confidence in the accumulation of confirmations provided by miners, a content-neutral determination of validity is reached. Miners act in response to an incentive disconnected from the content of the transaction whose validity they determine: they receive what is in effect a share of a transaction fee (payment in bitcoins) for a transaction whose further content is not within their responsibility or control. Instead matters such as validation of the eligibility of the transacting parties to conduct transactions is affected and determined elsewhere, e.g., national jurisdictions and their assertion of terms of contract law.

As miners enact their role in the consensus-driven determination of validity, the disconnected and content-neutral manner of their contribution to certification of validity means they need not have any knowledge of the content of the transaction. As with the question of the eligibility of transacting parties to transact, the question of the eligibility of the content of the transaction to be subject to transaction is equally outwith the role of the miner. Depending on

[84] See the Bitcoin FAQ at https://bitcoin.org/en/faq#why-do-i-have-to-wait-10-minutes.

an investigator's normative perspective, this may be viewed as a shortcoming or as a valuable feature of the Bitcoin approach – lack of a central or distributed control of the content of transactions may equally evade regulation of vice, or the reach of corrupt controllers. The absence of relevance of the miners' knowledge of the transaction's content is paralleled by the absence of relevance of the miners' attitudes towards even the role of Bitcoin in a scheme of social life. Indeed, those miners need not share anything but problem-solving capacity via control of processing units. Their identity, social positions and education are irrelevant and may be unknown. Their geographical location is irrelevant and possibly hidden. Their activity as a miner may be individual, or as a member of a pool, and may occur just once or as often as the miner chooses. Under close examination we must give up on the possibility of explaining the Bitcoin approach and its miners as subordinate to and explained within a system-centred, hierarchical view reliant on a cadre of officials accepting and enacting the system as they use powers, make determinations of law and so on. Mining is conducted by miners so broadly distributed, qualified and possibly intermittent in their participation that identification of miners as a class of actors seems without explanatory value insofar as there is by design no way to exclude willing participants from the mining process. The openness of the mining process to participation from diverse problem-solvers determining the validity of a transaction is a chosen feature of Bitcoin in its attempt to decentralize determinations of validity. The need for a class of officials is intentionally avoided and the possibility of an official-user hierarchy is both obviated and irrelevant. All who wish to bring technical capacity to bear on determinations of validity may do so without sharing knowledge, attitudes or an object of allegiance in the manner thought by many analytical legal theorists to be practically necessary to all but a primitive system of norms.

The nature of this example warrants recognition of several qualifications which puts its significance in fuller context. Bitcoin as an application of the new ICTs together with a community of users extends to a specific range of transactions and not further. As an ICT application in the hands of users, Bitcoin's independence from certain dimensions of norm-determination historically associated with a body of officials does not leave it altogether neutral in the sense of being independent of human intentions. As an instance of human-authored software then taken up and used in ways both intended and not intended by its authors, Bitcoin embodies in at least an early part of its life the normative commitments of its creators as those commitments are expressed in code permitting some inputs while rejecting others. Some may argue that Bitcoin's embodiment of its creators' commitments may last still longer. It might be the case that the elaborate lengths taken to obscure the real identity of Satoshi Nakamoto have been taken precisely because the creators recognize the difficulty of divorcing a piece of software and its use from original authorial intention and are attempting to accelerate that process by deliberately rejecting attention to the original author. Yet this may be part of a kind of in-community gamesmanship which is ultimately irrelevant, since it is a commonplace that technology is in a sense neutral to the extent that particular technologies can often be put to uses unimagined or unintended by their originators, particularly in combination with unforeseen other technologies. It may be sufficient to observe that Bitcoin's decentralization of determinations of validity is *de facto* networked and independent of hierarchical decision making even while Bitcoin as a socio-technical activity departs from code written by a particular author or group of authors.[85] This observation may be underscored by the observation that Bitcoin is the first widely recognized and effective proponent of the blockchain consensus validation approach, but it is not the only proponent. If Bitcoin comes to be perceived by users as non-neutral or undesirably controlled by a hierarchy, users may easily choose other Bitcoin-like options to conduct transactions with networked, non-hierarchical determinations of validity.[86]

A further qualification to the story of Bitcoin as a potential disruptor of official-constituted rules of recognition in state legal systems can be seen in the limited scope of Bitcoin as a transaction practice. The type of transaction to which Bitcoin applies is not novel, so Bitcoin is an alternative, or, depending on a particular transaction and its content as an instantiation of Bitcoin, Bitcoin is in some jurisdictions a competitor to or in conflict with existing transaction methods. This all means that Bitcoin and its validity determination method do not purport to be a comprehensive peer of or competitor to municipal systems of law. If anything Bitcoin resembles at first glance an international commercial legal order of a special type insofar as there is as yet no sign that its proponents wish to extend its scope beyond a specified set of transactions, or to develop a cadre of officials to accompany foundational norms expressed in code.[87]

85 J. Bonneau, A. Miller, J. Clark, A. Narayanan, J. A. Kroll and E. W. Felten, 'SoK: research perspectives and challenges for Bitcoin and cryptocurrencies', in *2015 IEEE Symposium on Security and Privacy (SP)* (San Jose, CA, 2015), pp. 104–121.

86 See generally R. Bollen, 'The legal status of online currencies: are bitcoins the future?', *Journal of Banking and Finance Law and Practice*, 1 (2013), p. 38. Available at http://ssrn.com/abstract=2285247.

87 Bitcoin might be usefully regarded as a modern *lex mercatoria* of the sort characterized by Dalhuisen as a 'non-territorial transnational law of a private law nature that has no state as originator and operates more in the manner of public international law'. See J. H. Dalhuisen, 'Legal orders and their manifestation: the operation of the international commercial and financial legal order and its lex mercatoria', *Berkeley Journal of International Law*, 24 (2006), p. 132.

Even with these qualifications and perhaps others introduced, Bitcoin is instructive as an example of present and future challenges to the presumption of state-law asymmetric supervenience. To the extent that Bitcoin and its cousins make possible decentralized determinations of law, the state (and its characteristic body of officials asserting and demarcating the state's claims to authority) is separated from law. As the above qualifications show, the present effect of Bitcoin is to diminish rather than to remove the extent of the asymmetric relation, whose details in any case remain an asserted best explanation in the face of plausible alternatives. This effect is nonetheless significant as a challenge to state systems' claims to authority, insofar as Bitcoin is not plausibly read as authored by states in its origin or authorized by states in its ongoing operation, notwithstanding some states' attempts to effectively ring-fence the operation of Bitcoin by regulating more closely the substance of the transactions Bitcoin otherwise addresses. At the same time, Bitcoin cannot plausibly be regarded as a sheer technical phenomenon to be marginalized and controlled as a whole, if not transaction-by-transaction, by states whose active consent and action is required for the functioning of the internet. Not only is it the case that no one state or set of states authorizes the internet now, but it seems that there are good reasons for state systems of law to seek to avoid attempting to govern all data exchanges and underlying technologies relevant to the legal system it asserts. The distributed nature of the internet means, on credible argument, that efforts by a state to render all data within some scope controllable by the state requires establishment of points of access and control equally liable to interference from non-state actors, creating from the point of view of assertion of exclusive authority a challenge to the extent that such an assertion creates a still greater governance challenge for a state which may be ill-equipped to respond to that challenge.[88] In other words, where the internet goes and where dimensions of social life are mediated by internet-carried applications of the new ICTs, state assertions of authority are easily challenged by competitors since code as the means of assertion of authority is unlike gunpowder and guns insofar as it is effectively universally distributed and cannot be hoarded. Where the state has limited capacity to exclude others from formation of normative institutions – institutions of law, in our framing, assembled into legal institutions – the status of state law as the basic instance of legality is under challenge. It may yet be the case that as Larry Lessig has argued at length, 'code is law'[89] occupying interstitial space between states and other legal orders, enabling novel social formations in

[88] http://dspace.mit.edu/handle/1721.1/97690.

[89] See generally Lawrence Lessig, *Code*, 2nd edn (New York: Basic Books, 2006). Available at http://codev2.cc/download+remix/Lessig-Codev2.pdf.

what is presently called 'cyberspace' but will soon be identified and spoken of differently as we come to realize degrees of connection between the internet and the world of things, and degrees of sophistication of social relation in the social web. Just as it is increasingly implausible to think of cyberspace as a world apart from the physical world, so the initially handy distinction between the internet of things and the social web is elided by recognition that daily social life can become so interconnected with internet applications that hard and fast distinctions between internet and other communications with normative effect in regulation of, e.g., obligations, property and use of force, hold no practical purchase. Instead, in a manner analogous to the community-driven emergence of lex mercatoria as the *de facto* commercial law of the middle ages across various forms of European political and legal order, Bitcoin and related socio-technical applications of the new ICTs offer a way for code plus community to generate law. Such law is not limited to the organization of cyberspace via matters such as address conventions, but may extend to express the purposes of new forms of community organization enabled by the internet as they are connected to new applications of the internet of things – whether currency exchange or other purposes and methods. Just what shape the 'ubiquitous web' may take as a combination of the internet of things, social web, mobile web and other technology applications we do not know and will leave to others to examine. It is sufficient for our jurisprudential purposes to observe that the notion of cyberspace as thoroughly separate from lived social space is far past obsolescence, and the degree to which the new ICTs have become embedded in daily life shows that norm-subjects do not leave meatspace behind to enter cyberspace. Instead, the reverse is occurring in something like the 'netification of meatspace', as evident in existing, quite ordinary applications of the new ICTs to critical infrastructure and to certain forms of transactions between norm-subjects. In the case of the examples we have examined, the emergence of a set of legal orders adjacent to state orders and practically ineliminable by them[90] is an indication that law's relation to the new ICTs as the currently most prominent technological drive of social change is a relationship which cannot be fully understood through the lens of system-centred legal theory.

LAW AND THE NEW ICTS: OPENINGS, CLOSINGS AND NEW QUESTIONS FOR LEGAL THEORY

Two particularly useful insights may be drawn from preceding analysis. The first is simple and general. It seems to us to be beyond question that advocates

90 For reasons ranging from benefits arising from coordination to the practical impossibility of closing virtual borders while benefiting from interconnection via the internet.

of system-centred approaches to legality must now recognize the existence of non-state forms of legality which are not usefully explained in terms of hierarchical subordination to or validation by state systems of law. A key next step for analytical legal theorists accepting this conclusion is to decide just what priority system-centred investigations ought to take in twenty-first-century theorizing about the nature of law. Where Raz sought to take up the law-state relation he thought Hart failed to recognize, but in doing so failed to specify the state-society-law relation adequately, a further shortcoming in both styles of approach to legality is now evident. Neither took up in any depth the possibility of what might be called internal pluralism within this relation. Neither took up, for example, the possibility that there might be a 'state plus international political union' relation to a given society and law, or that members of a given geographically located society might nonetheless conceive themselves to belong to further virtual societies creating adjacent legal orders. This omission has evidently been tolerable in a particular social situation – that of the modern municipal state most salient to the ordinary citizen of the twentieth century – and the legal theorists facing that situation. Now, however, the omission is intolerable. As our exploration of the relation between law and technology demonstrates, use of an observationally assessed official practice of recognition as a means to identification of a continuous legal order – whether systemic or otherwise – is ineffective in the twenty-first-century examples we have considered. The fact that some states are choosing increased interconnection in the form of features such as shared critical infrastructure weighs against attempting to modernize the account of a posited official/citizen distinction. Choice of increased interconnection renders systemic closure a less rather than more salient feature of the identity or identities of the legal orders present in some region where states interact and give rise to novel legal orders. Further attention to renovation of the notion of officials and a rule of recognition might even be viewed as an undesirable distraction, since it seeks to find boundaries where what is more interesting in light of law's salient relations in the twenty-first century is the way in which system closure is being intentionally breached.

This last observation gives rise to a second insight regarding next tasks for analytical legal theorists convinced by our arguments that there are novel phenomena in need of explanation unavailable from system-centred approaches. If analytical legal theorists accept that it is no longer sufficient to orient all or nearly all explanation to the presumed centrality of the state, those theorists are likely to accept also that the jurisprudential problems deserving of twenty-first-century attention are likely to be broader in number or nature than those accompanying explanatory focus on the law-state. Just how these problems might be re-framed is still under exploration. In the context of our relational approach and more particularly our examination of law's relation to technology, it seems to us that the problem of continuity is re-shaped by what we have seen, as understanding of the preconditions and conditions of continuity of a legal system (or other legal order) is joined by or becomes a problem of continuity *and transition*. That is to say that as our analysis of the relation between law and technology has shown the rise of legal orders adjacent to and overlapping with (and perhaps mutually constitutive with) legal systems, once relatively rare questions about the border between state and other legal orders are arising more frequently, and with more variation. Those questions are arising in a context where the legal orders under examination are not simply 'state and other' but instead, as we argued in Chapter 5 of *Legality's Borders*, intra-state legal orders such as those of First Nations in Canada, trans-state *lex mercatoria*, supra-state law of the European Union, and super state *jus cogens* norms.

Where the problem of continuity was once examination of the preconditions of the continuity of state legal systems, under the challenge of the new phenomena such as supergrids and Bitcoin, we encounter a different version of the question. We must take up what in Chapter 6 of *Legality's Borders* we called 'pathologies of legality'. We must continue to inquire into whether and how state legal systems are continuous or perhaps failing or failed or absorbed or enlarged; and investigation of this question must be supported by further investigation of the ontology of what is continuing in a particular form or taking another form, changing the problem of continuity into the 'problem of continuity of *what*?' This re-framed question can be usefully separated into two problems: the problem of continuity, and the problem of *transition* between and amongst legal orders each in need of characterization of its identity. In making the case for an expanded investigative scope for analytical legal theorists, the problem of transition arises as a consequence of recognition of the contingency of legal systems as one form of legal order, and the coincident contingency of the state law–society relation as the central object of general-level descriptive-explanatory legal theory. Where the problem of the continuity of momentary legal systems in the era of system-centred analytical jurisprudence permitted ready demarcation of boundaries between states and other forms of legality because the objects of analysis were in effect frozen in time, a quite different challenge is posed by an object of analysis whose interest lies in the fact that it is dynamic, composed of multiple forms of legal order and changing relations amongst them. It may be that analytical legal theory has yet to develop a technical vocabulary to address continuous legal orders subject to transitions. That challenge is much more worth facing, we think, than the task of fighting a rear-guard action defending a system-centred focus.

Such a focus risks failing to give due cautionary weight to Raz's caveat that legal system is a theorist's explanatory tool and not the name of a specific social phenomenon, and Weber's similar warning that the state as an ideal-type is useful as a heuristic, and again, not the name of a specific social phenomenon. Investment of effort in development of technical vocabulary seems to us to hold further value as legal theory's encounter with applications of the new ICTs has really only just begun. In closing *Legality's Borders* we suggested that further work may be needed in thinking through the nature of legal agency in an era where applications of the new ICTs provide for artificial agency, e.g., adaptive algorithms supporting automated trading in markets. Since our raising this topic, advances in computing have opened still more striking questions. Where we suggested giving attention to extensions of agency, scholars and practitioners concerned with artificial intelligence are now debating the possibility that it might give rise to agents competing with or outcompeting human agents. A recent open letter organized by the Future of Life institute advocates a set of research priorities for 'robust and beneficial artificial intelligence'[91] alongside investigation into unintended consequences of artificial agents including possible loss of control of artificial intelligence systems. While no one can yet say just how rapidly artificial intelligence will develop exhibiting what characteristics, it is clear that extensions and substitutions of agency will bring great changes to the conduct of social life. Legal theory as a reflection and instrument of understanding of that social life will be best off if well-prepared to engage those changes with well-adapted explanatory tools. We advocate increased attention to law's relation to technology now, in the near certainty that this relation will become only more significant in the future. Where once there was the problem of identity of momentary legal systems, we propose further investigation of the problem of continuity and transition of legal orders, and foresee in this new investigation only positive opportunities for legal theory to reach new audiences.

[91] See http://futureoflife.org/AI/open_letter and http://futureoflife.org/static/data/documents/research_priorities.pdf.

8

Beyond the Unsteady State

The final sentence of our introductory chapter set us the task of contributing to the 'destruction of the fiction of the centrality of the state to the nature of legality'. We set about our task by aiming at two goals. We sought first to demonstrate the implausibility of the view that a general explanation of legality is best derived from explanation of law's place in state systems of law, which by their nature claim to control fully and completely the operation of all legal norms within their territory. In addition to our identification of weaknesses in that view and its application to momentary legal systems, we sought in a second line of argument to demonstrate the inability of state-centred analytical approaches to respond to the problem of continuity. That problem is best understood as the challenge of explaining what forms the identity of a legal order over time and how we might best explain variations to that identity and form of legal order over time. We suggested that achievement of our goals might contribute to pulling off the mask of law, a mask whose existence was first announced by Jeremy Bentham. As we arrive at the conclusion of our argument, we believe we have identified several fictions and have offered better ways of approaching the phenomena previously left to fiction. We have not, however, succeeded in removing the mask of law, for reasons rather more interesting than our failure. We have failed because there is no mask to remove, no single most plausible story about the nature of law behind a single mask carrying many fictions. Rather, it seems that a better metaphor is one which conveys our finding that law has many faces, as a legal order changes over time while retaining its identity, or gives way seamlessly or through disruption to another legal order. As we sought to articulate the shortcomings of a state-centred approach to explanation of legality in an era where legality beyond state forms is just the beginning of the complexity of novel legal phenomena needing explanation, we developed a contextualized conceptual explanation of legality. That explanation aimed to be general yet history-sensitive and phenomena-responsive, neither too narrow nor too broad, and in its historical sensitivity intended to be capable of reflecting more than momentary snapshots of legal order as most famously found in unitary state systems.

Behind our new metaphor, an account of legality is beginning to emerge yet cannot be fully articulated here, and indeed ever, since it is under constant revision as it responds to novel phenomena. We have offered in place of a state-centred analytical view an institution-centred view whose application certainly finds state systems, but finds legality additionally in legal orders independent of the society-officials-state-territory amalgam. As was the case in *Legality's Borders*, we understand legal orders as consisting in institutions of law agglomerated in legal institutions whose mutual reference over time in varying intensities constitutes the order's identity. Some such orders may have a systematic character; others may not. Each has a history, and that history is key to understanding whether there are families of legal orders at any given time, whether there are forms of legal order typical of particular physical and social situations that arise from time to time, and key to ascribing a particular identity to a legal order. This may seem disappointing to those seeking a typology of legal orders, or a demarcation tool; but those interests are not those of our inquirer, who travels around the world in and through legal orders which sometimes meet the ideal of legal system and sometimes do not, in ways which matter to our inquirer's choices as realization of our inquirer's plans does or does not require the presence of a particular form of legal order. Our inquirer is likely to be satisfied by an account of legality which is as much a family tree as it is a reflection of practically prominent legal orders found in present state systems.

Our inquirer's predicted satisfaction with our view is derived from several sources. Our argument here builds on our positive account of the nature of legality in *Legality's Borders*. That account of the forms of legality in addition to state law is extended by our complementary investigation here of law's relation to environment, security and technology. Our inquirer is likely also motivated by the negative results of our attempt in the first part of this book to understand just how much we might carry from state-based analytical approaches to our concern with the problem of continuity. There we found that while the state system remains practically dominant in global life under law, a close examination of the elements of the state system in static form, undertaken as a precursor to examination of the system over time, tends to reveal articulated presumptions mistaken for explanation. While there is little question that these presumptions have enabled deeper understanding of state systems of law, their source in and application to such developed systems leaves them relatively unhelpful when inquirers seek to understand legality's continuity in transitions between forms of legal order. In a stable legal system, for example, there may be no motivation to worry about whether a norm of the system is presumptively valid subject to official recognition, or whether validity is in fact constituted by recognition and a moment of uncertainty precedes that act of recognition. Such uncertainty may be so brief as to be practically unimportant and of little theoretical interest because efforts are devoted to characterization of the system as a momentary system. Once outside the momentary system, however, presumptions regarding the ready identification of officials, of a legal system's functioning as a sub-system of a larger social system, etc., do not hold, and indeed, their not holding is the matter of interest needing explanation. Absent analysis to convert these presumptions into evidence-supported claims about general characteristics of social reality, our inter-institutional approach is preferable as a view which is inherently change-sensitive in its tracking frequency and intensity of mutual reference amongst institutions of law and legal institutions, all without presumption of particular society-legal system relations and legal system-territory relations as the mark and measure of legality.

The independence of our approach from a state system focus has enabled us to reach fresh insights into the role environmental change can play in transition between legal orders. We saw in Aceh an example of environment as an agent of systemic opening to hybridity. In Kiribati we saw environment as a source of systemic transformation, as the potential severing of the territorial dimension of statehood invites all Kiribatians to become legal theorists, as 'legal system' is for them much more than a legal theorists' term of art, when they ask what may become of their population, their culture, and their legal system if their territory is submerged beneath the ocean, and their participation in what we identified as the political ideal of legal system is diminished with uncertain consequences. As we bypassed thought experiments to consider the real experience of Kiribati as a potentially territory-less state and legal system, we opened the way to investigation of law's relation to security, where law's protection of expectations appears as protection of expectations of certain forms of control. Our exploration of security as control in the context of new ICTs enabled us to witness once again the fragility of system-centred explanations of legality, as we saw Bitcoin, a pioneer in what may be a long train of virtual currencies, creating a currency and means of exchange beyond the effective control of states. More pressingly and more personally, for many readers, our exploration of electrical grids crossing state boundaries demonstrated a broader version of the insight found in Lawrence Lessig's slogan that 'code is law',[1] that code-controlled instances of the internet of things make legal systems subject to their successful interaction with adjacent legal orders created by code's regulation of technologies upon which the systems are functionally dependent.

Our investigation of legal orders enabled by technology within them alongside legal systems has given rise to our suggestion that the problem of continuity is best understood more broadly as the problem of continuity and transition. Continuity of one legal system until replaced by another is not the only form of legal continuity we find in our experience of law. Whether a legal system arising from a simple customary legal order, a state contemplating continued existence without territory, or a virtual legal order governing virtual currency only loosely controlled, if at all, by state-based legal systems claiming to control currency within their boundaries, attention to the problem of continuity of legality matters to understanding the nature of state legal systems, and opens the way to jurisprudential territory as yet under-explored by analytical legal theorists.

We plan in our next work to follow the path of our imagined twenty-first-century inquirer who travels, and in travelling finds not just that state law is accompanied by other forms of law within and without state borders, but that the borders between states are just one kind of border shaping life under law. We, along with our traveller, are conscious that the twenty-first century is one of unprecedented domination of wealth, power and consumption by urban areas dominating regions within and across state boundaries. The most prominent example of this domination may be seen in the rise of mega-cities in excess of 10 million inhabitants, creating poles of global interaction between those cities, and the hinterlands which service them directly and contribute to global value chains. As political attention focusses on the demands and opportunities found in these centres, new opportunities arise for hinterlands to examine the differences found in their situation, and in some circumstances, to reassert identities and values at odds with those of urban centres. Autonomy-seekers of various kinds abound in these circumstances – whether indigenous peoples seeking increased autonomy within or across boundaries of states, groups in historic states such as Scotland seeking partial exit from the UK in anticipation of a better place in the European Union, or the regions and cities of the

[1] www.code-is-law.org/ and Lawrence Lessig, *Code*, 2nd edn (New York: Basic Books, 2006). Available at http://codev2.cc/download+remix/Lessig-Codev2.pdf.

European Union seeking their own influence on European law-making.[2] These familiar examples and sense of regionality are just part of our next exploration, which recognizes that the webs of connection between cities, and the webs between them and their hinterlands, are not the only webs of social interaction enabled and shaped by law. It may also be helpful to think of regions in relative terms, so 'relative regionality' refers to relative cores and peripheries in the context of some particular set of subject-born interests. Small island states, for example, may be peripheral to some global opportunities and challenges, yet at the core of others. In 2014 a symbolically important first step towards recognition of the special needs of these states was visible in the UN's declaration of an International Year of Small Island Developing States, 'a group of countries that remain a special case for sustainable development in view of their unique and particular vulnerabilities'.[3] These countries are presently only loosely aligned, joining together as what the Alliance of Small Island States describes as 'an ad hoc lobby and negotiating voice for small island developing States (SIDS) within the United Nations system'.[4] As international support for development of these 'special case' states enables policy choices implemented via supporting law, there is an opportunity and institution for sharing of lessons learned, and a further opportunity for best practice formalization in law. Should such formalization come to fruition, a new network of mutually referential legal norms would be created by a community of regions, warranting our attention as legal theorists concerned with legality's emergent traces in addition to its dominant manifestations. In this investigation familiar questions are brought to new phenomena. If virtual legal orders arise, or regional legal orders or global communities of regional legal orders, we shall still need to inquire into validity conditions for member-norms of those legal orders. We will be no less interested in relative institutional force of norms of those orders, and their relation to other legal orders and their norms – whether relations of incorporation, adoption without incorporation or otherwise. And as we encounter in regions the problem of identity as seen in continuity and transition of legal order within and without legal systems, we will no longer be satisfied with momentary characterizations of legality. Such characterizations no longer satisfy the interests of our travelling inquirer. Where we seek further application of our inter-institutional view to develop

[2] See, e.g., the European Union Committee of the Regions: http://europa.eu/about-eu/institutions-bodies/cor/index_en.htm.

[3] UNESCO Small Island Developing States Programme: http://whc.unesco.org/en/sids/.

[4] The Alliance of Small Island States: http://aosis.org/about/.

more satisfactory contextualized conceptual explanations of law, we take the problem of identity and transition over time as a new addition to the set of perennial problems, while remaining attentive to the possibility that still further innovation in the methods of analytical legal theory may be required. As Hart knew when setting off from his inaugural lecture, 'In law, as elsewhere, we can know and yet not understand'.[5]

[5] H. L. A. Hart, 'Definition and theory in jurisprudence', in *Essays in Jurisprudence and Philosophy* (Oxford: Clarendon Press, 1983), p. 21.

Index

CPSIA information can be obtained
at www.ICGtesting.com
Printed in the USA
LVOW01*2022210417
531716LV00009B/170/P

9 781107 134805